American Indians in U.S. History

THE CIVILIZATION OF THE AMERICAN INDIAN SERIES

AMERICAN
INDIANS
IN U.S.
HISTORY

Roger L. Nichols

University of Oklahoma Press : Norman

American Indians in U.S. History is volume 248 in The Civilization of the American Indian Series.

Library of Congress Cataloging-in-Publication Data

Nichols, Roger L.
  American Indians in U.S. history / Roger L. Nichols.
    p. cm. — (The civilization of the American Indian series ; no. 248)
  Includes index.
  ISBN 0-8061-3557-3 (hc : alk. paper)
  1. Indians of North America—History. I. Title. II. Series.

E77.N553 2003
973.04'97—dc21

2003047398

The paper in this book meets the guidelines for permanence and durability of the Committee on Production Guidelines for Book Longevity of the Council on Library Resources, Inc. ∞

2 3 4 5 6 7 8 9 10

To Katelyn Barr, Annie Nichols,
and Harvey G. Nichols

Contents

Illustrations

PHOTOGRAPHS

Following page 111
The Indian Fort Sasquesahanok, 1720
Return of the captives, 1760s
Indian halting wagon train
Monument to group hanging, in Mankato
Grass lodge, Kansa or Caddoan, at eastern edge of the southern plains
Teen-age Indian students at Carlisle Indian School in Pennsylvania, 1904
Indian children at the Cantonment School, Oklahoma, 1890–1910 era
Seminole family in traditional clothing, Florida, 1910
Example of Pacific Northwest totem-pole art, 1910
New Mexico Pueblo leaders' 1923 protest against land-title changes
American Indian Movement (AIM) protest poster, 1970s
Participants in the "Longest Walk," 1978

MAPS

Preface

The history of American Indians can be as appealing and exciting to general readers or to college students as reruns of 1950s western films are to twelve-year-old boys. As a result, since the 1960s authors and scholars have written to meet this appetite for adventure and excitement. Hundreds, perhaps thousands, of books and articles chronicling the lives of famous chiefs, the history of warfare, reservation stories, and tribal annals now line bookstore and library shelves. Some of this new work is excellent, but often the texts are lengthy. There are few comprehensive, interesting books for the general public. This briefer narrative is meant to highlight the main issues in American Indian history and to point readers toward more detailed analyses of events or people they find particularly interesting.

I make no pretense here of giving a comprehensive discussion of all the central questions—that would require many volumes. Rather, I present a broad outline of Indian experiences throughout American history. Generally the history moves through three stages. Prior to the European invasions, Indians enjoyed local independence, unless they had fallen under the domination of some other tribal group. From the start, they experienced, for lack of a better term, a frontier situation. That is, they had some contact, cooperation, competition, or conflict with their neighbors. Once the discoverers and those who followed them from Europe to the Western Hemisphere arrived, the situation changed. Gradually, as whites became more powerful, they began taking tribal lands and resources. By the last decades of the nineteenth century, Indians moved into the second stage in this broad history, becoming reservation dwellers. For many, this lasted until the twentieth century. The third stage begins with individuals and groups leaving their reservation bases to mingle with the general population, finding their way in contemporary society. Within this framework, my first chapter examines the precontact Indian world, and the rest of the book presents the post-1500 era, with five of the remaining seven chapters focusing on the period since American independence.

At first glance, the central issues seem clear. The Native people in the United States held the land and its resources, and the invading Europeans wanted those things. Although accurate, this version of the story is much too simple and gives the Indians no role other than that of victim. What actually happened from 1500 to the present proved far more complicated. During those five centuries, tribal groups and their European neighbors vied to control the situation. Indians wished to live their lives in traditional ways, and whites were determined to force them to change. Certainly both sides tried to impose their forms of government, diplomacy, and economic activity. Warfare gets lots of attention, but often the central disputes between whites and Indians focused on how people were to live. Issues such as social organization, family relations, language, food, clothing, housing, religion, education, and medicine were major points of conflict.

Tracing the history of American Indians in the United States presents several difficulties. With at least six hundred identifiable groups to consider, one faces hard choices. A general narrative cannot analyze the experiences of each tribe, trading partner, military ally or enemy, reservation, or particular leader, and this book makes no effort to do so. Another challenge is determining which events, spanning five centuries, to include. For many Americans, knowledge of Indian-related issues, events, people, or cultures may not go beyond what popular culture and the news media have offered, meaning that much of the story remains unknown. Then there is the question of which sources provide the most accurate and usable basis for understanding the events being discussed. Although prior to the twentieth century most Indians did not write, a variety of sources indicating their perspectives does exist. These sources include oral traditions, drawings, calendar sticks, and similar materials. Other information comes from a careful reading of non-Indian accounts of trade encounters, treaty negotiations, ceremonies, and even conflicts.

All this challenges the writer to uncover and analyze tribal points of view and then to place Native Americans at the center of the action, as they were at the time. The incorporation of tribal customs and practices into the narrative emphasizes ideas, movements, and individuals that often have not appeared in traditional American histories and also clarifies what motivated Indian communities to take particular actions. However, the historical record is opaque much of the time. Often little remains extant from those who could write, so scholars must depend on comments from angry pioneers, frustrated bureaucrats, missionaries, teachers, and ambitious army officers—and of course one must use extreme caution when examining such sources.

Americans have written a lot about Indians since the seventeenth century, with some of the first descriptions coming from the so-called captivity narratives. Often prepared after major wars, these narratives depicted tribal peoples as children of the devil, as heathen barbarians. Views about Native Americans became more varied in subsequent generations, but many Europeans and white Americans considered Indians to be savage and dangerous enemies down through the 1880s when the Apache Wars in the Southwest reinforced that idea. Novelists, radio authors, and film writers perpetuated stereotypes into the last half of the twentieth century, when the image shifted to an equally erroneous one of the peace-loving, ecologically aware victim of American national aggression. All of these views fall short of a usable analysis. Like people in any group, Indians fit into many categories—good, bad, or somewhere between.

Since the onset of "political correctness," officials, scholars, and Native American groups have debated which terms are the most accurate and appropriate for discussing American Indian history within the United States. When asked, many Indians prefer their tribal name, for example, Ho Chunk rather than Winnebago, but few use anything other than *Indian* for the entire group label. Anthropologists pale whenever they hear the word *tribe* because they insist that the Indians never belonged to tribes until long after encountering the European invaders in North America. Nevertheless, the federal government uses *tribe* as part of the legal definition of a group of Native people. *Native American* has some popular use, but technically all people born within the country are natives. *American Indian* has the most widespread acceptance, and many pan- or multitribal groups use it as part of their official names. The Indian Rodeo and Indian powwow circuits use it, and many universities have American Indian Studies programs staffed by people calling themselves Indians. All of these terms will be used in this book, simply to spare the reader what would otherwise be an endless repetition of any one of them.

Acknowledgments

When I was first asked to consider writing a book that presented the story of American Indian experiences from the beginning of time to the present, I laughed in surprise. The book was to cover the entire range of American history, yet it was to be brief. To these criteria my response was something like, "You have got to be kidding, right?" The answer sobered me. The University of Oklahoma Press really wanted such a book and asked me to consider the project. In a few weeks my initial lack of enthusiasm gave way to serious consideration of the request. Could the book be written, and was I the person to do it? Having recently recovered from the seemingly unending project that resulted in my 1998 comparative study of Indian experiences in the United States and Canada, I had vowed to steer clear of another far-reaching study. At the same time, it was that book which finally persuaded me to undertake this one, as a possibly less monumental project.

As with the writing of any book, many people and institutions provided support and encouragement. Jeff Burnham, then an editor with the Press, got me started. Jo Ann Reece took over the project in midstream. As project editor, Marian Stewart has guided it through production with care. Others on the University of Oklahoma Press staff have played important roles too, and all have my thanks and appreciation. Several of the scholars who read the manuscript for the Press made good suggestions and helped me to avoid both factual and interpretive errors. Among my colleagues, Leonard Dinnerstein read the entire manuscript, offering both support and trenchant comments as well. As usual, my wife, Marilyn Nichols, read the chapters more times than she would care to remember, and made telling comments that improved the manuscript.

Staff at the Library of Congress Reader Service Division and at Photographic Services there helped me locate material and illustrations that appear in the book. My home institution, the University of Arizona, assisted in a variety of ways. As always, the Interlibrary Loan staff located items beyond our collections. The aid provided by our technical support person, Jeff Block, proved to be of particular importance because this is my first book done entirely without a typewriter. Despite some grumbling on my part as pages disappeared into the ether, the manuscript came together well, if occasionally despite my best efforts. To the individuals and groups who assisted me throughout this process, I offer a sincere "thank you."

Chronology of Important Events

50,000 B.C.	Intermittent migrations from Asia (and Europe?)
15,000–10,000 B.C.	Evidence of early human occupation in the Americas
9000 B.C.	Date for Clovis points
3500 B.C.	Beginnings of agriculture in the Southwest
1400 B.C.	Poverty Point community in Louisiana founded
800 B.C.	Adena Culture develops in Ohio River Valley
100 B.C.	Hopewell Culture develops in Illinois
?–1300	Hohokam and Mogollon Cultures develop in the Southwest
700–1300	Anasazi appear in the Southwest
700–1400	Cahokia built in Illinois
700–1500	Mississippian Culture develops in the Southeast
1200–1400	Ancestors of historic tribes migrate to new locations
1513	Juan Ponce de León arrives in Florida
1534–41	Jacques Cartier visits St. Lawrence Valley
1539–43	Hernando de Soto invades the Southeast
1540–42	Francisco Vásquez de Coronado invades New Mexico
1565	Spanish found St. Augustine, Florida
1585–87	English establish Roanoke Island, North Carolina, settlement
1598	Juan de Oñate establishes colony in New Mexico
1607	English settle Jamestown, Virginia
1608	Samuel de Champlain founds Quebec
1609–14	First Anglo-Powhatan War in Virginia
1614	Dutch found Hudson River trading post
1616–19	Epidemics infect New England tribes

1774	Lord Dunmore's War
1775–83	American Revolution
1778	First U.S. treaty signed with Delawares
1779–81	Major smallpox epidemic in North America
1783	Treaty of Paris recognizes American independence
1789	Constitution gives federal government control of Indian affairs
1790	Alexander McGillivray signs Treaty of New York for Creeks
1790–94	War between Indians and United States in Ohio Valley
1794	Indians defeated at Battle of Fallen Timbers
1795	Treaty of Greenville
1799	Handsome Lake begins Long House religion among Senecas
1805	Tenskwatawa begins a new religious movement in Ohio Valley
1807–11	Tenskwatawa and Tecumseh work for a northwest confederacy
1811	Tribes defeated at Battle of Tippecanoe in Indiana
1812–15	Many tribes join British in War of 1812
1813–14	Creek or Red Stick War in Alabama
1817–18	First Seminole War in Florida
1819	Congress establishes Indian Civilization Fund
1821	Sequoyah develops Cherokee syllabary
1824	Office of Indian Affairs established in War Department
1827	Cherokees adopt a tribal constitution
1830	Congress passes the Indian Removal Act
1831	*Cherokee v. Georgia* finds Indians "domestic, dependent nations"
1832	*Worcester v. Georgia* finds state laws do not apply to tribes
1832	Black Hawk War
1835–42	Second Seminole War
1836	Creek Removal

1837	Smallpox epidemic in Missouri Valley
1838	Cherokee Trail of Tears
1848–49	California Gold Rush
1849	Office of Indian Affairs moved to new Department of the Interior
1851	Treaty of Fort Laramie
1861–65	American Civil War
1862	Minnesota Sioux War
1864	Sand Creek Massacre
	Navajo "Long Walk"
1866–67	Red Cloud's War closes Bozeman Trail
1867	Peace Commission treaties at Fort Laramie and Medicine Lodge
1869	Board of Indian Commissioners established
1871	Congress ends the treaty system
1872–73	Modoc War in Oregon
1874–75	Red River War in Texas
1876–77	Great Sioux War and Custer defeat
1877	Nez Perce War
1878	Indian police forces begun
1879	Carlisle Indian School established
1881	Sitting Bull surrenders
	Sun Dance outlawed
1882	Indian Rights Association founded
1883	Lake Mohonk Conferences begun
	Courts of Indian Offenses established
1884	Beginning of modern Peyotism
1885	Major Crimes Act passed
1886	End of Apache Wars in the Southwest
1887	Dawes Allotment Act passed
1890	Ghost Dance and Wounded Knee Massacre
	Sitting Bull killed
1903	*Lone Wolf v. Hitchcock* rules that Congress can end treaties

1908   *Winters v. United States* defines tribal water rights

1911   Society of American Indians founded

1917–18   United States enters World War I

1918   Native American Church established

1924   American Indian Citizenship Act passed

1928   Meriam Report published

1934   Indian Reorganization Act passed

1930s   Navajo Livestock Reduction Program

1941–45   Twenty-five thousand Indians serve in World War II

1944   National Congress of American Indians founded

1946   Indian Claims Commission established

1953   House Concurrent Resolution 108 and Termination

1956   Relocation Program begun

1961   American Indian Chicago Conference and Self-Determination

       National Indian Youth Council founded

1966   Navajo Rough Rock Demonstration School founded

1968   American Indian Movement (AIM) founded

       Indian Civil Rights Act passed

1969   Activists seize Alcatraz

       Navajo Community College opens

1970   Taos Pueblo regains Blue Lake

1971   Alaska Native Claims Settlement Act

1972   Trail of Broken Treaties and occupation of BIA building

1973   Sixty-seven-day confrontation at Wounded Knee, South Dakota

1974   *United States v. Washington* (Boldt decision)

1975   Indian Self-Determination and Educational Assistance Act

       Council of Energy Resource Tribes founded

       Leonard Peltier conviction

1978   American Indian Religious Freedom Act

       Tribally Controlled Community College Act

       Federal Acknowledgment Program established

1980   Penobscot/Passamaquoddy claims settled (Maine)

1985   Wilma Mankiller becomes principal Cherokee
        chief

1988   Indian Gaming Regulatory Act

1990   Native American Grave Protection and
        Repatriation Act

        Employment Division v. Smith decision

1992   Mashantucket Pequots open Foxwoods Casino

1994   Tribal Self-Governance Act

2002   Thirty-two tribal colleges in operation

2004   National Museum of the American Indian
        schduled to open

American Indians in U.S. History

Chapter 1

PEOPLING THE LAND

Debating Human Origins in America

 At a hydroplane race along the Columbia River in June 1996, two students watching the competition saw more than they had expected. What later proved to be part of a skeleton was poking up through the mud, and so they hurried to call the local sheriff. At first the authorities assumed the bones were those of a recent murder victim. Soon, however, James C. Chatters, who did skeletal forensics work for the coroner, realized that the remains were much older, and in fact the bones ultimately proved to be those of a prehistoric man from approximately 9,300 years ago. News of this discovery might have attracted only modest media attention except for one startling fact: Kennewick Man, as he became known, had no physical features that might link him to the ancestors of modern American Indian groups. Rather, the skeleton showed similarities to modern-day Europeans or Pacific Islanders. This discovery brought immediate public attention to long-standing academic and scientific debates over how and when humans had reached the Americas.

Until well into the 1990s most scientists agreed that humans crossed the modern Bering Sea by walking from Siberia to Alaska on land that now lies far below the ocean surface. According to this theory, during the last Ice Age, the nearly unending cold locked much of the world's water in vast glaciers that stretched across large parts of the Northern Hemisphere. With so much water removed from the oceans, their levels dropped hundreds of feet, exposing an 800-mile-wide land bridge called Beringia that connected Asia and North America. To call this route a bridge is deceptive because at that width it was broader than the expanse from the Mississippi River to the Rocky Mountains. Clearly, people could cross Beringia without ever seeing the oceans at all.

Supporters of this overland-migration theory note that sometime between 35,000 and 15,000 years ago the earth's climate began a gradual change. Warming initiated glacial melting, and as the ice sheets shrank, gaps opened in what may have been impenetrable barriers of ice. The newly formed passes allowed groups of hunters from northeastern Siberia to follow the herds of big game animals into the Americas. For several thousand years, small bands of people from Asia trekked eastward and southward, taking advantage of the passages around and through the ice fields. By about 13,000 years ago these Paleo-Indians had spread across North and South America. Time erased most signs of their presence, but ancient sites where they killed large game have provided scientists with stone spear points found resting among the bones of their prey. Around 10,000 years ago the gradual climatic warming and perhaps the increasing numbers and skills of the hunters combined to drive such large animals as mammoths, giant camels, and ground sloths to extinction. Prehistoric man stood supreme!

This version of the prehistoric settlement of the Western Hemisphere now faces challenges from several quarters. Many traditional Indian accounts offer versions of tribal origins and history, explaining how their ancestors came to be in America, that differ vastly from this one. Most groups have creation stories that say little or nothing about traveling great distances to reach their modern locations. A sampling of those accounts reveals differing descriptions of ancient events and actions. Often these say that "the People" or "the only True Men," as they called themselves, came from under the earth. For example, the creation story of the Zuni people who live on the Arizona–New Mexico border describes how they "first emerged out of Mother Earth's fourth womb at a sacred place deep within the Grand Canyon." From there they migrated slowly along the Colorado River, building and abandoning villages as they went. Finally they came to what they call the "Middle Place" near the headwaters of the Zuni River, where they still live.

Although many tribal origin stories recount similar tales of coming up from the underworld, others tell of descending to earth from above. The Iroquois of New York describe human origins as beginning with a pregnant woman who fell to earth through a hole in the floor of the sky. A Maidu version has the creator descending from the sky to a water-covered earth, where he used mud brought by a turtle from the sea floor to make the earth's land and its people. The Cherokee version also describes the earth as covered with water. After a water beetle brought mud to the surface, the land grew so that the animals, plants, and people could descend from the sky to live on the earth. Except for the Paiute story in which the raven helped to crack ice that blocked their ancestors' travels, these legends include nothing that suggests the tribal people had any memory of living anywhere other than in the Western Hemisphere.

Whatever cultural or religious value these tribal accounts have for their listeners, like accounts of Moses descending from Mount Sinai with the Ten Commandments, they offer little real data for scientists seeking clues to prehistoric migrations or settlement. As a result, scholars in such fields as archaeology, paleontology, geology, and linguistics continue their efforts to learn about humans in the early Americas through other means. The 1990 passage of the Native American Grave Protection and Repatriation Act by the federal government accelerated their efforts. That legislation called on museums, universities, and historical societies to examine their holdings of tribal artifacts and funerary remains to determine if present-day Indian groups had any religious or other claims on these materials. This demand focused renewed attention on items long locked away in collections but rarely studied. As curators and scientists studied these items, often for the first time in decades, they made discoveries that challenged not only tribal ideas about their ancestors' location of origin but also existing theories of early human activities here.

At the beginning of the twenty-first century, repeated and sometimes acrimonious debates have focused on several issues. The first of these is "When did early man first arrive in the Americas?" The long-accepted theory held that between 15,000 and 10,000 years ago small bands of hunters moved east from Siberia. Their descendants left behind spear points found at Clovis, New Mexico; thus they came to be known as the Clovis people. Early skeletal remains found at their kill sites in the Southwest date to 11,000 B.C., but the hunters spread rapidly across North America, reaching the Atlantic coast of Nova Scotia in Canada as early as 8500 B.C. and eastern Virginia at about the same time. Until the 1990s, most scholars accepted the theory that the Clovis people represented the earliest group of what were called Paleo-Indians to arrive in North America.

Since then, a variety of new techniques, including work with human DNA taken from skeletal remains and discoveries of implements that predate Clovis materials, have pushed back estimates of early migrations and settlement. At a site named Monte Verde, in Chile, researchers located a village of about thirty hunters who lived in mastodon-hide shelters some 14,500 years ago, which predates by a full one thousand years any Clovis materials found thus far. Thomas Dillehay, chief archaeologist at the site, faced such opposition to his findings that eventually he invited a blue-ribbon panel to visit Monte Verde and evaluate his data. To their surprise, the "experts" came away persuaded that Dillehay was correct.

Meanwhile, other scholars working at sites in the eastern United States began to present evidence that pushed early human occupation of those areas farther back in time than the Clovis era. At Saltville in Virginia, archaeologists have uncovered tools of stone and bone amid mastodon bones thought to be at least 14,000 years old. Farther east at Cactus Hill, Virginia, scientists decided to dig below the earth level containing Clovis era spear points. To their amazement, they found, in layers, different and older weapon points and the stones used to make them now estimated to be at least 15,500 years old. Still older dates have been suggested for the Meadowcroft Rockshelter in western Pennsylvania. For several decades researchers there have sifted through remains that include implements, charcoal they believe to be the residue of cooking fires, and even woven materials dating to at least 17,000 years ago. A dig in Kenosha County, Wisconsin, has found piles of bones from butchered mammoths that are at least 13,500 years old. Other sites, ranging from eastern Brazil north to Florida and west to Alaska, have yielded prehistoric items that scientists agree push back by centuries the previous estimated time frame for early human occupation of the Western Hemisphere.

The evidence of pre-Clovis settlement has increased the debate over a second issue: "Where did the early peoples originate?" If the glaciers remained in place, blocking migration across Beringia until nine or ten thousand years ago, how did the early people get here? On this issue researchers have found little evidence. Small boats, whether of wood or skin, have long since disappeared, and coastal lowlands that might provide evidence of human activities now lie under the oceans. Yet it seems clear that some of the migrants must have traveled by water. Recent findings suggest that they probably journeyed from island to island or along the edges of the ice fields, hunting for maritime animals and following the flights of land birds to find their way across the oceans. In response to their skeptics, those who support this interpretation note that humans traveled from mainland Asia to Australia at least 40,000 years ago. There seems little reason to reject the possibility that early hunters worked their way along the edges of the ice fields across both the

North Pacific and the Atlantic Ocean while finding their way to the Americas.

The theory that people might have worked their way west from Europe has only recently found some scientific acceptance, or even a willingness among scientists to consider the idea. This theory is based on at least two kinds of archaeological data. Evidence of pre-Clovis occupation in both Virginia and South Carolina raises interesting questions. The spear points found at several sites differ markedly from the later Clovis workmanship. In fact, they resemble artifacts from the Solutrean culture of southern France and Spain far more than anything now recognized as having come from Asia. The discovery of red-ocher burial sites containing non-Mongoloid skeletal remains also raises questions. Such burial practices also existed in Western Europe but not in Asia. If these materials have been dated correctly as having been laid down hundreds or even thousands of years before Clovis era people occupied those sites, then they must have come from migrations that predated the land-bridge migrations or from Europe, because the glaciers blocked land migration from Asia at that time.

Scientists have unearthed specific sets of bones which suggest that some of the early people who came to the Americas might not have come from northern Asia at all. For example, the Spirit Caveman, found near Fallon, Nevada, dates to 9,400 years ago. Had he been a part of the overland migrations of Asian hunters to Alaska, he should resemble modern Indians, but he does not. Rather, he appears to have descended from the ancestors of the aboriginal Ainu of modern Japan or groups from Southeast Asia. The Buhl Woman, found near Buhl, Idaho, is thought to be 10,600 years old. She too bears almost no physical resemblance to members of any modern tribal group. These tentative identifications resulted largely from the 1990 federal order requiring museums to examine the burial items in their holdings and when possible, to return these materials to the tribes considered to have descended from the ancient groups. That action brought archaeologists and other scientists into direct confrontations with Indians and with the federal government.

As a result of the federal directive to examine their holdings carefully, scientists developed a highly detailed set of ninety measurements for each of the nearly two thousand skulls held in various museums. Often, however, their findings have angered nearly everyone involved in the issue. While individual tribes demand that the bones be returned to them for proper burial, the archaeologists insist that physical evidence proves the skeletons came from individuals who could not have been the ancestors of modern Indians. Not only do the skulls bear little or no resemblance to present-day Indian physical types, but they clearly have more in common with Ainu, Polynesians, or even early Europeans than they do with contemporary groups in the United States. As arguments escalated, they led to threats of suits in the federal courts and produced rulings by the Department of the Interior that particular skeletons be given to individual tribes.

The suggestion that early settlers in America might not be the direct ancestors of modern Indians angered many. Pointing to their creation stories, many Native Americans believe that they have always lived in North America. Certainly they never consider the possibility that others may have arrived here first. Elders have taught that Indians have not always looked exactly as they do now, and some scientists agree. They accept the possibility that during the last 10,000 years the appearance of humans in North America most likely changed, perhaps drastically. That claim provided the basis for demands that museum skeletal holdings be turned over to the tribes for interment. The Shoshone-Bannock tribe of Idaho pressed their claim to the Buhl Woman successfully and reburied her. Both the Northern Paiute from Nevada, who asked to be allowed to rebury the Spirit Caveman, and the Umatilla of Washington, who demanded that the Kennewick Man be turned over to them, moved aggressively to assert what they considered their tribal rights. However, in both cases the skeletal profiles scientists developed do not support the tribal claims, and so the debate continues.

The ongoing story of the Kennewick Man bones since their uncovering shows how contentious the issues surrounding the treatment of skeletal remains have become. Shortly after the discovery, researchers judged the skull to be that of a non-Indian, perhaps a Pacific Islander or even a European. Within two months of that announcement, the Army Corps of Engineers took possession of the skeleton. When scientists asked for permission to examine the engineers' study of the bones, the Corps denied them access. This led quickly to the publication of notices that the Confederated Tribes of the Umatilla were to get the skeleton for reburial. In October 1996 scientists filed a complaint that challenged the actions of the Corps of Engineers. What they wanted was a chance to do Carbon-14 and DNA testing on a tiny portion of the bones. Meanwhile, archaeologists, physical anthropologists, tribal leaders, and bureaucrats all argued about what was to be done with the remains. The major news outlets and television networks ran interviews and articles, all of which brought the question of early human presence in the Americas to public attention as never before. In August 2002, Judge John Jelderks of the U.S. District Court in Oregon ruled against those who wanted immediate reburial of the skeleton. So the research on Kennewick Man continues.

The newest and in many ways most interesting part of the search for early man in the Western Hemisphere has arisen from the recent tracing of the human genome. DNA researchers now claim that all humans descended from early peoples who came from sub-Saharan Africa as recently as 100,000 years ago. From there they migrated across Asia and Europe to the rest of the world. More specific studies of DNA have uncovered a rare genetic factor called haplogroup-X-DNA that is passed down through women. Some geneticists claim that this factor shows that the earliest migrants to the Americas had "no obvious ties to any Asian groups." They could have been earlier pioneers to the New World from Asia, or they could have come from

Europe, where the haplogroup-X still exists among a small portion of the population. Whatever scientists make of the new evidence, it seems clear that the older theory of a migration over the land bridge and the tribal ideas about their ancestors' origination in the Americas are too simplistic. The prehistoric process of peopling the Western Hemisphere was far more complex.

The scientific findings have received their sharpest criticism from Lakota Sioux writer Vine Deloria, Jr., who objects to both the methods and the theories scientists have developed when studying early human presence here. Mercilessly heaping ridicule on the Bering Sea–crossing theory, Deloria asks how the herds of Pleistocene animals the hunters supposedly followed east from Asia could have crossed Beringia when ice covered the region. He also says that scientific data based on Carbon-14 dating techniques are flawed or even entirely wrong. Deloria agrees with some scholars when he claims that early man may have been in the Americas much earlier than the Clovis era, but he asserts that a human population lived here for several hundred thousand years and may even have evolved here independently from those peoples in the rest of the world. With the recent DNA findings, few other researchers still accept the multisite theory of human development, but debate continues over how and when humans came to this continent.

Though the disputes remain unresolved, the new evidence has convinced many researchers that the story of prehistoric migrations to America is much more complicated than previously thought. It now appears that repeated movements of small groups took place over thousands of years, stretching back much farther in time than earlier findings had suggested. Many of those migrations brought people not just from Siberia, but also from Southeast Asia, the Pacific Islands, and possibly even Western Europe. As scientists continue to locate artifacts and reexamine Clovis era sites to see if further evidence lies beneath them, they continue seeking a more compete understanding of how, when, and from where early man came.

THE ARCHAIC ERA

Whatever direction these debates take, at this point the issue of human occupation and development in North America after 9000 B.C. is less contested. Scientists have concluded that the climate in the Northern Hemisphere moderated around that time, and the ice fields gradually melted. Most agree that these climatic changes drove such large mammals as mammoths, sloths, and camels to extinction, although a few scholars claim that the early hunters destroyed them. As people sought new animal sources for food, they spread across the continent rapidly, and by 8500 B.C. they had migrated as far as the Atlantic coast of Nova Scotia in Canada. Wherever they lived, Paleo-Indians faced a variety of environments. Archaeological remains suggest that during what scientists call the Archaic Era (8500 B.C. to 1000 B.C.), these people developed a relatively common culture. Most lived in small family groups or bands. Together they hunted, fished, gathered, and used food sources found within an area perhaps one hundred miles across. They made their tools out of stone, bone, or wood and fashioned household implements out of wood, shells, and reeds.

Scientific data for the Archaic Era remain modest as few artifacts have survived. This means that archaeologists must work chiefly with weapons, pottery, and tools, and these items provide only a limited amount of information about how early people lived. Because researchers unearthed mostly weapons from that era, they began to name groups of people according to the sites where their spear points were found. Thus, one can read that people such as the Sandia, Clovis, Folsum, or Cascade made unique implements and lived in towns or regions bearing those names. The first three of those sites lie in present-day New Mexico, where the dry climate preserved the evidence. The Cascade people got their name from an area along the Pacific coast. All of these groups left behind implements and weapons, and some of these can be dated by various methods. Scientists consider the Sandia items to be among the oldest in the West, assigning them dates of between 15,000 B.C. and 10,000 B.C.

Of these early groups, the Clovis people left the most extensive remains. Scholars have found their delicate, well-crafted stone spear points at sites ranging from the Southwest to the Atlantic coast. Discovered near Clovis, New Mexico, early in the twentieth century, these items took their name from that locality. Their makers lost or abandoned the weapons among the bones of the large animals they hunted. Based on clues from existing remains, archaeologists depict these people as wearing animal skins and fiber sandals, using their long, slender, fluted spear points successfully for thousands of years, and subsisting primarily on meat from their hunting. Clovis artifacts have been found from New Mexico eastward to coastal Virginia and South Carolina—clear evidence that the people adapted to life in various geographic regions.

Gradually the Clovis people disappeared or mixed with others who made Folsum points, first discovered during the 1920s near Folsum, New Mexico. Nomadic hunters like their predecessors, these people tracked early bison, deer, and elk. They may have been more numerous than earlier Paleo-Indian groups, based on evidence they left of cooperative hunts. Tactics such as driving animals over cliffs or into marshy river bottoms made their food-gathering more effective than the efforts of earlier small hunting bands. Like the Clovis people, the Folsum groups spread over much of North America and left evidence of their activities all the way to the Atlantic coast. Except for a different type of spear point, the items researchers have found from these groups suggest that the roving hunters shared a similar culture and a similar level of technology.

Sometime between 7000 B.C. and 4500 B.C. the Folsum disappeared or evolved into people who developed the Plainview culture, a group scientists see as a sort of link connecting the early hunting cultures with their more modern Indian descendants. These Plainview or Plano people began hunting the increasingly large herds of bison on the plains. They learned to preserve meat by drying it in the hot summer sun and mixing it with fat, seeds, and berries that they packed into containers made from animal intestines. This produced a sort of trail mix—called Pemmican today—that resembled sausage but without much of its meat. Another climatic shift occurred between 5000 B.C. and about 3500 B.C. This seems to have reduced the herds of large animals the hunters followed, and so the Plano people migrated after the animals or changed their subsistence patterns. For whatever reasons, their culture disappeared, and almost no evidence of human occupation of the Plains for the next thousand years has been discovered.

Artifacts from approximately 3000 B.C. suggest that people living in America at that time had developed new skills for using the environment effectively. They had begun making and using pottery, which allowed them to store and prepare food. Some groups had begun to cultivate grains and squash as well. Although physical evidence for that era is limited, what has been found suggests continuing improvement in hunting weapons and an increased knowledge of edible plants, as well as more efficient fishing and harvesting of seafood along the coasts. All of these changes resulted in a gradual expansion of populations. In every part of the country, people settled into routines that depended on their local resources. For generations, even centuries, they lived in what became accepted as their home areas, becoming "Natives" in their particular locales.

Because humans reached North America at different times, separated by hundreds or even thousands of years, the cultures that emerged differed widely. The societies that developed depended on the individual groups' knowledge and technology, but also on available local resources. Groups that settled along the Pacific coast from Oregon north to Alaska established the Cascade culture, making their living from the products of the rich coastal waters. Some became seafarers, hunting whales and sea lions often far from shore. Others dwelling near the coast or along the rivers that flowed into the ocean depended heavily on the annual salmon runs for their basic food supply. Inland bands living near the mountains spent less time fishing and subsisted by hunting deer and elk and gathering seeds and bulbs. All of these peoples depended on roots, berries, nuts, seeds, and plant fibers to make their lives comfortable.

Vastly different lifestyles emerged among those who dwelt between the Sierra Nevada Mountains and the Rockies farther to the east. Sparse resources there limited the population. The arid climate meant that hunters had little choice beyond small animals such as rabbits and ground squirrels. As a result, these people lived in small bands and supported themselves by hunting and by gathering seeds, fruit, and nuts whenever possible. Working with reeds and other plant fibers, they made baskets, twine, nets for trapping birds and small animals, and sandals. Excavators have unearthed baskets and twine dating to roughly 9000 B.C. made by these desert peoples. The Spirit Caveman found near Fallon, Nevada, was an early inhabitant of this culture, one that lasted for at least five thousand years in parts of the desert West.

Other hunting groups lived at the fringes of the plains, gradually coming to depend on the herds of bison that grew to dominate the central grasslands. These people hunted cooperatively, using drives to frighten large numbers of animals over the cliffs of ridges, into pens or corrals, or toward the marshes and quicksand bogs along the major rivers. They obtained meat, hides, bones, horn, and sinew from the shaggy beasts, yet the bison herds often held less attraction for them than one might expect. The Plains dwellers hunted on foot and had only dogs to help them transport the hides and meat from the hunting sites. Also, the animals moved frequently, often staying hundreds of miles from the hunters' villages. As a result, the bison provided an erratic food supply at best for those who lived at the edges of the Plains or at the base of the Rockies. This encouraged people in those places to begin cultivating food crops in order to supplement their diet. Centuries later, their descendants would acquire horses from the Europeans, revolutionizing their lives.

THE GOLDEN AGE

By about 1200 B.C., the inhabitants of America entered an era that scholars have labeled the Golden Age of prehistory. The term is employed because by that time many of the early societies had learned how to use local resources effectively. Not only did they plant and harvest crops, but they also developed the use of repeated and large-scale fires to shape their environment. In the Pacific Northwest they burned grasses and bushes, clearing land to encourage the growth of bracken and camas. In the Midwest and East other groups burned the undergrowth to open the forests and thus encourage the growth of berry bushes and other shrubs, which attracted large numbers of browsing animals such as white-tailed deer. On the prairies people used fires as part of their hunting, driving animals into traps, over embankments, or into marshes where they might be caught and killed more easily. These activities developed over several centuries and at different speeds, bringing long-term, substantial changes to the landscape. By this era the Native peoples in many parts of the country had learned to process and store foods for several years at a time, so they no longer had to worry continually about their daily supply. Certainly by 1000 B.C. agriculture had spread from west to east, and across much of North America large-scale, well-organized societies emerged. Some of these societies still functioned at least a thousand years later, but several disappeared "mysteriously," or at least for reasons not yet determined.

During the Golden Age, ancestors of later desert dwellers of the Southwest struggled to settle in that region because of the limited resources they found. Between 1000 B.C. and A.D. 1000 at least three distinct cultures developed there. The Hohokam settled on riverine lands that stretched southward from the Gila River in southern Arizona into the Mexican state of Sonora. There they built towns with square buildings on or near the river floodplains and irrigated hundreds of acres of land, raising corn, beans, pumpkins, and squash. Like other early peoples, they welcomed traders who brought such things as sea-turtle shells and turquoise from California. Highly successful farmers, they continued to live in what is now southern Arizona until after A.D. 1300, when their society appears to have disintegrated. Why this happened is not entirely clear, but scientists offer several possible explanations. During the 1200s, gradual climatic changes and a series of droughts brought chaos to these sedentary communities. Heavy winter rains flooded the fields, and silt blocked the irrigation canals that had taken so much labor to construct and maintain. Because the people had watered the same fields for generations, the soil became clogged with mineral salts, which led to smaller crops. The crop shortages and an increasing population apparently overwhelmed the people's ability to feed themselves. As a result, by A.D. 1400 they had left the large towns, scattering across the countryside for survival. Their descendants, the present O'odham groups, referred to them as the Hohokam, people "who are used up."

At about the same time, a second desert culture, the Mogollon, developed in what is now central Arizona. These people lived in the mountains east and north of Phoenix, which today bear their name. Another farming people, the Mogollon produced some of the most beautiful prehistoric pottery made in the Southwest. Active participants in the extensive trade networks that then existed, they had many connections with other early peoples in northern Mexico and in California. These influences appear in their pottery designs, which include many kinds of ocean fish not found within hundreds of miles of their settlements. Archaeologists have identified artifacts from at least twenty Mogollon villages along the Mimbres River, marking these people as the producers of the most varied and beautiful ceramic work in the region. Like the Hohokam, this culture faded from the scene during the A.D. 1300s, and scholars assume that the climatic changes of that era and perhaps Apache raids explain the disappearance. No one is certain which modern Indians may have descended from the Mogollon.

Perhaps the most intriguing of the prehistoric people in the Southwest, the Anasazi or "ancient ones" or "ancient enemies," as the Navajo call them, appear to have been the ancestors of modern Puebloan groups. By A.D. 700 they had settled at the southern end of the Colorado Plateau and in what are now desert lands in Arizona, New Mexico, and Colorado. Expert basket-makers, they hunted, gathered, and farmed across the rugged countryside. Between A.D. 900 and 1000 they constructed modest adobe and stone buildings, and during the next several centuries they erected large towns with multistoried stone buildings. A series of well-paved roads stretched out from their apparent cultural center at Chaco Canyon in New Mexico, connecting them to many other communities. The seven pueblos there had at least thirteen hundred rooms and housed some six thousand people. Pueblo Bonito, the largest of these, stood four stories high and included four hundred rooms.

Communities that size depended on agriculture. The residents at Chaco Canyon farmed small plots of ground that they watered by hand as well as others they managed to irrigate using a series of canals. During the thirteenth century, regional droughts devastated the crops, and in a few generations this society had collapsed. At Chaco Canyon the thousands of people split into smaller groups and scattered across the region. Until the 1990s, scholars attributed the abrupt collapse of Anasazi culture almost entirely to the recurrent droughts that struck the Southwest. More recently, however, some have suggested that warfare may have been part of the drama as well. Substantial evidence of human slaughter and cannibalism has been found. For example, specimens of human tissue in preserved samples of ancient human feces found at an Anasazi site provide incontrovertible evidence that some cannibalism took place. Large numbers of human bones bearing marks that could only have resulted from their having been butchered and stirred in cooking pots have been found there as well. Whether the cooking and eating of people resulted from invasion and conquest, was part of symbolic religious ceremonies, or occurred for other reasons is uncertain. What remains clear, however, is that, whether because of these actions or despite them, by A.D. 1300 this culture had collapsed and the people had left Chaco Canyon.

In the Mississippi Valley region far to the east, the later Archaic Era population developed what is known as the Woodland culture. Unlike the West, which offered only limited amounts of good cropland and lacked dependable water supplies, this area had a variety of resources. As a result, many small settlements developed, often connected by wide-ranging traders who carried items for exchange over hundreds of miles. The earliest known settlement of any size stood at Poverty Point, Louisiana, so named because these people left so few pottery shards behind for scholars to examine. Apparently the people preferred to carve their bowls out of soapstone rather than to fire them. Perhaps they never found clay that made good ceramics. Begun shortly before 1400 B.C., this community built large-scale earthworks that are among the earliest known north of Mexico. There, near the Mississippi River, they built a series of six octagonal earth ridges that enclosed more than ten square miles of land. On the terraces inside the ridges they built conical and bird-shaped earthen mounds ranging from twenty to seventy-five feet high, where they buried some of their leaders.

The inhabitants situated many of their houses on the earth ridges, and the community seems to have used most of the enclosed space for ceremonies, public business, and play. Some scholars contend that the leaders and merchants from Poverty Point were Olmec people who had come from Mexico. In what is present-day Louisiana, they dominated the local population and patterned their community on what they had known at home. They built earth mounds like those common in parts of Central America at the time. Wherever these people might have originated, they were skilled stone workers, making axes, hollow drills, and other tools as well as pendants shaped like humans, birds, and insects. The community had considerable astronomical knowledge, identifying the equinoxes and solstices that marked the changing seasons. There is evidence that they understood magnetism, and it appears that they used magnetic stones in some ceremonies. Whether they developed their skills and knowledge independently or learned from trade and other contacts with people across the Gulf of Mexico is unclear.

Like most of the prehistoric cultures in America, the Poverty Point people disappeared or merged with groups that later became prominent. By 800 B.C. another Woodland culture, the Adena, emerged in the Ohio River Valley to the north. Their villages dotted riverbanks in present-day Ohio, Kentucky, and West Virginia, and they too built earth mounds sometimes more than sixty feet high. Often these covered burial huts or chambers. Like the Poverty Point people, they laid out earthen ridges or embankments but on a smaller scale than their predecessors. The Adena buried some of their dead in mounds, which they built by the hundreds in the Ohio Valley over a period of more than a thousand years. They enjoyed a varied diet that included seeds, nuts, fish, shellfish, birds, and animals. Their technology resembled that of other late Archaic Era people, including stone axes, chipped weapon points, and stone pipes, as well as bone, wood, and copper personal ornaments.

By about 100 B.C. a new Woodland group, the Hopewell, emerged in Illinois. They seem to have benefited from a gradual warming trend that made farming more successful than it had been several centuries earlier. Using hoes made from the shoulder blades of deer or other large animals, they planted and raised corn in several of their communities. Hundreds of Hopewell villages stretched along the major rivers in the East, as these people came to dominate the area from western New York to the edge of the plains and from the Gulf of Mexico north to the Great Lakes. The use of mounds begun by earlier cultures continued, as the villagers built embankments often stretching several miles in length. These people buried wealthy and powerful individuals in earthworks too, but now often included wives, retainers, servants, and personal goods as part of the rituals. While some mounds stood sixty to seventy feet high, others took the shape of birds, animals, and snakes and could stretch for hundreds of yards and contain thousands of tons of dirt.

Throughout the early Woodland cultures the leaders wielded enough authority to persuade or force extraordinary amounts of toil from their citizens. All of these vast engineering projects resulted from hand labor. These Indians had no domesticated animals to assist with the work. Such control over the common people could not achieve everything, though, and by A.D. 350, when the climate began cooling again, the Hopewell villagers saw their orderly world begin to unravel. In Illinois and the Ohio Valley region the shortened growing seasons endangered food supplies, and individual villages began taking independent action. It seems likely that intervillage warfare occurred as the people faced increasing competition for diminished resources. The efforts needed to erect and maintain defensive walls around the villages took much of the time previously used for mound-building. Farther to the south, where the climate remained mild, Hopewell villages continued to function in the old ways. Sites in Tennessee, Louisiana, and Florida all suggest that some mound-building continued there long after it had ceased in the North.

The cool, wet climate that initiated the Hopewell decline encouraged other Midwestern Indian farmers to develop crops that required a shorter growing season. Gradually the weather shifted again so that by A.D. 800 the Mississippi Valley was experiencing warmer and drier weather. By this time, maize cultivation had spread, and corn became an essential staple for feeding people in existing villages and towns. A new society evolved into the Mississippian Culture, which remained in place until the eve of contact with intruding Europeans centuries later. Again, scholars lack evidence to pinpoint the origins of these people, but they theorize that this culture grew out of the existing societies in the lower Mississippi Valley.

CAHOKIA

The city of Cahokia, standing near the Mississippi River but across the water from the site of present-day St. Louis, became the center of this society. Established as early as A.D. 950, it appears to have resulted from an intrusion onto the local scene, for it featured a strong log palisade for defense against attacks by local groups. The people there enjoyed trade and cultural contacts with others in eastern Texas, Mississippi, and Illinois. They chose the site for the community wisely: an area with excellent soil, a dependable water supply, and plentiful stands of timber. These qualities attracted people, so that by the time the city was strong enough to dominate the entire center of the country, large subsidiary towns had grown up along major streams nearby. Cahokia itself covered nearly five square miles and had a population of nearly 30,000. At that size, it represented the largest urban center to develop north of Mexico in the prehistoric era.

To its neighbors, Cahokia's stout defenses, large population, and obvious powers had to have been impressive. However, the huge earthen mounds built by its inhabitants characterize the community more than anything else. Some of them still dominate the local landscape. Monk's Mound, so called because a small monastery once stood atop it, reached a height of more than one hundred feet. Even today, it covers an area larger than a football field and includes some 22 million cubic feet of soil. It is by far the largest of all extant earthworks found within the United States. Built entirely of dirt, it grew in stages over several hundred years. More than one hundred other mounds of various shapes and sizes remain as an indication of the power Cahokia's leaders exercised over their community.

By A.D. 1000, the city had grown to its full size and served as the economic, political, and religious center for a vast network of towns and villages that reached across half of the continent. As they spread their influence outward from Cahokia, the Mississippians established communities as far apart as Red Wing, Minnesota, and Etowah in

Georgia. Their expansion, however, brought resistance from some groups living at the edges of the Cahokia sphere of influence. Evidence from one site includes the skeletal remains of young men, presumably killed in fighting, that had been chopped to pieces and then dumped into the refuse piles. It is not possible to know whether the victims came from the ranks of the victors or the vanquished, or perhaps from prisoners executed later. Nevertheless, their presence indicates that some local groups resisted stoutly. Scholars think that by A.D. 1400, Cahokia had collapsed. The large population had denuded the nearby hills, taking all the timber for housing and fuel. This increased flooding and erosion, thus damaging food production. It seems likely that centuries' worth of refuse, garbage, and sewage polluted local water sources and brought disease and occasional deaths.

AT THE END OF THE ARCHAIC ERA

When the Golden Age cultures went into decline or disappeared, life for most aboriginal groups continued, often taking several centuries to change. Between A.D. 1000 and A.D. 1500, many of the ancestors of modern American Indians moved into the regions they were occupying when the first Europeans arrived. In the Southwest, descendants of the earlier desert cultures dispersed and became the Puebloans of northern Arizona and New Mexico or the desert dwellers of southern Arizona. At the same time, small groups of Apacheans drifted southward east of the Rocky Mountains and moved gradually into the region. Ancestors of the Utes and Navajos followed, apparently reaching the area only a short time before the earliest Spanish invaders arrived.

On the plains the culture that had developed by A.D. 1500 would give rise to such later tribes as the Blackfeet, Cheyenne, Arapaho, Comanche, and Siouan groups. These people followed the bison, and that activity led them into a mostly nomadic existence. Long before they acquired horses from the Spanish or their tribal neighbors, they had become effective hunters. Some groups like the Lakota Sioux came to the plains from their previous home north and west of Lake Superior many generations after the hunting cultures had attained predominance there. Because of their numbers, they retained the nomadic way of life longer than some others and so came to represent the hunting cultures of the region in popular culture.

East of the plains along the Missouri, Platte, and Kansas Rivers, other groups settled during this era. To the south, the Wichita and later the Kansa combined buffalo-hunting with farming along the rich river-bottom lands. They built lodges of grass and reeds in summer and sturdier earthen dwellings for winter. Each year after planting their fields in late spring, they hunted on the plains. By late summer they returned to their villages for the rest of the year. North of them, Caddoan groups, who became the Pawnees of Nebraska and the Arikara of South Dakota, followed a similar annual cycle. The Arikara villages became some of the major trading centers in the upper Missouri Valley. Plains hunters traveled there to exchange surplus meat, hides, and horns for food crops the villagers raised. These trading patterns continued well into the nineteenth century.

East of the Mississippi River, three cultural groups—Muskogeans in the South, Algonquians along most of the Atlantic coast, and Iroquoians in New York, Tennessee, and Georgia—came to dominate the area. All three lived in agricultural villages, although the Iroquois had substantially larger towns than the other groups. They combined farming, hunting, and gathering, but the coastal Algonquian groups also obtained much of their food from the rivers and nearby ocean. The presence of strong palisades used for defense of some Iroquoian villages suggests that raiding and war played important roles in their lives. All three cultures shared economic practices and technology, but their languages and religious practices kept them apart as competitors if not enemies.

Like people in other parts of the country, the eastern villagers shifted their locations gradually, depending on hunting success, the presence or absence of enemies, and modest climatic changes. Ethnologists estimate that by A.D. 1500, nearly six hundred distinct groups had emerged across the country. Numbering perhaps four or five million people, these groups took part in wide-ranging trade networks that made available ocean shells from each coast, mica from the Appalachians, copper from the Great Lakes area, precious stones from the Far West, and even tropical feathers. Yet, despite the extensive trading, suspicion resulting from raiding and warfare continued to separate groups. Actually, few Indians lived as part of formally organized tribes at the time. Rather, most dwelt in nearly independent villages. Occasionally they joined with nearby communities that shared their language and culture for trade or war. By A.D. 1500 dozens of cultures existed that linked the prehistoric people with the groups who occupied what would become the United States several centuries later.

SUGGESTED READINGS

Cordell, Linda S. *Prehistory of the Southwest*. Orlando, Fla.: Academic Press, 1984.

Deloria, Vine, Jr. *Red Earth, White Lies*. Golden, Col.: Fulcrum Publishing, 1997.

Dillehay, Thomas. *The Settlement of the Americas: A New Prehistory*. New York: Basic Books, 2000.

Fagan, Brian M. *Ancient North America*. New York: Thames & Hudson, 1995.

Jennings, Jesse D. *Prehistory of North America*. Mountain View, Cal.: Mayfield, 1989.

Kehoe, Alice Beck. *North American Indians: A Comprehensive Account*, 2d ed. Englewood Cliffs, N.J.: Prentice Hall, 1992.

Parfit, Michael. "The Dawn of Humans: Hunt for the First Americans." *National Geographic* 198, no. 6 (December 2000): 40–67.

Preston, Douglas. "Cannibals of the Canyon." *New Yorker*, November 1998, 76–89.

[Staff] "Who Were the First Americans?" *Newsweek*, 26 April 1999, 50–57.

Young, Biloine Whiting, and Melvile L. Fowler. *Cahokia: The Great Native American Metropolis*. Urbana and Chicago: University of Illinois Press, 2000.

Chapter 2

MEETING THE INVADERS, *1500–1700*

 They came from all directions. Some had fur on their faces and looked like dogs, others gazed out through eyes the color of the sky, while a few had hair the color of sand or dried grass. Often word of their arrival raced ahead of them, so that even villages far from any ocean learned something about the strangers. Few Indian accounts of early contacts with the invaders have survived, and some of those come down to the present only in garbled form; but when the Europeans described what happened, they claimed that their presence awed the tribal people. For example, a member of the 1539 de Soto expedition to Florida characterized the Indians of the Southeast as being terrified by the Spaniards. Given the explorers' frequent cruelty and the destruction they brought, this should have come as no surprise. Nearly a century later, in 1630 New England, a colonist claimed that local Indians thought the first ships bearing settlers were floating islands. Clearly that was nonsense, because the villagers there had dealt with explorers, fishermen, and traders sailing along the coast for a half-century by then. A traditional Sauk story described their first encounter with whites rather differently. After dreaming for several decades of meeting a white man, the leader, Na-na-ma-kee, met the French. They gave him a medal, shirt, blanket, and other presents and promised to remain friends. At this first encounter, the Indians were not awestruck or terrorized. The variety of experiences produced widely different accounts.

Wherever they met, the two peoples brought vast differences in thought and custom to the encounter. While European societies operated within guidelines laid down by centralized governments, authoritarian religious groups, and often well-defined class structures, societies in aboriginal America had little in common with them or with each other. In widely scattered places tribal and even multitribal organizations existed, such as the Five Nations Confederacy of the Iroquoians in New York, the confederation led by the Powhatans in Virginia, and the chiefdoms in the Southeast. Otherwise, most groups operated one village at a time, each having a council of respected elders that made recommendations for the group but held only modest enforcement power. A reverence for nature stood at the center of Indian thought and practice, as the villagers assumed that the earth, sun, and moon as well as the plants and animals around them all had spiritual powers. Obviously, this belief put them at odds with the Europeans, who saw nature as a set of resources to be developed and used, and certainly not as entities having spiritual powers. In fact, to Christians then, that idea was heretical. Because at least six hundred distinct groups inhabited the land in 1500, making valid generalizations is difficult. Still, from almost any aspect, tribal life differed from that of the newcomers.

Whether Indians realized it or not, the European invasions of North America would alter their lives forever. In fact, one scholar who studies the relations between the tribal people and the English in colonial Virginia and Carolina wrote that the arrival of the English created a New World, not just for the invaders but also for the Native peoples. Generations of villagers had mastered their environments. They knew the countryside and its resources, plant and animal. When vegetation threatened prized hunting areas, they simply burned the offending shrubs. If the soil in their fields became depleted, they moved

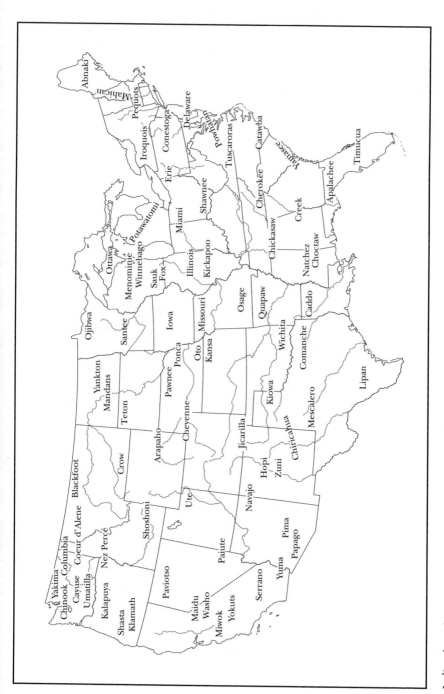

Indian America, 1500

a few miles away, allowing the ground to lie fallow as it recovered. They knew how to deal with their neighbors. The European arrival meant that in many regions the early Indian patterns of subsistence, trade, and warfare changed abruptly. Certainly villages near the coasts or other entry points for the newcomers encountered them first and may have suffered the most consequences, but the invaders' impact spread across the continent. They came from several directions, and nearby tribes had little chance to avoid contact for long.

Actually, even groups living hundreds of miles from intruding Europeans could not escape the disruptions, as new patterns of trade, diplomacy, and warfare developed and came to affect everyone. More important, new diseases, animals, and plants forced Indians to remake their lives. Epidemics of smallpox, influenza, and measles ripped through Native communities, often killing many of the most productive adults who held the villages together. Repeated waves of contagion moved across the countryside, destroying entire populations in places and thoroughly disrupting village societies repeatedly. Demographers have estimated that in the heavily populated areas in central Mexico and on some of the islands in the Caribbean, up to 75 percent of the Native population died from epidemic disease during the first several generations after the Spanish arrived. Although tribes in the south-eastern U.S. had extensive populations, many of the people lived in modest-sized villages; so, the epidemics that swept through that region seem to have killed somewhat fewer people there.

The farther people lived from regions the Europeans visited, the less impact imported diseases had. Yet, even tribes living hundreds of miles from colonial settlements suffered, as visiting Indians and white traders carried sickness with them. At the same time, domesticated animals such as cattle, horses, and hogs changed the landscape forever. Some cattle trampled village cornfields while eating much of the crop. Hogs rooted through marshes, destroying long-used clam beds along the coastal waters. Grazing and browsing animals competed with the native deer and later with the bison on the plains, reducing the supply of food available for Indian hunters. Eventually the introduction of firearms and alcohol brought other difficulties. So, groups far beyond local contact suffered as well as those who lived near the Europeans.

ENCOUNTERING THE SPANISH

The Indians' first experiences with the Spanish proved more violent and disruptive than their meetings with most other Europeans. By 1513, when Ponce de León's expedition reached Florida, some villagers along the Atlantic coast already had met Europeans. As much as five hundred years earlier, Native people on the coast of Newfoundland encountered these strangers. Skraelings, as the Norsemen called the Indians there, fought so well that they drove the Greenlanders away. Other villagers met small numbers of fishermen, traders, and men hoping to seize people they could carry off into slavery, long before the Spanish reached Florida. Those minor incursions alerted some coastal groups to the dangers newcomers posed, and in the Southeast violent clashes marked the meetings between Spaniards and Indians from the start. Ponce de León's Florida experiences illustrate this clearly. When he first landed on the Florida coast in 1513, the Calusa tribe there attacked almost immediately. Eight years later, in 1521, Calusa arrows gave the explorer a mortal wound and drove his men back to Cuba.

Other southeastern tribes had less luck defeating the Spanish a generation later, when Hernando de Soto invaded the region. In 1539 de Soto landed at Tampa Bay leading an army of six hundred men plus an interpreter who had lived with tribes in the region for several years, and hundreds of horses, mules, pigs, and dogs. This force crisscrossed the region during the next four years, bringing misery to each group it met. Many of the village societies there had descended from the earlier Mississippian cultural groups. They lived in multitribal chiefdoms that had prosperous farms, large populations, and well-built communities constructed around temple mounds. Despite their wealth, they lacked the gold or silver de Soto craved, and his demands brought repeated violence. The expedition seized a town abandoned by the Apalachees, and then had to fend off several attacks there. The next summer, when they met the Cofidtachequi people near Camden, South Carolina, the young female leader of those people welcomed the invaders, giving them clothing and freshwater pearls. Not satisfied with these gifts, the Spanish looted the villagers' graves and temples and seized the "queen" before marching away.

The invaders left a trail of destruction as they murdered, looted, raped, and enslaved Indians throughout the entire four-year expedition. Certainly not everything went as they had hoped. The tribal "queen" slipped away from her captors, and as news of the Spaniards' violence and greed spread, villagers along their route all resisted or fled. This enraged the Europeans, who feared that it decreased their chances of finding gold or other precious items. Repeated Indian attacks against de Soto's party reduced its numbers steadily. Several times the tribes attacked successfully, inflicting heavy casualties. In 1540 the Tascaloosa people assaulted the Spaniards, killing and wounding many. The next spring the ancestors of the Chickasaw mauled the weary invaders again. In a surprise raid, they killed many of the horses and hogs and also burned clothing, food, and equipment. Despite these setbacks, the leaders' greed kept the tiny army going in its futile search for wealth. When leaders of the Natchez tribe ridiculed de Soto's claim that he had descended from the sun and rejected his demands, the weary Spanish continued down the Mississippi River. By May 1542, their leader had died and the remainder of the contingent struggled back to Mexico. Their four-year invasion of the thickly settled Southeast brought violent deaths and the spread of European diseases that weakened many of the Native societies. Aboriginal life was permanently disrupted, as the ancestors of the upland tribes such as the people who later became the Choctaw and the Chickasaw moved into areas that had been depopulated by Spanish violence and disease.

Although far from any coast, tribes in the Southwest did not escape Spanish incursions. Continuing stories of richly clad Natives who lived in wealthy cities far north of Mexico caught the interest of authorities in northern New Spain. In 1540 Francisco Vásquez de Coronado led the largest expedition up to that time into the future United States. With some four hundred Spaniards, another three hundred servants and slaves, one thousand Indian allies, and at least as many horses, cattle, mules, and sheep, he traveled north into present-day New Mexico. Having followed the advice of Fray Marcos, who had visited the region earlier, the invaders faced bitter disappointment when they reached the first of the Zuni pueblos, what they thought was the legendary city of Cíbola. This was no city of gold. Rather, it was a three-story mud adobe structure that looked less inviting than some of the farming villages Coronado's men had passed in New Spain. The Zuni offered some food, but when they asked the Spanish to leave, violence erupted. During the fighting, the soldiers' armor protected most of them from injury, and after their defeat, the villagers had to accept the invaders' presence for some time. It seems likely that the Zuni resistance stemmed from rumors they heard from people who had met the invaders earlier about what to expect from the strangers.

Although Coronado seems to have been less greedy and destructive than de Soto, who marched through the Southeast at the same time, his force entered a region with a smaller population and a much weaker economic base. With less fertile land to cultivate, little water for irrigation, and violent Apachean neighbors, the New Mexico tribes experienced severe demographic shocks from the Spanish invasion. Meanwhile the explorers continued their hunt for riches, with one party finding its way north and west to the Grand Canyon. The rest of the expedition reached the vicinity of Albuquerque, where they robbed the nearby Indians repeatedly. When men from various pueblos raided the Spaniards several times during the winter of 1540–41, the invaders struck back. In a vicious attack, the soldiers destroyed the pueblo of Arenal and immolated its defenders. By spring they had destroyed about a dozen of the nearby villages. Soon afterward, in 1541, Coronado led his force east onto the plains, seeking the fabled city of Quivira, but somewhere in Kansas he quit. Instead of a golden city, he found Caddoan people living in villages of grass shelters. Having failed to do anything more than bring destruction and disease to the Indians, he returned to Mexico.

While the Indians probably celebrated when the unwelcome intruders left, their freedom lasted only another fifty years. In 1598 Juan de Oñate led some five hundred soldiers, settlers, and friars up the Rio Grande Valley into New Mexico. These people had no intention of hurrying through on a search for gold; they had come to stay. Pueblo leaders welcomed the Spanish cautiously, soon moving out of one Tewa town to make room for them. When the newcomers also demanded laborers, food, fuel, and clothing, the villagers reluctantly complied. After a short time, some of the soldiers complained about their inactivity and lack of opportunities to find wealth in the new land, and so Oñate sent them exploring. At Acoma Pueblo the soldiers' actions quickly outraged the Indians, who attacked, killing the commanding officer and twelve of his men. At first it seemed that they had succeeded in driving the Spanish away, but the soldiers returned quickly. Seventy well-armored fighting men stormed into the village, and in bitter combat killed nearly eight hundred people. Then the victors hacked off one foot of all the surviving adult males and enslaved the women and children for the next twenty years.

At least temporarily this barbarity seems to have terrified the Puebloan groups in New Mexico and others nearby. The uneasy peace that followed allowed the Spanish settlers along the Rio Grande to spread slowly, as they established small farming communities near the river and its tributaries. Friars lived at many of the pueblos, and troops strove to retain control over the region. Repeated efforts to disrupt and destroy Indian religious practices and to seize and burn sacred items enraged the villagers, but their varied languages and differing cultures often kept them from taking cooperative action against their oppressors. Still, individual pueblos rebelled, and the Spanish had to subdue outbreaks at Zuni in 1632, Taos in 1639, and Jémez in 1644 and 1647, as well as among the Tewa in 1650. These Indian efforts to regain their independence taught the Spanish little, because neither civil nor clerical practices changed. In fact, the invaders continued to impress labor and food from the Indians and to interfere in every way possible with Native ceremonies and cultural practices.

This intolerance helped generate the one successful, multitribal revolt that took place in colonial New Mexico, although other factors played parts too. From 1660 to 1680, the Southwest experienced repeated droughts and higher than normal temperatures. For the agricultural Puebloans, this meant crisis, if not disaster. Each year they produced skimpy crops, and each year Spanish demands for labor and food continued. The droughts also affected their nomadic Apachean neighbors. As the aridity continued, their hunting and gathering became less successful, and so they stepped up their raiding of their sedentary neighbors. Responding to these issues, the village shamans blamed their troubles on the acceptance of Spanish cultural and religious ideas, and they strove to re-energize the kiva religious ceremonies. Whenever Spanish friars or priests learned of this, they seized sacred items and had the Native priests arrested, frequently whipping them publicly and executing several of them.

Outraged by this treatment, in 1680 a Taos shaman named Popé persuaded leaders in almost all of the pueblos that they had to join together and annihilate the Spanish or their own gods might destroy them. On 10 August 1680 a concerted attack on the intruders began, with nearly all of the 17,000 Puebloans cooperating. In the first few days, fighting broke out in almost every town or village and the Indians killed hundreds of Spaniards. They focused much of their fury on the churches and clerics, burning buildings and killing the priests whenever they could. Those settlers who could flee did so, and early in the fighting over one thousand people straggled south to El Paso. In the days that followed, the Indians drove the rest of the population into

Santa Fe. There, after a bitter siege in which the attackers cut off the water supply and burned much of the town, the survivors broke through Indian lines and fled southward. At this point Popé and the other leaders halted the fighting. They wanted to drive the hated invaders out of their pueblos, and once the Spaniards left, they had achieved that goal. In the months that followed, they destroyed more of the invaders' property, particularly the churches and any religious objects discarded earlier.

The Spanish considered the Pueblo Revolt of 1680 to be a nativist and anti-Catholic event. In their view, Popé and the other shamans represented Satan, and their fight was just a part of his battle with Christianity. Given the strong ties between church and state in the Spanish empire at the time, the authorities assumed that they had to avenge their military defeat and the desecration of church items. So, twelve years later, in 1692, Diego de Vargas led troops north from El Paso to reassert control over the New Mexico tribes. By this time the Indians' earlier unity had unraveled, and their short-lived freedom ended. Another rebellion, this time in 1696, failed. According to Indian testimony, the priests' actions against Pueblo religious ideas and practices lay at the center of the Puebloans' anti-Christian bitterness. Once they learned this, the clerics wisely chose to ignore many Indian kiva activities, and a sort of standoff between the clerics and the shamans developed. By the end of the seventeenth century, Spanish settlement efforts among the Indians slowed markedly. To colonial leaders in Mexico City, the northern regions appeared distant and produced little wealth, and so their interest in expansion waned. As a result, tribal people saw only a slow increase in the number of their oppressors.

ENCOUNTERING THE FRENCH

The tribes of Florida may have been the first to face intruding Europeans, but within a generation the French followed the Spanish to North America. Although Jacques Cartier and his companions avoided the wanton brutality exhibited by de Soto and his army, Indians along the St. Lawrence Valley of eastern Canada still faced danger when dealing with the strangers. In July 1534, Micmac people fishing along the Atlantic coast saw the explorer's ship near shore. Quickly they launched their canoes hoping to trade, but their eagerness frightened the French, who fired warning shots to keep them at a distance. A day later, by "holding up . . . some furs on sticks," the Indians convinced the French that they only wanted to trade, opening the way for peaceful meetings between the two. Before they returned to France, the explorers captured two young sons of the chief, Donnacona, whom they decided to take back to Europe so that the youths could learn French and serve as translators.

These almost peaceful first relations continued the next year. That summer Cartier returned, sailing his three ships up the St. Lawrence to Stadacona, a village near the site of modern Quebec City. There the captives rejoined their father after promising to lead the French farther upstream. Later they refused to do so and warned the villagers that the explorers could not be trusted. This left Cartier's party to travel farther inland alone. Most of that winter the Indians ignored their unwelcome visitors, until the French became sick with scurvy. The Indians taught them how to cure this affliction by using a tea made from tree bark and leaves. In the spring of 1536, Cartier kidnapped Chief Donnacona and his two sons and sailed away to France with them. Living there further exposed the captives to common European diseases, and the chief died before he could be returned to his home. The French explorer came back yet a third time, in 1541, but that year the Indians avoided the strangers whenever they could. Mutual suspicion led to some violence that winter, and in the summer of 1542 the French party gave up and sailed away.

During the next few decades a modest fur trade along the Atlantic coast began. When the Indians went east to enjoy the warm weather and to fish, they met European fishermen, and by the 1580s they had begun exchanging furs for tools, weapons, cloth, and jewelry. By that time fashions in Europe had changed and the easily workable beaver pelts became central for successful trading. While furs were commonplace for the tribal hunters, metal goods and comfortable fabrics were not; so, often the Indians began the trade. Clearly the hunters thought that the trade items they got from the French had at least as much value as the animal skins the strangers welcomed so eagerly, and they traded willingly. In fact, they often thought that they got more from the trade than did their partners. One French cleric reported that his acquaintances laughed about the value the Europeans placed on the furs. They told him that "the Beaver does everything to perfection. He makes for us kettles, axes, swords, knives, and gives us drink and food without the trouble of cultivating the ground." Here the Indians did not consider the trade as exploitation.

The exchange continued and became the economic base for relations by the early 1600s, when Samuel de Champlain established the tiny settlement that became Quebec. Both the villagers and the newcomers wanted the trade to continue, so they worked to avoid violence or war that might disrupt it. However, the new alliance that evolved brought warfare anyway, with different groups. In 1609 the five nations of the Iroquois Confederacy in western New York became bitter enemies of the French after Champlain and a few of his men helped the Hurons attack and defeat a Mohawk force that year. The Iroquoians saw Champlain's friendship with their Huron enemies as a major threat. This relatively minor incident set the stage for more than a century of fighting between the French and their tribal allies in Canada and the Native people in New York.

For much of the 1600s those tribes dealing with the French came to view them as either trading partners and diplomatic and military allies, or as competitors and enemies. Even though only a few would-be settlers built homes or established farms in the St. Lawrence Valley or south of the eastern Great Lakes, the newcomers' presence and actions had serious immediate and long-term impacts on the villagers.

Within only a generation after Champlain had founded Quebec, the Hurons of southern Ontario dominated a trade network that included tribes living hundreds of miles farther inland. Each spring they brought bundles of beaver pelts down the rivers to the French settlement, and in return got and distributed household items such as pots and pans, needles, knives, and textiles for the women, as well as axes, knives, guns, and traps for the men. Missionaries moved into some of the larger villages, and Frenchmen crisscrossed the countryside learning the tribal languages, becoming familiar with routes west, and meeting more and more village leaders.

Although careful not to antagonize their trading partners, the new-comers exerted an influence far beyond mere barter, introducing such things as Catholic Christianity, epidemic diseases, sharp trading practices, and new alliances. Over time these changed Indian societies dramatically. Yet aboriginal practices and ideas remained. For example, when a canoe convoy of Huron traders accompanied by a Jesuit priest tried to force its way upstream over the objections of Algonquian villagers who demanded a toll, the local chief ordered that the priest be hanged "from a tree by the arm-pits" to enforce the customary right of the village leaders to control passage on "their river." Tribal groups living near the trading posts soon learned how to manipulate the exchanges to their advantage. They refused to bring in their furs until several French ships arrived, and then they bargained until they got good prices for their furs. Experience taught them to be skeptical of the traders' claims and of the priests' urgings that they accept the Europeans' beliefs. Repeatedly they criticized the French while defending their own customs. At one meeting they rejected a Jesuit's claims of superiority by assuring him that they were "not thieves, like you."

During and after the 1630s, when Jesuit missionaries fanned out among the villages, diseases—usually smallpox, measles, or influenza—swept through each tribe they visited. Indian leaders blamed the epidemics on the Black Robes, and the continued French presence caused bitter divisions within some societies. The shamans considered the Jesuits to be witches and charged that when the priests administered the last rites to the dying, they were actually killing their patients. When the clerics carried life-size images of Jesus and the Virgin Mary during a particularly virulent epidemic, the Indians blamed the images for the sickness and death. Jesuit efforts to stop Indian torturing of prisoners in one village so enraged the chiefs that they ordered holes burned in the hands and feet of the victims to mock the crucifixion story. Throughout the seventeenth century, traditionalists strove to keep their allies from destroying tribal religious, cultural, and economic practices. Often how well they succeeded depended on how far they lived from French settlements and whether or not any missionaries came to their villages.

Over the decades Native peoples living south of the Great Lakes and along the major rivers in the upper Midwest and the Mississippi Valley all met French traders, government officials, or priests. Usually the villagers cooperated by holding councils, negotiating alliances, and frequently encouraging the strangers to marry young women and become part of the community. As a result, French influence and presence grew as they built tiny trading posts, missions, and forts throughout the region. Not all Indian groups there welcomed the Europeans, but most wanted access to the trade goods that came during times of peace. Others such as the Iroquois tribes in New York fought the French and their tribal allies for much of the century. These conflicts, often called the Beaver Wars, brought destruction to many groups. Wide-ranging Mohawk and Seneca war parties moved out of New York, attacking tribes from Pennsylvania west to Illinois and Wisconsin as they tried to smash the French-Huron trading system and the alliances that had evolved. Their assaults forced their tribal enemies to flee or to accept Iroquois domination whenever the French proved unable or unwilling to help defend against the raids.

The experiences of many northeastern tribes, then, differed markedly from that of groups who encountered the Spanish. The Spaniards came to conquer, to exploit, and to convert, by force if necessary, but the French usually came to trade first and to bring Christianity later. For most of the seventeenth century the fur trade dominated relationships between the northern groups, and the Europeans there had to remain mostly peaceful for trade to continue. Certainly the Jesuits brought their full energies and skills to the challenges of converting Indians to Christianity, but they lacked the military support that the Spanish often gave their missionaries. The interethnic contacts in New France brought disease, economic change, village disruption, division, and forced movement. Yet many of the village societies came to terms with the intruders, adapting some European ideas and practices while forcing the French to do many things the Indian way. Richard White, who has studied these relationships extensively, labels the results of the blending of cultures south of the Great Lakes as a "Middle Ground," where the two societies met and each changed by accepting practices of the other.

ENCOUNTERING THE DUTCH

For tribal people living along the coasts of present-day New York, New Jersey, and Delaware before the 1660s, the Dutch posed a formidable threat. Although they never invaded in large numbers, their determination, greed, and ethnocentrism caused more than their share of misery. By the early 1620s the Dutch West India Company brought settlers to the Hudson River Valley, and they moved quickly to build Fort Orange, near present-day Albany, New York. More than a century later, one account reported that when they saw the Europeans' ship, the Indians thought that it was "a large canoe or house, in which the great Mannitto [great or Supreme Being] *himself* was, and that he probably was coming to visit them." Rather than the Supreme Being, the ship carried Dutchmen. Another description noted that "our visitors were white [and we thought that they] must be sick." The Algonquian tribes of the region often competed with or fought each other as well as their Iroquoian neighbors, and so when the out-siders arrived, the tribes could not unite easily against them. Early trade pleased both sides, but by the 1630s the company directors decided to enlarge their enterprise and soon were shipping hundreds of farmers and townspeople to the settlements. This changed relations between the villagers and the colonists quickly. As long as trade drove their con-tacts, the two sides needed each other. Once Dutch farmers arrived, however, they wanted land, and the Indians' cleared, well-tended plots looked too attractive to resist.

This led to bitter fighting from the 1640s until the English ousted the Dutch authorities two decades later. When colonial farmers spread onto lands being used by Indian families, anger and violence followed. As happened later in New England, the newcomers' unfenced live-stock destroyed tribal crops. If the Lenape villagers objected or dared to kill the cattle or swine, Governor William Kieft encouraged the settlers to retaliate. Determined to clear the nearby lands of Indians, in 1642 he supplied the farmers with arms and sent them marching through the countryside to intimidate the villagers. The next year he launched a destructive attack on the village of Pavonia, triggering a series of raids and widespread destruction of Native groups. During the negotiations that ended the fighting, tribal leaders protested Dutch aggression vehemently. They reminded the colonial negotiators that the Indians had welcomed the Dutch into their villages, given them young women to marry, and traded with them. "Why," they com-plained, "did you villainously massacre your own blood?"—referring to the mixed-race children who had been born. The victors could say little in response, but their aggression continued. From 1657 to 1664, raiding and warfare between the Esophus tribe and the Dutch kept the region in turmoil.

The New Netherlands settlement had a broad and long-term impact on tribes of the Northeast that went far beyond the destruction of the coastal groups. Operating out of Fort Orange near Albany, Dutch traders opened a solid trade with the nearby Mohawks. When the

Mohawks began their attacks on the French and their Huron trading partners along the St. Lawrence Valley in the 1640s, they needed weapons, and despite company objections to a firearms trade, the local authorities acquiesced. That relationship remained profitable for the businessmen, but, more important, it bound the authorities in what became New York to a trade and diplomatic alliance with the Five Nations. For the Iroquois, that meant a steady supply of arms and other trade goods in the bitter competition with their French and tribal enemies. At the same time, it made them dependent on whichever group controlled the trade at Albany, and during the next century it dragged them into the imperial wars between the French and the British.

ENCOUNTERING THE ENGLISH

For American Indians, the English colonists who began arriving in the late sixteenth century eventually became the most important and most dangerous of the invaders. By the time tribal peoples met them, these aggressive outsiders had acquired plenty of experience in attacking and subjugating others. First they had defeated and conquered the Scots. Then they invaded Ireland, where they tried to subdue the "savage" inhabitants and developed ideas and practices used later in North America. In the long run, however, the English movement into North America posed the most serious threat to the aboriginal societies because the English came to settle the land. Although the other invading Europeans may have hoped to do that, only the English ever got large numbers of people to cross the North Atlantic. As a settler society, they needed land, not just furs or hides, and when they took it, their actions brought irreversible changes to the Native societies that faced them.

In the summer of 1584 the Roanoke and Croatan tribes who lived on the North Carolina coast first encountered English sailors near present-day Roanoke Island. Men from the two ships sent by Sir Walter

Raleigh landed, hoping to find a site for future trade and settlement. The Algonquian people there welcomed the visitors cautiously, as they traded minor items and tried to make themselves understood. After a few weeks, as the crewmen prepared to leave, they took "two of the savages being lustie men, whose names were Wanchese and Manteo," aboard the ships. Apparently one of the pair volunteered, but it seems likely that the English kidnapped the other man.

Despite that, when Raleigh sent seven ships carrying six hundred men to America in 1585, the Indians remained peaceful. In June of that year, after the tribesmen visited one of the newcomers' ships, a silver cup belonging to Sir Richard Grenville turned up missing. The Indians denied having stolen it, but the English decided to punish them for theft. Like the Spanish, Dutch, and later the Russians, they attacked first by destroying the nearby cornfields and then by burning the closest village. The shocked tribesmen took no immediate action, but soon retaliated. This led to English counterattacks and further Indian raids. Not all of the colonists supported the aggressive tactics their leaders used. In late 1585 one colonist complained that "some of our companie . . . shewed themselves too fierce, in slaying some of the people" over minor matters they should have ignored. During the 1585–86 winter, fears of Indian attacks kept the English worried. When ships expected to bring people and supplies failed to arrive in June 1586, the leaders decided to abandon their settlement. Before giving up, however, Governor William Lane launched another series of attacks, killing and decapitating one chief and scattering the nearby villagers.

The Algonquians had little time to recover or to celebrate their enemies' departure, because just a few weeks later Sir Richard Grenville returned with a fresh batch of settlers. When he learned that the colonists had evacuated the site, he decided to leave only eighteen men to continue the English presence there and then sailed back to Europe. Soon the Indians attacked, killing or driving the men away. In 1587 the last group of colonists arrived, but they needed support from home, and so the Governor returned to England to gather more people and supplies. A war between Britain and Spain cut off the colony until 1590, by which time the Roanoke Island settlers had disappeared. Apparently, continuing hostilities with local tribes reduced the settlement, and the survivors migrated north to settle among tribes near the Chesapeake Bay. Whatever happened, this first English colonial venture failed. The experience warned the coastal Indians of the potential dangers the strangers posed.

The Algonquian peoples of coastal Virginia encountered the next English arrivals. In the spring of 1607 three small vessels sailed nearly sixty miles up the James River to what is now Jamestown. After a peaceful meeting with the Paspahegh tribe, the colonists began to build temporary shelters. As soon as they realized that the strangers meant to stay, the villagers "fell to skyrmishing & killed 3" of the newcomers before a volley of English musketry drove them off. The local Indians belonged to a powerful chiefdom of thirty tribes with nearly two hundred villages, all under the direction of a leader the colonists called Powhatan. When he learned about the intruders, he sent a war party of 160 men to drive them away. Once again the Europeans' small arms, this time aided by cannon fire from the ships in the river, ended the attack.

Having decided that the English offered valuable metal items, Powhatan soon shifted his tactics from military confrontation to diplomacy. Perhaps he hoped to incorporate the newcomers into his confederacy or to become allied with them against his tribal enemies. Despite his efforts, relations remained strained at best, as frequent raids by whites and Indians alike kept the region in turmoil. By 1608, John Smith, a colonial leader, began an aggressive policy of demanding that the villagers stop raiding and also provide corn and other food to the settlers. He led armed bands into nearby villages, often taking food and hostages at gunpoint. Smith infuriated Opechancanough, leader of the powerful Pamunkey tribe and later Powhatan's successor, publicly humiliating him by holding a gun to his head and forcing his followers to fill a boat with corn for the invaders. The young chief's hatred of the English remained hidden for years, but contributed to two devastating wars against the colonists. Unaware of this threat, Smith boasted that in 1609 the aging Powhatan had begged him for peace, asking "what will it availe you to take that by force you may quickly have by love, or to destroy them that provide you food." Despite such bragging, the sporadic fighting continued.

Tired of continued warfare with the English, Powhatan sued for peace in 1614, and the next few years remained calm. Like their European competitors in North America, the Jamestown colonists talked of bringing Christianity to the tribal people. After Pocahontas, one of the chief's daughters, accepted the new religion in 1614, she married John Rolfe, one of the planters. Their marriage signaled a brief era of cooperation and peace between the races. During that time missionaries began planning for an Indian college named Henrico, to be supported by contributions from England and by profits made by farming land in Virginia set aside for it. Although the Algonquians had no interest in the foreigners' gods, Opechancanough promised to allow some of his people to listen to missionaries in exchange for muskets, powder, and lead. As a result, a few families moved from their villages into the English settlements, but only briefly. At this point, colonial leaders foolishly allowed young Indian men to learn the use of muskets and to drill with the militia.

While the tribes gained European military equipment, a virtual tobacco craze swept through the colony. With high profits for the crop, English farmers rushed to plant on open land wherever they found it, often on the cleared fields of the Native farmers. This increased tensions between the races dramatically. Then in early 1622, several Englishmen murdered Nemattanew, a charismatic shaman and close associate of Opechancanough. For the angry Indians, this was the last straw, and on 22 March 1622, the Powhatan Confederacy forces overwhelmed outlying settlements and isolated farms. They killed so many colonists that the authorities called the attack the Massacre of 1622.

Fighting raged for much of that year, and as late as the spring of 1623 tribal forces annihilated a militia company that had marched out from Jamestown against them. They defended their homeland so stoutly that at one point warriors in sixty canoes attacked the *Tiger*, a small ship in the James River. These actions led the English to recognize Opechancanough as the "Great General of the Savages," but did nothing to end the hostilities. Sporadic warfare continued until 1632, when the confederacy leaders accepted colonial terms for peace.

For the next decade, the Virginia tribes watched as the colonial population grew and the whites spread ever farther from Jamestown and into the villagers' home areas. This movement went mostly in one direction, because the colonists built log palisades between the James and York Rivers to keep Indians away from the settlements. Because of the continuing incidents between his people and the pioneers, the aged Chief Opechancanough reinvigorated the Powhatan Confederacy and, although he had to be carried on a litter, in 1644 led it into another all-out war. Once again the tribal forces caught the Virginians by surprise and inflicted heavy casualties, but in the long run the warriors ran out of weapons and ammunition. As the war ended, the English captured the Indian leader and held him briefly at Jamestown. Then they shot him, claiming that he was trying to escape. By the 1670s, when Bacon's Rebellion swept through the Virginia back-country, the Indians had been reduced to serving as an excuse for pioneer aggression in what became a civil war within the colony. When that conflict ended in 1677, the scattered tribes signed a peace agreement at Williamsburg, which reduced them to dependency on the Virginia authorities.

Tribal experiences in New England varied somewhat from the violence and confrontation in the Chesapeake region. There no major chiefdom stood ready to challenge the intruders. Rather, the tribes had been in competition and conflict for generations. Also, in the years 1616–19 visiting fishermen and traders had introduced epidemic diseases that swept through many coastal villages, severely depopulating some areas. One early observer reported seeing entire villages standing vacant, with the once cleared fields filled with waist-high brush, and the "bones and skulls of the dead" lying about where the wild animals had left them. Those same sailors who had carried the plagues kidnapped men from several tribes, and if those individuals ever got home, they spread anti-English stories wherever they went. Thus, even before the English tried to establish colonies, coastal people had reasons to fear and hate them.

Whether they realized this or not, early English colonists certainly feared the New England peoples. Pilgrim leader William Bradford, before he ever got off the *Mayflower*, described the Indians as a "savage people, who are cruel, barbarous and most treacherous." When the coastal Algonquian people saw the English ship offshore, they sent scouts to observe, keeping their distance for weeks. Then, late on 7 December 1620, the villagers came up to the Pilgrims' stockade, making what the terrified whites described as "a great and strange cry" before loosing a rain of arrows into the camp. As in Virginia, when the whites replied with musket fire, the attackers withdrew. The Indians ignored the sickly colonists through the winter of 1620–21, except for taking a few tools left in one of the fields and shouting unintelligible words from a nearby hilltop. The Pilgrims responded by placing several of their cannons on the hill.

In March 1621, Samoset, an Abenaki sagamore or chief, walked into Plymouth. Speaking English to his astounded listeners, he described some of the nearby tribes and promised to bring other chiefs to the settlement. On 22 March, Chief Massasoit (Yellow Feather) of the Wampanoag tribe led sixty of his men into the settlement. This terrified the Pilgrims, but at that moment the English-speaking Tisquantum or Squanto stepped forward. He had been kidnapped in 1614, enslaved by the Spanish, and worked as a crew member on an English trading ship, where he learned the language. Having escaped, in 1621 he lived with Massasoit's people and served as a valued interpreter for several years. Talks between the colonists and their visitors soon led to a formal treaty. The Wampanoag leaders feared the powerful Narragansett tribe just west of them and wanted assurances of help, while the English desperately needed peace and trade. The agreement the two crafted worked and proved durable as well. In it the chief agreed to help enforce peace between Indians and whites, end the petty theft of the colonists' tools, and punish those who hurt or robbed the English. John Carver, the colonial governor, agreed that the Pilgrims would aid their tribal allies if anyone else attacked them. This mutual defense pact lasted for the next forty years.

For the next several decades the Wampanoag-Pilgrim treaty was reasonably successful, but beginning in 1630 the far more numerous Puritans began their Massachusetts Bay colony at Boston. During the 1630s thousands of Puritans came to Massachusetts, and their arrival put immediate strains on peaceful dealings with the Indians. Apparently their religious scruples and fears of an Indian war restrained the whites' greed for land at first, because for a time colonial leaders tried to protect the villagers' property and rights. They punished pioneers who ran roughshod over the Indians, and one small community even had to pay for damages English hogs did to tribal crops. As the colonial population grew, self-confidence replaced wariness, and by the mid-1630s Puritan authorities became more aggressive.

That change in attitude led to a major war in just a couple of years. English entry into the Connecticut River Valley brought the Pequot tribe there face to face with the intruders. They could not have arrived at a worse time for the Indians. By the early 1630s, Chief Uncas had led his Mohegan followers out of the tribe, and the nearby Narragansetts used that move as an excuse to undermine the Pequot middleman role in the trade with the Dutch. In 1633–34 several epidemics swept through the villages, and soon after that, John Stone, a dishonest English trader, appeared. He tried to kidnap some of the villagers to hold for ransom. Enraged, the Indians stormed aboard his ship, killing Stone and eight of the crew. It is not entirely clear that the Pequots carried out the attack, but Massachusetts authorities forced tribal leaders to accept a treaty in which they agreed to capture and turn over the murderers to the English, pay reparations for the killings, and accept colonial settlement in their homeland.

In this first contact with the Puritans, Pequot chiefs recognized that the newcomers threatened their independence, but they had no idea how aggressive and brutal their new neighbors would become. Tribal leaders would not surrender Stone's suspected killers and paid only part of the demanded reparations for his death. In 1636, with English settlement moving into the Pequots' homeland, a second incident brought the two sides into conflict. In July, Indians on the coast near Block Island attacked and killed another trader, John Oldham. At that point Puritan leaders demanded that the Pequots surrender those who had killed the two traders and began raiding Indian villages. When the inhabitants fled, the troops burned crops and dwellings. Angry warriors struck back, raiding outlying towns and carrying off isolated farm families as prisoners.

Tribal leaders saw few options and defended their villages vigorously. At the same time, they tried to strengthen ties with neighboring tribes, but with little success. Although land hunger rather than genuine piety drove many settlers, the Puritans considered the challenge to their authority at least partly in religious terms. They characterized the tribal actions to block English expansion as being the work of the devil. They called for all-out war, and in May 1637 militia leader John Mason led a combined white-Indian army against the largest Pequot village on the Mystic River. Slipping through the palisaded entry in the predawn light, Mason's troops set fire to many of the lodges. When the villagers awoke, they ran out of the burning lodges into a combined barrage of gunfire and arrows from the force surrounding the village. The Pequots were destroyed. So many died that morning that the slaughter appalled even Puritan witnesses. Describing the scene, one of them wrote that "it was a fearful sight to see them thus frying in the fire . . . and horrible was the stinck & sente thereof." The survivors found themselves sold into slavery in the West Indies or placed under the authority of their tribal enemies.

Other tribes avoided that kind of desperate confrontation, but not easily. Although the Wampanoags and other smaller groups had remained at peace since their 1621 treaty with Plymouth, the Puritans wanted to dominate the region. They viewed Indian shamans as spokesmen for the devil, passed laws to control daily activities, and urged whole villages to move into "praying towns" where teachers and missionaries could turn them into good Christians. At the same time, the authorities brought the villagers under the colonial legal system. Frontier settlers moved their animals into the forests, often near unfenced Indian fields. Instead of building fences to keep the livestock from destroying crops, the whites blamed their tribal neighbors for leaving their fields unprotected. As long as Chief Massasoit remained alive, the two societies avoided war, but in 1661 he died. His son Wamsutta lacked the luck or skills his father had enjoyed, and only a year later Plymouth authorities brought him into town at gunpoint for questioning. They soon released him, but he died before returning home.

While being pressured to accept English political dominance, the New England tribes also faced a cultural offensive led by missionaries and teachers determined to remake them as copies of Englishmen. By the middle of the seventeenth century, John Eliot, Thomas Mayhew, and Mayhew's son (also named Thomas) had brought Christianity to the villagers of Massachusetts and the nearby coastal islands. Between 1650 and the 1670s, Eliot established eleven so-called praying towns that drew their populations from some of the most threatened villages. He modeled these communities after Old Testament accounts and developed strict regulations for the new communities. The rules prohibited drunkenness, polygamy, Sabbath breaking, and other activities. English authorities supervised the actions of village magistrates, and so, while the Algonquian towns seemed to have local autonomy, the Puritans supervised almost all aspects of life. In Massachusetts the authorities paid to send at least twenty Indian boys to school, hoping to prepare them for entrance to Harvard. That university established an Indian College in 1658, but it failed. Despite mixed feelings about their Puritan neighbors, some tribal groups participated in these religious and educational activities.

The central dispute between the tribal people and the colonists focused on Indian efforts to retain their culture and their independence. Plymouth leaders rejected that idea out of hand, and when young Metacomet (King Philip) succeeded his brother as the tribal chief in 1661, the dispute worsened. Fending off repeated demands for Wampanoag land, Metacomet came to regard the English as harsh aggressors. Ongoing damage of village crops by the colonists' animals remained a contentious matter as well. As Indian resentment grew, colonial leaders feared that the tribes would unite and attack frontier settlements. To prevent this, English officials demanded that Metacomet surrender his followers' weapons. He objected that this left his people nearly defenseless against their tribal enemies and greatly reduced their hunting abilities. When the magistrates waved such arguments aside, he told them, "I am determined not to live until I have no country." In 1674 a Christian Indian named John Sassamon told the colonists that the Wampanoag chief had begun to prepare for war and to form anti-English alliances. A month later the authorities found Sassamon's body under the ice in a nearby pond. They arrested three men from Philip's band. After being tortured, one of the men confessed, and all three were executed.

Scattered violence continued for much of the next year, and in 1675 what is now called King Philip's War began. Most of the Rhode Island and Massachusetts tribes joined forces against the English, destroying farms, overrunning entire villages, and killing or capturing hundreds of colonists. The English struck back with an army of one thousand men against the Narragansetts and called on their Mohawk allies from New York to attack Philip's forces too. As usually happened, the Indian soldiers ran out of ammunition and had to resort to using bows, arrows, and lances against colonial troops who were

wearing some body armor and using firearms. In the early summer of
1676, colonial militiamen captured Metacomet's wife and son and
quickly shipped them off to slavery in the West Indies. On 11 August
they surprised and killed the Indian leader. After cutting off his head,
they displayed their grisly trophy atop the town gate for years. The
war had pitted tribe against tribe as well as tribal groups against the
English. When it ended, Indian villages stood vacant and many English
towns lay in ashes. The efforts to coexist with the colonists had failed,
as the whites smashed all resistance. By the late 1670s, surviving
Indians had to accept colonial domination or slip away to join related
groups far from the settlements.

For much of the seventeenth century the Carolina tribes had less
contact with the English than did groups in either Virginia or New
England. The first settlers arrived in 1670, and ten years later they
founded what became Charleston. The early outpost resembled French
settlement actions in the North, as the pioneers began a trade-based
economy. For the coastal tribes this proved advantageous for two
reasons. They gained coveted European goods, and they served as
middlemen for the trade between the English and tribes farther from
the coast. However, some Indian groups nearby had not settled
permanently, and so the English presence disrupted their movements.
This resulted in bitter competition among the tribes, particularly in
1674, when the Westos, a group new to the coastal region opened
successful trade relations with the newcomers. In 1680, minor incidents among the Indians and between tribes and the whites led the
Charleston traders to ally themselves with the Savannahs to defeat and
enslave the surviving Westos. Thus, in Carolina, even though few actual
settlers contended for tribal land, in a short time Native people there
became enmeshed in trade and military alliances with their dangerous
neighbors.

As the seventeenth century drew to a close, Indians in many parts
of the country had encountered Europeans. Explorers, traders, diplo-

mats, soldiers, and settlers had arrived, forever changing the face of aboriginal America. Some people benefited from the manufactured goods they obtained. Certainly fabric made some clothing more comfortable. Both men and women enjoyed metal implements, the women in the lodge and the field, and the men for hunting, land clearing, or warfare. At the same time, trade relations with the whites brought other responsibilities and dangers. Epidemic disease followed the traders' steps closely, and many Native groups also faced unwelcome missionaries. In the Southwest the Pueblo Revolt had been undone. In the North the Iroquois and French finally agreed to peace, while in New England and Virginia the local tribes had suffered crushing defeats. Only in the Southeast did most village groups manage to avoid such disasters. Their apparent good fortune resulted from the slowness of European penetration into their home region. In the century that followed, Indians in all of these areas would have to come to terms with vastly altered circumstances. The outsiders who now occupied some of their lands were numerous, dangerous, and here to stay.

SUGGESTED READINGS

Bourne, Russell. *The Red King's Rebellion: Racial Politics in New England, 1675–1678*. New York: Oxford University Press, 1990.

Jennings, Francis. *The Invasion of America: Indians, Colonialism, and the Cant of Conquest*. Chapel Hill: University of North Carolina Press, 1975.

Merrell, James H. *The Indians' New World: Catawbas and Their Neighbors from European Contact through the Era of Removal*. Chapel Hill: University of North Carolina Press, 1989.

Rountree, Helen. *Powhatan Foreign Relations 1500–1722*. Charlottesville: University Press of Virginia, 1993.

Salisbury, Neal. *Manitou and Providence: Indians and the Making of New England, 1500–1643*. New York: Oxford University Press, 1982.

Trelease, Allen W. *Indian Affairs in Colonial New York*. Ithaca, N.Y.: Cornell University Press, 1960.

Trigger, Bruce G. *Natives and Newcomers: Canada's "Heroic Age" Reconsidered*. Montreal: McGill—Queen's University Press, 1985.

Vaughan, Alden T. *New England Frontier: Puritans and Indians, 1620–1675*. Rev. ed. New York: W. W. Norton, 1979.

Weber, David J. *The Spanish Frontier in North America*. New Haven, Conn.: Yale University Press, 1992.

White, Richard. *The Middle Ground: Indians, Empires, and Republics in the Great Lakes Region, 1650–1815*. New York: Cambridge University Press, 1991.

Wright, J. Leitch, Jr. *The Only Land They Knew: The Tragic Story of the American Indians in the Old South*. New York: Free Press, 1981.

eighteenth century, major wars erupted frequently and brought young Indian men into cooperation and conflict with the English, French, or Spanish. Sometimes tribal soldiers traveled hundreds of miles from home, meeting and working with strangers. Other times, invading armies marched through Indian homelands, depleting game and timber and destroying village dwellings, fields, and even crops stored for the next winter. Honor-bound by diplomatic ties and fur-trade connections, the villagers entered many of these conflicts to help their allies. In some instances, particular tribes persuaded their colonial allies to assist them against their Indian competitors or enemies. More often, however, the imperial conflicts among the invading powers pulled Indians into fights where they had little stake in the outcome. By the time of American Independence in 1783, many village societies were well experienced at trying to survive the upheavals the invaders brought.

TRADE AND TECHNOLOGY

Often when Indians first met white men, it seemed that they wanted to barter immediately. Certainly exchange was nothing new, because long-standing trade networks had tied far-flung groups together in North America for centuries. Yet what the Europeans often saw as tedious routines and time-wasting speeches had important cultural and diplomatic roles in the village societies. There tribal leaders welcomed the strangers with speeches, prayers, dancing, and feasting, and by smoking the calumet or peace pipe and exchanging gifts. In these early meetings, Indian ceremonies and customs dominated. To the villagers, these acts created a relationship as allies, even as distant family, with their guests, and they repeated at least some of the ceremonies each time their new "relatives" visited. It seems to have taken the whites several generations to recognize that their welcome in each village went beyond an eagerness to trade.

Having accepted the newcomers as allies, Indians sought manufactured goods such as metal implements, textiles, weapons, and even

Chapter 3

LIVING WITH STRANGERS, *1700–1783*

 By 1700, except for Native groups in Alaska and along the Pacific Northwest coast, few people living near the oceans or north of New Spain could escape some contact with the European invaders. The seventeenth-century encounters had brought fundamental changes to North America. Some groups gravitated toward the newcomers for trade, defense, and help against their enemies. Others fled from the disease, warfare, and cultural destruction the whites brought to their villages. Whatever their response, Indians faced new issues. Early plagues reduced their populations, often carrying off leaders, shamans, hunters, and others with special skills. Because of those losses, many small tribes disappeared as their survivors fled, joining nearby villages with a similar culture or language whenever they could. For much of the eighteenth century, Native groups struggled to absorb these refugees. They also developed ways to protect their own social customs, economic practices, and military-diplomatic alliances while dealing with the expanding imperial networks of Britain, France, and Spain.

The European newcomers brought such basic changes that a return to aboriginal ways became impossible. During the paints and dyes, which made an immediate impact on their lives. The men recognized that steel knives and axes cut better and lasted longer than stone ones. Women found that iron and brass cooking pots outlasted stone or ceramic pottery and made food preparation easier. With the colorful fabrics traders brought, it was easier to make comfortable clothing. Much of the time, except for alcohol, firearms, and mirrors, the trade goods coming into the villages offered little that was really new. Rather, the items were better, longer-lasting, or easier to use than the Native products they replaced. Because many people wanted the trade goods, the exchange that grew from the early contacts soon included Native groups from the Aleutian Islands in the North Pacific to Hudson's Bay in eastern Canada, and from southern Arizona and New Mexico to the East Coast.

In their efforts to acquire trade goods, the villagers became part of a cycle of hunting or trapping, carrying the pelts and hides home, and then preparing them for use or sale. Each autumn the hunters left home to gather the furs. At first men shot or trapped almost any furbearer, but soon beaver pelts became the most desired items except in the Southeast. There the hundreds of thousands of white-tailed deer proved more important than the smaller fur-bearers. When the hunters returned home, the village women cleaned and prepared the hides for trade. Although their work increased, neither the men nor the women were doing things entirely new. Hunters had always left the villages for weeks. Now they might be gone for months. The women had always worked with the hides and furs, but now they had more of them to clean. At the same time, the trade brought important changes to the villages. With many of the men absent for longer periods, the women faced extra duties in the villages beyond just having more furs to work. Also, because the men got their traps, firearms, and ammunition on credit each fall, an unsuccessful hunt might push Indian families or even whole villages into debt that they would never be able to pay. These issues introduced new, long-term pressures to tribal life.

The trade brought new challenges to the Europeans as well. At first they failed to realize that when they shared food and exchanged goods for furs in front of or inside smoky lodges, they were entering into a diplomatic agreement with their trading partners. Indian leaders assumed that they had forged an alliance with the Europeans and expected them to live up to tribal customs. The traders and diplomats had little understanding of this. Young Indian women chose to marry the newcomers to help strengthen ties between the groups and to improve their family standing. At times village elders encouraged their daughters or other female relatives to live with the visitors. This was to benefit both sides, as the trader would become a member of his wife's clan, gaining access to the leading families in the village, and the Indians would, presumably, gain closer ties to the whites. The practice had a direct impact on trade because although some English traders had Indian wives, their French competitors took village brides more often. This meant that even though French goods could not compete with English wares in either price or quality, personal connections within many groups kept the competition between the two nearly even. At times this allowed the tribal hunters to play one European power against another.

Much of the time trade brought more violence and misery than benefit to the Native people. For example, in the Southeast bitter competition among the English colonists and between them and the nearby Spanish and French enclaves, as well as fundamental disagreements over Indian policies between the English Proprietors and colonial leaders, brought disaster to some tribal people. The Carolina officials proved so dishonest and brutal that a commission set up to help the Indians there did just the opposite, acting for their "oppression [rather] than protection." As a result, warfare racked the area for decades. When several tribes joined them to defeat the Westos tribe in 1680, the English profited by selling the captives into slavery in the Caribbean. Within just a few years traders began to seize women and children in villages where the hunters could not pay their debts. Then they held the captives for ransom or sold them as slaves. The Carolina merchants also encouraged intertribal warfare, urging their allies to capture and enslave other people. As they tried to keep peace and encourage settlement, the Proprietors denounced these actions repeatedly. After one of the wars they charged that the Carolina leaders had induced the Savannah tribe "to ravish the wife from the Husband, Kill the father to get the Child and to burne and Destroy the habitations of these poore people into whose Country wee were Ch[e]arefully received by them . . . [and] never have done us hurt." Their words had little impact, and the wars and slave trading continued for another generation.

The English aggression in Carolina had many parallels elsewhere. For example, far to the northwest the Aleuts, Inuit, and other Indians living in Alaska and along the northern Pacific coast faced invaders at least as greedy and vicious as those from Charleston. There, by the early 1740s, when Russian traders from Siberia reached the Aleutian Islands, the Aleuts launched their boats and frightened the newcomers away temporarily. At a nearby island the Russians met skilled hunting and seafaring people. Their stores of luxurious sea otter pelts attracted the traders' attention, and within just a few months trouble ensued. While camped on the island of Attu, the Europeans abused some of the women. When the victims' husbands objected, the traders killed all of the men on the island and then raped and enslaved the women. This incident, at what is still called "Massacre Bay," set the tone for relations between the Alaska Native groups and these invaders for generations to come.

The islanders resisted the Russians whenever they could, and between 1762 and 1766 they attacked repeatedly. At Umnak and Unalaska Islands they lured the traders inland away from their ships with stories of vast collections of furs and then killed them. Next they boarded and burned four of the five Russian ships in the harbor. Once news of this reached Siberia, the enraged traders smashed their way through the Native settlements, destroying all of the villages on one of the islands and eighteen on the other. This brutal repression worked, as the surviving Aleuts never again dared to retaliate for the ongoing Russian atrocities. Twenty years later Gregory Shelikhov, a leading trader, forced his way ashore on Kodiak Island near the Alaska mainland, where he wanted to set up a permanent base. Knowing what had happened to the Aleuts earlier, the Inuit or Eskimo people there tried to repel Shelikhov's men but failed. He reported that "the savages came down from their rocks in great numbers, and fell upon us with . . . fury." After a bitter fight, the Russians' muskets won the day, and they occupied the site.

In the region around the Great Lakes the fur trade brought Indians, English, and French into uneasy relationships that shifted frequently and kept all of the groups off balance from time to time. Prior to the peace negotiated by the French and Iroquois in 1701, tribal remnants from Pennsylvania and western New York had migrated into the Ohio Valley. Algonquians such as the Shawnees, Delawares, Ottawas, and Miamis moved about Ohio, Indiana, and even Kentucky, while the Senecas and a few other Iroquoians headed west too. Although they had sought to escape fur-trade violence and competition, the same issues followed them. The Fox Wars, stretching from 1710 into the 1740s, illustrate the disruption and confusion European trade and diplomacy brought to the Native peoples. At one time the Fox or Mesquaki people lived in Ontario, Canada. From there they gradually moved westward, first into lower Michigan and later into Wisconsin and Illinois. Shortly after 1700 they began trading with the French at Detroit, but soon the relationship became strained and then turned violent. By 1712 heavy fighting had broken out, and the French killed more than a thousand members of that tribe. By the end of the 1730s the Mesquaki had almost disappeared, with only remnants living among their relatives, the Sauks, in Illinois and Wisconsin.

RELIGION AND CULTURE

Even though trade brought Indians and colonists together, other factors also played important roles. At one time or another, most of the European powers talked about bringing Christianity to the heathen in America. This idea sparked an attack on tribal cultures and beliefs that continued for centuries, and some Indian traditionalists insist that this is still the case. For Native peoples during the eighteenth century it meant being looked down upon by whites as heathen savages. Often village shamans faced ridicule from visiting clerics, who did everything they could to disrupt the tight circle of village life. Missionaries denounced tribal medical practices while offering useless treatments and often bringing diseases that destroyed entire groups. Catholic priests may have brought the most misery to their hosts, because they lived with the villagers more frequently than did the Protestants. Which particular religious groups caused the most damage is hard to judge. Together the missionaries directed generations of cultural destruction from which most Native people have yet to recover. At best, their actions present a tragic story of good intentions going terribly wrong.

The Indians considered their own ways clearly superior to the whites'. The Europeans had a more well-developed technology, but their dependence on it showed both weakness and ignorance. The tribal people practiced rites that differed dramatically from those of the missionaries. They disliked many things about the Black Robes or Catholic priests from the start. A proper man took great pride in his hair, but the Jesuits wore theirs cropped short. Their robes caused much rude jesting because they appeared effeminate. Facial hair alienated the villagers too. Travelers, traders, and missionaries reported similar reactions among many tribes. Indians described a beard as "a monstrosity," and "the greatest disfigurement that a face can have," and men wearing them as "very ugly" and "deformed" or looking like dogs. Although only the Catholics had taken vows of poverty, few if any missionaries had much property. In Indian villages, sharing and gift-giving were part of everyday life, so the lack of goods created another barrier between the clerics and their intended audience.

The variety of Indian languages protected the villagers from all but the most determined missionaries. Few white men had the time or inclination to learn another dialect for each small group of villages or each tribe; translations therefore remained necessary. Often only the traders could speak tribal languages passably, and they saw little reason to help the meddling clerics disrupt their relationships and business in each village. Few Protestant clergymen lived with the Indians for long, and they had even more difficulties in communication than did their Catholic competitors. When a Yale graduate named John Ogilve won approval to minister to the Iroquois in New York, one thing in his favor was that he spoke Dutch. His supporters thought that anyone who spoke it could learn Mohawk. Certainly English speakers could never "utter those Barbarous Sounds [of the tribal languages] unless Accustom'd to them from their infancy." A more basic difficulty was that often the tribal languages lacked words for religious ideas that had no place in their belief structures. This frustrated generations of clerics but failed to stop their efforts.

Rarely did many of the villagers accept the new religion. Their shamans attacked it, and often acceptance of the new practices brought personal and family disputes. Indians had their own set of ethnocentric ideas, and these led many to resist the missionaries' teachings. Frequently the colonists demanded that their listeners learn English, but they refused to learn the villagers' tongues. Tribal religious practices remained tied to group welfare and sharing. Protestant teachings tended to emphasize individual actions and decisions. Glaring differences between professed beliefs about how people should act and the colonists' dealings with the Native peoples led some chiefs to suggest that the missionaries first convert their own people before preaching to the Indians. Disputes among competing Christian groups puzzled tribal leaders as well. In one case they sent a missionary on his way, saying that the "Indians could not tell what religion to be of, if they had a mind to be Christians."

Once the tribes had rejected the white man's religion, most colonial powers tried other means to acculturate at least some of the villagers. The Europeans reasoned that if the Indians could speak their language, trade disputes could be reduced and opportunities to make religious converts improved. That meant that the colonial authorities had to educate at least some of the villagers. The 1693 charter for the College of William and Mary in Virginia called on the new school to do just that. However, when it opened in 1700, tribal leaders refused to send any of their children, fearing that the whites might enslave them. So, instead they sent captured young people from enemy tribes to the college. Despite this, the Virginians remained optimistic and in 1723 erected Brafferton Hall to house Indian boys at the college. During the frequent wars and scares in the Southeast, colonial authorities forced tribes such as the Catawba and the Pamunkey to enroll young people at the college, where they kept them as hostages. Elsewhere, when colonial authorities urged the Iroquois to send young men to school, Onondaga Chief Canasatego refused. He denounced colonial schools because they made the students "absolutely good for nothing." When the boys returned home, he pointed out, they lacked the necessary skills for "killing deer, catching Beaver, or surprising an enemy." Rather than send Onondaga boys to the white man's school, the chief offered to take some English boys and "make men of them," but he got no response from his listeners.

Exchanging young people had been a long-established tribal practice, but usually the Europeans ignored Indian offers to do so, expecting to acculturate their tribal neighbors instead. As early as 1715, Virginia funded a school at Fort Christanna, where the Quaker missionary Charles Griffin worked with seventy children. Here too, once they realized that the colonial schools offered only English and some religious instruction, tribal leaders decided that such education threatened the children's health and culture; so, by 1717 they withdrew the students. These earlier meager results seem not to have discouraged the educators, and in 1756 the Reverend Eleazar Wheelock founded Moor's Indian Charity School in eastern Connecticut. He raised money in both England and the Northern colonies and then moved the school to New Hampshire, where later it became Dartmouth College. Few Indian young men got past the preparatory school, but Wheelock's efforts demonstrate the continuing pressure Native communities faced over controlling both their children and their future.

Despite their failure to educate many tribal children, some French and English willingly lived among the tribes, absorbing their customs and culture, but often even these bicultural men expected to return someday to their own societies. In places both Indians and some colonials welcomed intermarriage as a way to bridge the cultural gaps between them. Although people in each group talked about the practice, few actively supported it. French religious authorities objected to the irregular nature of such unions, and the English found the practice distasteful. Most English colonists lived in family-dominated settlements that had few unattached men. Nevertheless, some leaders thought that the colonists' aversion to intermarriage caused difficulties with the tribes. William Byrd of Virginia complained that the tribes would never consider the colonists as their friends, because whites had refused to marry Indians even when the settlements lacked enough women. At the same time, few tribal women saw colonials as potential spouses, because they lacked the hunting and other skills necessary to support a family.

DIPLOMACY AND WAR

During the first century and a half after the Europeans arrived, new diseases, missionary efforts, and economic changes disrupted aboriginal America as it had long existed. Gradually some early traders and government officials became not just economic partners, but diplomatic and military allies too. Others became competitors and enemies. Prior to the 1680s, this left tribal leaders facing two kinds of war. They fought against their traditional tribal competitors and enemies, but except for the Iroquois wars of the mid-1600s, those conflicts usually had only modest fatalities. However, when they defended themselves against the aggressive colonial people, their casualties and destruction rose so dramatically that often these conflicts became desperate struggles for tribal survival.

By the 1680s the situation changed, and from then until the end of the colonial era the villagers living east of the Mississippi River became enmeshed in the new imperial wars involving Britain, France, and Spain. In some cases this involvement grew out of trading alliances in which they joined their economic partners against their competitors. In other instances local issues persuaded them to help one European group against another. Although some tribes benefited at times from helping European groups, alliances with the colonial powers did little more for other tribes than disrupt trade, bring devastation to their villages, or force them to move away from their home areas. This meant that during much of the eighteenth century, violence and warfare brought by the colonial powers swept across eastern North America repeatedly. The major European conflicts gave Indian leaders few choices. Indians could join one of the combatants, try to stay neutral, or move. Whichever path they followed, their lives became more complicated and dangerous than they had been previously.

Bitter competition between France and Great Britain to gain colonies and expand their power led to decades of fighting around the world. In North America, Indians chose one side or the other in most of these colonial wars. Usually European dynastic or imperial issues lay behind the conflicts that engulfed the tribes and colonists alike. The first of these, called King William's War in American history, began in 1689 when the king of France refused to recognize William of Orange from the Netherlands as the new king of England. This conflict proved to be a major turning point for Indians. It lasted for eight years and dragged tribal people into a situation that tied international issues to local trade. Some members of the Five Nations Iroquois Confederacy in New York renewed their intermittent war with the French. At the same time, the nearby Abenaki and Wyandot tribes joined the French in attacking Schenectady, and the Mohawks retaliated by sending a fifteen hundred-man army to the gates of Montreal. They sacked the nearby village of La Chine and carried off over one hundred prisoners. Brutality marked the actions of both sides, as they burned villages, farms, and crops and tortured and killed hundreds of people. The Indians gained little from this war except a reputation as merciless and bloodthirsty savages, a label that tainted their relations with whites for the next two centuries.

The ink had barely dried on the treaty that ended the hostilities when in 1702 Queen Anne's War began. This strife grew out of long-standing European rivalries, as the French and Spanish joined forces against the English. In America, fighting over trade issues opened the conflict. By 1704, French-led Abenaki and Caughnawaga fighting men swept into settlements in western Massachusetts. At Deerfield they killed fifty colonists and led another one hundred away as prisoners. The English and their tribal allies marched north into northeastern Canada to attack the French there. Often during these wars tribal leaders joined their European allies in order to hurt their own tribal enemies and not because they had much interest in imperial affairs except to help their trading partners. For example, in the South, Creeks and Choctaws joined with the French to attack British traders from Charleston and their Chickasaw allies because these tribes had been enemies for generations. In this conflict the Chickasaws suffered most, since their enemies lived between them and their English allies. They begged for help: "We have not had the liberty of Hunting these 3 Years," they complained, "but have had to defend our Lands and prevent our Women and Children from being Slaves to the French." How much their appeal helped is not clear, but the ongoing raids encouraged the destruction of villages and crops as well as the frequent enslavement or butchery of prisoners by all sides. This conflict seems to have brought little wealth or glory either to the colonial powers or to any of the tribal people.

Three decades later, by the early 1740s, King George's War began. For a change, few tribesmen joined the campaigns, as colonial troops fought across New York and New England, attacking back and forth over the English-French border there. By this time most eastern tribes had suffered repeated casualties and remained neutral. Even so, the conflict had immediate local consequences. The most important result for many Indians grew out of the Iroquois' agreement to abandon their claims to dominance in the upper Ohio River Valley. By this time, bands of Delaware, Shawnee, and small groups of Iroquois who called themselves the Mingo had moved west into that region to escape Iroquois domination and the continuing flood of white pioneers. For the next several generations they would join the Miami and other tribes there as they tried to keep the area for themselves.

They had only a decade to enjoy relative peace in their new home region, because in 1755 skirmishes leading to the French and Indian War began in western Pennsylvania. There both the British and the French wanted control of what they called the Forks of the Ohio River, the region around Pittsburgh, because from that location they could then dominate the fur trade in the entire upper Ohio River Valley. When the English learned that French troops were building a fort and trading post there in 1755, the English General Edward Braddock led British and Virginia troops accompanied by Cherokee allies west to attack the partially completed Fort Duquesne. The English leader had little respect for his local Indian scouts, and as a result the Cherokees went home and the Delawares and Shawnees left his army to join the French. Without the tribesmen for guides, Braddock led his men into a devastating ambush that destroyed most of his army. When General Braddock and many of his officers died in the fighting, young George Washington directed the retreat to Virginia. The French had many fewer troops than the English, and as the war went on they could not supply or reinforce them effectively. Yet they benefited from the villagers' anger over repeated encroachment on their lands by colonial pioneers. When English negotiators asked the Delawares for help against the French, a tribal spokesman denounced both nations bitterly. "Why do you and the *French* not fight in the old Country . . . ? Why do you come to fight on our land?" he asked. "This makes every body believe, you want to take the land from us by force, and settle it." Obviously the Delawares had no intention of siding with the British. Even without their help, however, by 1760 most of the fighting in America had ended. The 1763 Treaty of Paris removed the French troops and governing officials and turned over present-day eastern Canada to the British. For some tribes in the region, that ushered in another brief time of peace.

STRUGGLES FOR INDEPENDENCE AND SURVIVAL

Although these international wars brought frequent destruction and suffering to the Indians, other more local conflicts proved at least as important during the eighteenth century. Whites' cruelty and greed in the fur trade infuriated the villagers in many parts of the country, yet most bitterness and violence resulted from the pioneers' encroachment on tribal lands and the colonial governments' unwillingness and inability to police the frontier. Tribal leaders throughout the East complained repeatedly that the colonists never lived up to their agreements. They protested that no matter what the treaty agreements said, the pioneers ignored them and the colonial authorities took no action. The intruders killed the Indians' game, cut their timber, and stole their land. After the Cherokees' defeat in 1777, their chief, Corn Tassel, chided the American negotiators that whenever the tribe parleyed, the whites' "whole cry is *more land!*" "Indeed," he said, for years they demanded "what they know we durst not refuse."

Surrendering their land struck at the heart of tribal culture and identity. For generations Native people had lived in their villages, and when treaty cessions or warfare drove them away, they lost local religious sites, knowledge of usable resources, and some of their shared memories. Village leaders differed over how to deal with this continuing invasion of their lands. In most communities the elders or peace chiefs counseled negotiations, but that rarely halted the whites' demands or ended the discussion. Often the less patient younger men demanded action, calling for war to drive the invaders away. At other times, village shamans approved and encouraged the warriors' approach. In fact, from the early 1600s through the early 1900s, tribal religious leaders called on their listeners to avoid the corrupting influence of all whites, be they traders, diplomats, missionaries, or settlers. Frequently the cultural leaders' actions led to direct confrontations when the colonials failed to understand the Indians' religious ideas or practices. In the eighteenth century, tribal people struggled to hold on to their land, but equally important, they strove to keep their cultures alive and working.

Often tribal struggles to maintain independence led to bitter wars against the colonists, whose actions threatened that independence. In Carolina the Tuscarora War in 1711 grew out of such Indian fears. Serving as active middlemen in the coastal fur trade, the tribe dealt with both Virginia and Carolina frontiersmen. These contacts brought not only European goods but also epidemic disease. When smallpox ravaged the tribe in 1708, village leaders correctly blamed the English. The traders further alarmed the chiefs when they bypassed them and began direct dealings with smaller regional tribes. This undermined the Tuscaroras' prestige and economy, so in 1711 Chief Hancock led hundreds of fighting men against the colonists. The English responded with an army of nearly five hundred whites and Indian allies, but with little success. In fact, they fled when the defenders of one fortified village rushed out to attack them. As they ran, several Carolinians were "deservedly shot . . . in their arses." Despite that failure, the next year an army of nearly one thousand men defeated the tribe, killing or enslaving hundreds. At first the survivors agreed to live on a small reservation, but most fled to New York and joined the Iroquois Confederacy as its sixth nation.

Although English destruction of the Tuscaroras frightened other Native groups, the steady encroachments by pioneer farmers caused immediate anger and violence between village farmers and the expanding colonial population. The nearby Yamasee tribe suffered repeatedly from colonial mistreatment and violence. For example, village hunters complained that the Charleston traders often refused to pay them promised wages after they had carried bundles of furs for hundreds of miles. They also demanded that criminal whites be stopped from raping their wives and enslaving their children during the men's absences from the villages. When the abuses continued, Yamasee messengers called for an all-out war against the pioneers and traders. Because other tribes had similar experiences, in April 1715 they joined the Yamasees and attacked farms and outlying settlements. On the first day the raiders killed more than 160 colonists. Within a few weeks they controlled most of the countryside. Catawbas from the North and Apalaches from the South joined in the fighting, and a terrified clergy-man wrote that hostile groups "surround us on Every Side but the Sea Side." After bitter fighting for nearly a year, the colonists won, and the Yamasees fled south into Florida rather than face enslavement.

At this same time, the tribes in the Mississippi Valley confronted new challenges from French colonists. Far to the north in New France, few of the Indians were farmers, and so when colonists took land, there was no one to dispute its use. By the early eighteenth century, however, French pioneers in Louisiana encroached on Natchez tribal lands. Their differing customs led quickly to misunderstandings and then to violence. French leaders there offended Indian sensibilities by ignoring the customary meetings, calumet or peace-pipe smoking, and exchanging of gifts, and by not showing proper respect to their chiefs, Great Sun and Tattooed Serpent. Divisions within the tribe also affected relations with the Europeans. Most of the Natchez villages traded with the French, but a few made alliances with English traders from Carolina. This strained their dealings with the intruding whites and provoked isolated violent incidents.

By 1722 more than one hundred French colonists had settled among the Indians, taking some of their best land. Daily contacts between the two groups led to more trouble. When pioneers gave Indians things such as fabric or pots and pans, their hosts considered them presents. The whites saw the manufactured goods as trade items and demanded something in return. In October of that year, in the anti-French Apple Village, a sergeant killed two of the villagers in just such an argument. When the chiefs got word of the murders, they ordered an attack in retaliation. By the time pro-French tribal leaders halted the attacks, angry warriors had killed or wounded a dozen settlers or their slaves and had slaughtered or stolen some of their livestock. Because the colonists built part of their settlement on the sacred land of a worn-down former temple mound, Indian raids disrupted the shaky peace. In response, the colonial leader Jean-Baptiste Bienville led a six-hundred-man force to the Natchez villages, where they joined their trading partners in destroying the pro-British bands.

Peace proved only temporary. The pioneer settlers carried smallpox with them, and soon an epidemic struck the villagers. As they recovered from its effects, changes in leadership along with continuing French incursions triggered renewed violence. In 1725, Tattooed Serpent, one of the most cooperative leaders, died. Several years later during the Great Corn Feast, the Indians' most sacred ceremony of the year, the commander of the local French garrison ordered the Natchez to move their villages so that French farmers could use their croplands. This infuriated tribal leaders, and they struck back quickly. Pretending to need weapons and ammunition for hunting, they borrowed these items from the settlers. In November 1729 armed warriors attacked the fort, killing its commander and other settlers. In a single day they slew 237 Europeans and placed the victims' severed heads on the Fort Rosalie palisade. Then they took the surviving pioneers off to their villages as slaves. Determined to control the region, French officials opened a war of extermination, and in the next three years they killed, scattered, or enslaved most of the Natchez. This conflict combined issues such as disease, competing trade networks, and quarrels over land, as well as differing cultural practices and religious ideas. When neither side had any clear understanding of why their strange neighbors acted as they did, war resulted.

While the southern tribes tried to keep their land and independence, those in the backcountry of New England also experienced English encroachment. There the Eastern Abenaki sought to hold their lands along the Kennebec River between French Quebec and the Maine settlements. Perhaps acting with French encouragement, in 1722 they canoed down the river to attack settlements near Brunswick, Maine, opening hostilities now called Dummer's War. Massachusetts leaders blamed the Jesuit missionary Sébastien Râle for the attack, and in 1724 they sent militiamen to the Indian village where he lived. When the troops stormed into their village, the Abenaki resisted, and in the melee that followed the priest and several Indians died. The whites destroyed the village, scalped their victims, and returned downriver. This incident touched off a series of raids and counterattacks that lasted until 1727, when the fighting ended. For the next several decades the tribe resisted English domination publicly, blaming the colonists for the troubles. "It is you, brother, that always attack us," a tribal spokesman said. "Your mouth is of sugar but your heart [is] of gall." Rejecting Massachusetts's claims to their land, the Abenaki speaker Atiwaneto warned that "we expressly forbid you to kill a single beaver, or to take a single stick of timber [from our territory]." At the same 1752 meeting, he criticized the survey crews then working on tribal land and demanded that they be punished for trespassing.

In the southeast the Cherokee fought for their independence. During the French and Indian War they sent six hundred men north to help the English in Pennsylvania. While the Cherokee campaigned there in 1757, English authorities built two new military outposts: Fort Prince George among the Lower Cherokee villages and Fort Loudoun among the Overhill groups. When colonists learned of the new forts, they flooded onto lands still owned by the tribe. Then, when the men who had gone north to join the war against the French started for home, pioneers in western Virginia attacked, killing forty of them, apparently to collect the scalp bounty the colony paid. Tribal customs about clan retribution demanded that the families of the victims attack the English. To settle the continuing disputes, Carolina Governor William Lyttelton met a Cherokee delegation at Charleston. When talks bogged down he seized Chief Oconostota and several more men as hostages until other tribal leaders captured and surrendered those accused of killing pioneers. This action set off the Cherokee War of 1760–61.

Indian customs prevented their doing what the governor demanded, and eventually he released the hostages. However, his action so enraged Oconostota that the chief led an ambush against the soldiers at Fort Loudoun, and in response the garrison commander murdered the hostages still being held there. At this point, raiding parties swept across the southern frontiers killing, burning, and routing the pioneers. They forced troops at Fort Loudoun to surrender and later killed most of them because the commander had executed the hostages. In 1760 English authorities sent an army of thirteen hundred regulars, supported by colonial rangers and Indian allies, smashing into the Cherokee homeland, where they destroyed crops, burned villages, and drove the fleeing Indians into the wilderness. This failed to end the raiding, however, as the villagers fought to retain their land and to retaliate for what they considered colonial aggression. That in turn led the British commander, Sir Jeffrey Amherst, to send another expedition of some three thousand men through the Cherokee country, where they destroyed fifteen villages completely and damaged many others. Lacking enough guns and ammunition to resist effectively, tribal leaders sued for peace. So, in late 1761 the Cherokee War ended. At that point many villages lay in ruins, and the victorious colonial leaders extracted a harsh treaty that included Indian acceptance of new British forts in their country and a major land cession. Thus, for the tribal people, their alliance with the colonists against the

French had failed completely. Not only did they get nothing positive for their help, but by the time the French and Indian War ended, they had also tasted bitter defeat at the hands of their own allies.

In each of the disputes that led to Indian wars for independence, the tribes lost at least in part because their traditional competitors or enemies sided with the Europeans against them. Although intertribal conflict continued, by the middle decades of the eighteenth century chiefs, war leaders, and shamans began calling for anti-European cooperation. As early as the 1740s, refugees from villages that French, British, or colonial forces had attacked came together in the Ohio Valley. There Delawares, Miamis, Mingos, and Shawnees struggled to bring some order to their communities. They had few options. They could agree to a single set of leaders in each village and promise to support them. They could also find ways to cooperate with people in other villages. Even as early as the late 1730s, shamans had called for tribal people to pull back from their contacts with the colonists. Prophets came onto the scene and then disappeared, but gradually their ideas began taking hold. Often they denounced the whites as witches and as representatives of evil who contaminated Indian life.

By the 1750s, Indian leaders focused most of their attention on the British and on the American colonists, pointing out that these people brought disease, introduced alcohol, and encouraged hunters to become dependent on trade goods. At a meeting that same decade, the Catawba leader Hagler attacked the whites for the rum trade. The liquor, he said, "Causes our men to get very sick and many of our people has Lately Died by the Effects of that Strong Drink." A few years later the Delaware shaman Neolin also preached against alcohol, and by 1760 his ideas had spread through the disgruntled tribal societies. He reported that the spirits told him that the Native people had to strengthen their societies by returning to traditional practices or be destroyed. They had to abandon their use of white trade goods and even their contacts with the whites. Ultimately, his effort to develop a multi-tribal or pan-Indian movement failed, but it represented something

new. By this time some Indians saw their world as having two irrecon-
cilable civilizations, theirs and that of the invaders. Many eastern
villagers never saw Neolin, but his ideas spread rapidly. Yet even here,
tribal divisions and competition limited the impact of those ideas.
Shamans who represented other beliefs or who saw Neolin as an inter-
loper objected to his teachings whenever they could.

Neolin's preaching became important when the Ottawa war leader
Pontiac used them in his calls for war. Whereas other prophets had
denounced the impact of trade goods, Neolin's distinctly anti-English
rhetoric gave Pontiac phrases that helped him to mobilize anti-British
feelings among the groups near Detroit. In 1763 the British and French
had signed the Treaty of Paris, which surrendered French claims to
North America. More important to the Indians, the agreement left
them at the mercies of the British and their colonial allies, the very
people who posed the biggest threats to tribal survival. So, early that
year the Ottawa warrior spread Neolin's idea that the tribes had to
join forces against the invading whites. According to Pontiac, the Master
of Life described the English as people "who have come to trouble
your country," and he ordered the Indians to "drive them out, make
war on them!" If they did that, the spirits would help them to regain
what they had lost in the preceding generations as they dealt with the
English. That summer, as traders fanned out across the frontier with the
news that their French brothers had left, many tribes joined in the
fighting that came to be called Pontiac's Rebellion. Fort after fort fell
to attacking war parties, until only Detroit and Pittsburgh remained.
As usual, in just over a year the Indians' individualism and the need to
feed their families caused many to return home, and by 1765 the
British and their colonial allies had won. Yet, almost for the first time,
Neolin and Pontiac succeeded in getting differing tribal groups to
cooperate, as they sought to blunt the English encroachments on and
destruction of their village societies.

Unfortunately, the pioneers ignored tribal complaints in their violent and unrelenting movement west. Their repeated incursions onto

tribal lands, destruction of game, and frequent mistreatment of Indians increased tribal bitterness along the frontier. At the same time, shamans reported visions in which voices from the spirit world urged them to break off all contacts with whites. These anti-English and anti-American teachings rarely called for war but did nothing to ease tensions. An Assinsink prophet named Wangoment urged villagers to avoid the pioneers, to quit trading animal skins for alcohol, and to return to more traditional practices. Joining other shamans, he taught that the spirits had punished the Indians for allowing the corruption of tribal society through contact with the whites. Teachings such as these divided many tribes. Traditional chiefs and shamans had come to terms with the whites, and some owed their influence and power to the very trade being denounced. So the prophets encouraging a return to traditional values divided their own societies at a time of renewed stresses.

By the 1770s, Indians had come to see most pioneers as their enemies, so violent incidents and raids continued. As whites surged into Kentucky, the Delawares, Mingos, Shawnees, and Cherokees all objected, and in 1774 Cherokees attacked traders on the Ohio River. The Virginia authorities retaliated, indiscriminately attacking innocent as well as guilty people. In April 1774, frontiersmen welcomed a small Mingo party into their camp, got them drunk, and slaughtered them. The Mingos' Shawnee neighbors took up arms, and this set off a major war scare. Terrified pioneers hurried to fortified villages or fled. Virginia Governor John Dunmore sent three militia forces into Ohio and Kentucky, where they burned crops and destroyed villages. After early victories, Shawnee leader Cornstalk sued for peace. In the Treaty of Camp Charlotte, signed later that year, the Indians surrendered their Kentucky hunting grounds, and hundreds of frontier families hurried to the newly opened region. Angry anti-American feelings remained, and during a meeting at Fort Pitt in western Pennsylvania one tribal spokesman denounced the colonists' actions. "You have feloniously taken possession of part of our country," he charged. Therefore, he threatened, "we now tell you in a peaceful manner to quit our lands . . . or blame yourselves for whatever may happen."

IN THE AMERICAN REVOLUTION

News that the colonists had declared their independence from Britain did little to change relations between the frontier peoples. The long knives, as Indians called the Virginia pioneers, had made it clear that they considered all Indians their enemies. As a result, when the American Revolution began, most eastern tribes remained neutral or joined the British as a way to fight for their own continued independence. In the Southeast the pioneers in the Watauga region of east Tennessee encroached steadily on Cherokee land. When many established tribal leaders took no action, Chief Dragging Canoe denounced them as Virginians, not Cherokees, and in April 1776 he led an attack that set off another vicious frontier war. His men fought alongside Choctaw and Muscogee or Creek allies, but their efforts failed to halt the tide of settlement. Rather, militia armies from Virginia, as well as from North and South Carolina, invaded Cherokee country, destroying dozens of villages, burning crops, and taking hundreds of prisoners. With their shelter and food supply gone, tribal leaders asked for peace. At the 1777 negotiations Chief Corn Tassel objected to the colonists' demands. "It seems misterious to me why you should ask [for] so much land near me," he remarked, at first refusing to cede more land. Yet soon after this the chiefs signed the treaties of DeWitt's Corner and of Long Island, surrendering their lands east of the Blue Ridge Mountains as well as the areas already occupied by the pioneer settlers. Despite this defeat, later, when it looked as if the British would defeat the colonists, Chief Dragging Canoe launched new attacks along the frontier. Response came quickly, as militia forces smashed through the Cherokee country again. They destroyed crops and villages, leaving the Overhill towns in shambles. In 1781 the discouraged chiefs had to sign a second Treaty of Long Island, surrendering more of their home territory.

In the North, most tribes either sided with the British or remained neutral. Like villagers in the South, they faced constant pressure to cede their land even when that was the last thing they wanted to do. Many wished only to be left alone, but they could not escape the whites' demands for land. The Iroquois Confederacy in New York split when the Revolution began, as the Oneidas and Tuscaroras sided with the colonists and the Senecas and Mohawks joined the British. Under Mohawk leader Joseph Brant, the tribesmen ambushed and defeated Gen. Nicholas Herkimer. In May 1778, Brant led his force along the Mohawk River, while other tribesmen joined Colonel John Butler in raiding across the Wyoming Valley in Pennsylvania. Later that same year the British and Indians swept through the Cherry Valley, driving terrified pioneers away. These raids brought repeated invasions of the Iroquois home territory. In these raids the Americans burned or destroyed whatever Indian property and crops they could, leaving the northern tribes few options. Some fled west to the Ohio Valley, and many Mohawks joined Brant when he moved to Canada.

In Kentucky and the Ohio Valley the Shawnees, Delawares, Mingos, and Wyandots all attacked the pioneers. These raids kept Daniel Boone's followers penned in their small palisaded villages. In 1777 the Shawnee chief Blackfish attacked the Kentucky settlements, disrupting the pioneers' farming and hunting and reducing their winter food supplies to dangerous levels. Early the next year, Shawnee raiders captured Boone and about thirty other Kentuckians as they were gathering salt. They took their prisoners back into Ohio and Indiana, where they adopted Boone and several others. Despite their precautions, Boone escaped and raced back to Boonesborough to warn of another attack. Fortunately for the settlers, the Shawnee and their allies delayed until September 1778, when they besieged the village. This attack failed, and for the next several years parties of Delawares, Wyandots, Shawnees, and others raided settlements beyond the mountains. Fighting there continued into 1782, when the warriors defeated a colonial force under William Crawford. Seeking vengeance for the murders of peaceful Christian Indians by Pennsylvania pioneers, the victors burned Crawford to death slowly.

By the time the United States gained its independence, the tribal groups within its borders saw little to celebrate. When the Iroquois learned that the British had abandoned them in signing the 1783 Treaty of Paris that formally ended the war, they complained bitterly. "Brother . . . we were greatly alarmed and cast down when we heard the news," Mohawk leader Joseph Brant wrote. His people had good reason to feel betrayed and angry. Their experiences with the Anglo-American governments and people of the late colonial era offered them little hope for the future. The victors represented everything that had brought misery to the villagers. Whiskey peddlers, land-grabbing pioneers or land companies, and a new government whose officers treated tribal people as defeated enemies presented only bleak prospects for peaceful relations. Even the most optimistic chiefs had to feel some uncertainty, even dread. Encroachments on their lands continued, alcohol-induced violence disrupted most villages, and divided leadership and religious confusion undermined village unity. The preceding century of living with the intruding Europeans had brought many changes, but few of those changes represented positive results for the Indians. Now Indians had to face a self-confident and aggressive government whose citizens feared or hated them.

SUGGESTED READINGS

Dowd, Gregory Evans. *A Spirited Resistence: The North American Indian Struggle for Unity, 1745–1815*. Baltimore: Johns Hopkins University Press, 1992.

Edmunds, R. David, and Joseph L. Peyser. *The Fox Wars: The Mesquakie Challenge to New France*. Norman: University of Oklahoma Press, 1993.

Hatley, Tom. *The Dividing Paths: Cherokees and South Carolinians through the Era of Revolution*. New York: Oxford University Press, 1993.

Hulley, Clarence C. *Alaska, 1741–1953*. Portland, Oreg.: Bibfords & Mort, 1953.

Jennings, Francis. *The Ambiguous Iroquois Empire*. New York: W. W. Norton, 1984.

McConnell, Michael N. *A Country Between: The Upper Ohio Valley and Its Peoples, 1724–1774*. Lincoln: University of Nebraska Press, 1992.

Merrell, James H. *The Indians' New World: Catawbas and Their Neighbors from European Contact through the Era of Removal*. Chapel Hill: University of North Carolina Press, 1989.

Naske, Claus M., and Herman E. Slotnick. *Alaska: A History of the 49th State*. Norman: University of Oklahoma Press, 1987.

Saunt, Cladio. *A New Order of Things: Property, Power, and the Transformation of the Creek Indians, 1733–1816*. Cambridge, England: Cambridge University Press, 1999.

Usner, Daniel H. *Indians, Settlers, and Slaves in a Frontier Exchange Economy: The Lower Mississippi Valley before 1783*. Chapel Hill: University of North Carolina Press, 1992.

White, Richard. *The Middle Ground: Indians, Empires, and Republics in the Great Lakes Region, 1680–1815*. New York: Cambridge University Press, 1991.

Chapter 4

CHIEFS, SHAMANS, AND WARRIORS FACE THE USA, *1783–1840s*

The Postwar Era

 The 1783 Treaty of Paris that ended the war between the British and their American colonies granted the rebels independence. However, the English negotiators ignored their tribal allies when they wrote the treaty. This left Indian leaders facing angry pioneers and a new government that viewed them as dangerous, but defeated, enemies. The tribes and colonists had fought each other repeatedly for nearly two centuries. By this time the two sides feared and hated each other and sought revenge for past wrongs. When American officials could not keep the pioneers away from tribal lands, wartime violence continued. Sensing its own weakness, the new government acted as if it owned all the lands between the Appalachians and the Mississippi River by right of conquest. For the villagers this meant immediate confrontation. They asserted their independence, rejected American claims of victory over them, and demanded that the pioneers get off their land. This put them in direct conflict with the United States. For the next half-century tribal leaders negotiated, prayed, fought, and continually relocated as they struggled to keep their identities, customs, and lands from their ever more aggressive frontier neighbors.

The issues that brought Indian-white conflict before and during the War for Independence remained, as hunting parties of the villagers and the pioneers clashed repeatedly, from western New York, west of Pittsburgh in the Ohio Valley, and south into Tennessee and Georgia. Tribal chiefs wanted peace and hoped that the commissioners they met would agree to keep settlers away from tribal lands. At the same time, the American government had to sell western land to survive, and it hoped to acquire the region that the Indians used. With the two sides each wanting what the other could not or would not give, the situation remained chaotic for the next ten or twelve years. During this time Indian leaders tried to protect themselves through multitribal confederacies, negotiations with the Americans, religious and cultural revivals, diplomacy with the British and Spanish, and warfare. Some of these tactics succeeded for a time, but even with these options, chiefs struggled to keep their people from being overrun and destroyed by the advancing frontier population.

STRUGGLES IN THE OHIO VALLEY

In the first few years after American independence, the Native people west of Pittsburgh failed to deal effectively with government agents. Those negotiators extracted harsh treaty concessions from the Iroquois at Fort Stanwix in 1784, from the Delawares, Wyandots, and Ojibwas at Fort McIntosh in 1785, and from the Shawnees at Fort Finney the next year. Tribal leaders denounced government attempts to treat them as conquered enemies, because many of the groups had not been defeated. They considered themselves British allies, not subjects, and rejected the idea that diplomats in Europe could deed away their lands. Their bitter objections persuaded officials in Canada to offer some help and encouragement. Those officials promised to support Indian land claims and refused to move their troops out of forts that now stood within the United States. From those posts, English military and civilian officers assured their allies of continued support and urged them to resist any American settlement in their territory.

Some chiefs ignored the British effort because they feared that their allies would not live up to these new promises, but others sought to use any help they could get. Still, rather than depend on the Europeans, Mohawk leader Joseph Brant soon became the leading Native spokesman, as Indians worked to create a multitribal alliance against the Americans. In December 1786, representatives of at least nine tribes met on the Detroit River to plan a unified approach. When the discussions ended, they sent a message to Congress, promising to work for peace. However, they insisted that all negotiations about land be held in public and that any treaties with the United States require that all tribes of the confederation agree. Any other negotiations they would consider "null and void." Having said that, they prepared to defend their lands and homes, as runners traveled south to forge new ties between the confederation and the Muscogees and Chickamaugas there.

By 1787, while the Constitutional Convention debated how a new government should operate, young Indian men raided isolated settlements and attacked travelers. Mingos and Miamis now joined the Delawares, Wyandots, and Shawnees in the fighting against pioneers in Kentucky, West Virginia, and along the Ohio River. The frontiersmen retaliated, raiding north into Ohio and Indiana, burning crops and leveling villages. While pioneers denounced their government for not destroying the tribes, Indian leaders asked the British for continued support. Officials in Canada urged the Ohio Valley groups to defend their homeland and supplied them with trade goods and weapons. By 1789, when George Washington became president, the region west of Pittsburgh had become a war zone.

Pioneers in western Pennsylvania and in Kentucky begged the new government to help them against the Indians because the raids had brought settlement almost to a stop. The president ordered Gen. Josiah Harmer to mobilize frontier militia units and then attack the villages

in Ohio and Indiana. In September 1790, his force of about 1,450
men marched north from present-day Cincinnati, burning crops and
villages. Miami Chief Little Turtle and Shawnee leader Blue Jacket had
their men drop trinkets along the trail to persuade the pursuing whites
that their people were in full retreat. The ruse worked, and on 17
October Harmer's force blundered into an ambush while trying to
cross the Eel River. The terrified militiamen broke ranks, threw down
their weapons, and fled. When reinforcements stopped them, one
soldier cried out, "For God's Sake retreat—you will Be all killed—
there is Indians enough to Eat you all up." Four days later, the reor-
ganized troops launched a second attack on the Miami village of
Kekionga, but the tribesmen defeated them again in heavy fighting.
Despite Harmer's report of success, the Indians had killed more than
10 percent of his men. The two victories persuaded the tribesmen
that they could resist the Americans.

Once the federal officials realized how thoroughly the warriors
had defeated Harmer, they planned a follow-up expedition for the
next summer. Arthur St. Clair, the territorial governor, received
command and led about 2,300 men north into the Indian country.
The Miami victory the preceding summer encouraged resistance, and
fighting men from at least ten tribes united against the American
force. By October 1791, the army had moved north, building several
forts as it made its way slowly into Indian territories. General St.
Clair posted his men with care, but the warriors surprised them
anyway, attacking on the morning of 4 November and focusing their
heaviest fire on the clearly marked officers and the artillerymen
whose weapons they rightly feared. When St. Clair ordered his forces
to retreat, the undisciplined militiamen fled, leaving the regular
troops to face overwhelming numbers of attackers. The retreat turned
into a rout as soldiers abandoned the artillery, their other equipment
and weapons, and wounded comrades. When Little Turtle halted the
slaughter, more than six hundred soldiers lay dead and hundreds
more had been wounded. What the Miamis called "The Battle of a

Thousand Slain" was the worst defeat that Indians inflicted on U.S. forces in American history.

This stunning victory elated tribal leaders, who had now twice defeated American armies in little more than a year. At this point the British urged them to demand that the Ohio River become the boundary between their lands and those of the pioneers. The chiefs had already decided to make this their goal, so they rejected government efforts to reach a peace agreement. In fact, they became so confident that in 1792 they murdered two American negotiators who had traveled west to meet with them. The next year confederation spokesmen again insisted on the Ohio River as the only boundary they would accept. At the council they assured the visiting diplomats that they wanted peace but also told them, "We have therefore resolved to leave our bones in this small place to which we are confined" rather than surrender more land to the United States. This clearly stated determination to resist persuaded the government to halt its negotiations. It had to have the land and had to protect the settlers there, so Washington and his advisors decided to rebuild the army and take the region by force.

While Washington worked with his army, confederation leaders met with British officials who urged them to continue their demands for all of Ohio as Indian country. The U.S. government rejected this idea out of hand. Instead, Gen. Anthony Wayne trained a new army and in the summer of 1794 led his troops north along the Ohio-Indiana border. Blue Jacket and Little Turtle gathered between fifteen hundred and two thousand men to oppose the Americans, but this time they faced well-led and well-trained regular troops, not just militiamen out to shoot a few Indians. General Wayne knew that Indian fighting men fasted for at least twenty-four hours before going into battle, so he announced the day he expected to fight. Rather than attacking as promised, however, he waited several days until the hungry warriors scattered to get food. He assaulted the Indian force on 21 August at a place called Fallen Timbers near present-day Toledo.

Because of Wayne's delaying tactics, only about eight hundred Indians remained to oppose his troops, and this time they had to flee. When the retreating warriors reached the nearby British fort, its officers refused to protect or help them, and the tribal leaders realized that they stood alone. Their resistance broken, the next summer they signed the Treaty of Greenville, ceding much of Ohio and parts of Indiana as well.

SOUTHEASTERN DISPUTES

In the South, the Cherokees and Muscogees, or Creeks, faced the encroaching pioneers in Tennessee, Georgia, and Alabama. These groups struggled as well to keep their lands and independence, but because of their long-standing rivalries, they found it difficult to form defensive alliances against the Americans. Instead they tried a combination of negotiations and violence to gain their objectives. Federal officials gave the region little attention because some of the states still claimed land there, and often this left the tribes to deal with the pioneers alone. When squatters in east Tennessee settled illegally on Cherokee land, they created the state of Franklin to protect their territorial claims. Then in 1785 they persuaded a few minor village chiefs to sign the Treaty of Dumplin Creek, which ceded the land in dispute. Most Cherokee leaders objected, and later that year U.S. officials wrote a new agreement, the Treaty of Hopewell, which repudiated the earlier cession and recognized tribal independence. Both the Indians and the federal officials hoped this would slow pioneer intrusions, but that did not happen.

Whites continued using the rivers flowing through tribal lands and settled illegally beyond the treaty boundary lines. When minor incidents continued, the Cherokees called for a new treaty. In 1791 some forty chiefs met with U.S. negotiators at Knoxville. There they agreed to the Treaty of Holston, which surrendered more land and allowed pioneers to travel through tribal territory. In return, the federal government sent troops to remove squatters who had refused to leave Indian lands. These actions infuriated frontier citizens, and soon white volunteers began raiding Cherokee settlements, looting and burning crops and buildings, and shooting peaceful villagers. For the next several years Indians and whites attacked each other, until news spread of Anthony Wayne's victory over the Ohio Valley tribes at the Battle of Fallen Timbers. Once Cherokee leaders understood the determination of federal officials to impose their will in the frontier regions, they decided that they had to make peace. In 1798, at Tellico in Tennessee, they signed yet another agreement, ending their raids.

While the Cherokees tried to hold off the aggressive pioneers in east Tennessee, the Muscogees or Creeks in Georgia and Alabama faced demands from aggressive Georgia officials for ever more land cessions. When chiefs from just a few villages signed several agreements, the rest of the tribe objected. They repudiated these treaties and asked the Spanish, who then controlled Florida and the Gulf Coast, for help. In 1784 Alexander McGillivray, a mixed-race spokesman for the villagers, asked the nearby Chickasaws and Choctaws to join the Creeks in signing the 1784 Treaty of Pensacola with Spain. The Spanish promised to supply trade goods and to help the Indians protect their lands. They also paid McGillivray to keep them informed of American moves in the region. Because of bitter divisions among the Creeks, some other village leaders decided to reopen talks with the Georgians, and during 1785 and 1786 they surrendered most of the tribal land near the state border. Objecting to the new cessions, McGillivray rallied his supporters and struggled to gain control of the tribal government. His followers formed a vigilante-like group of constables to suppress his Creek rivals and then began raiding outlying frontier settlements.

The war parties cleared the settlers from their eastern lands in 1787, and their success brought at least the possibility that the United States might intervene. This frightened Spanish officials in Florida, who tried to persuade McGillivray to end the raids. When he ignored their requests, they cut off the supply of arms and ammunition as well as other trade goods the tribe depended on, and the violence diminished. The new U.S. government began operations in 1789, and soon American negotiators visited the Creeks. When they told their hosts that the United States expected to enforce the earlier treaties between Georgia and the tribe, an infuriated McGillivray disrupted the council meeting. "By God I would not have such a Treaty cram'd down my throat," he shouted, shutting down the talks abruptly. The next year President Washington invited Creek leaders to reopen negotiations in New York; McGillivray and Hopoithle Miko agreed to work together there. That summer they concluded the Treaty of New York, which recognized some tribal claims to the disputed lands and allowed the Creeks to expel illegal settlers from their territory. In return, the Indian negotiators agreed that their lands lay within the United States. To get the treaty, the leaders surrendered over half of the disputed border lands, and that decision caused continuing disputes within the tribe for several decades. Yet this agreement eased relations between the villagers and their greedy neighbors, thus averting major wars like those in the Ohio Valley.

PACIFIC COAST TRIBES

Although the United States reached only as far as the Mississippi River, groups beyond that boundary could not escape the expanding European presence in their homeland regions. By 1790 the czar had granted the Russian-American Company an exclusive charter to trade in Alaska and along the Pacific coast. That same year, company traders began moving south. There they met the Tlingit Indians, who were already trading successfully with the British and the Americans. Ignoring the villagers' objections, company leaders founded Sitka as their headquarters. After just a few years of mistreatment by the high-handed intruders, the Indians attacked. In 1802 they killed at least 150 Russians and their Aleut workers. When it appeared that neither side could win, the two negotiated a truce. Ten years later the Russians decided that they needed an agricultural settlement in California in order to obtain food for their Alaska trading posts. They sent 175 men to build what became Fort Ross, about 90 miles north of San Francisco. As elsewhere, the local villagers attacked when the traders took land for their crops and demanded that the nearby Pomo tribe give them labor, women, and food as well. The raids limited the Russians' crop yields, but the Europeans' violence and the diseases they carried caused sharp population declines within just a decade or two.

Decades earlier, Spanish authorities had grown alarmed at the Russian activities along the California coast, and in 1769 they began a countermove from the south, meant to discourage other powers from claiming much of the Pacific coast. By early that year, two small ships and an overland expedition reached San Diego. The invaders set up camp near a village of Kumeyaay people there. Father Junípero Serra led a small party of Franciscans, while the accompanying soldiers and workers set about building permanent quarters. Their plan included bringing Christianity to as many of the coastal tribes as possible and solidifying Spanish economic and political control over the region. The local villagers watched the invaders' activities for a little more than a month. By then they realized that the strangers intended to remain, so they attacked but failed to drive the newcomers away. Resistance continued, and in 1775 a larger revolt occurred at San Diego as well. Within less than a decade the soldiers and friars marched up the coast, founding twenty-one missions accompanied by presidios or forts along the way. By the late 1770s they had extended their occupation of the coast as far north as San Francisco Bay.

For the California tribes, the Spanish missions brought disaster. Although at first the mission fathers worked with volunteers, within a couple of years the soldiers rode out into the countryside to "recruit" Indian laborers. They rounded up people and herded them from their villages to the missions, where the clerics forced them to change every aspect of their lives. New food, work, clothing, and strange religious practices disrupted their lives. The Spanish segregated men and women, often crowding them into cramped buildings, a practice that fostered the spread of disease. As a result, within the next two decades the mortality rates shot up, with many more people dying each year than were born. Within just a few years, most of the missions became virtual prisons where the priests forced their Indian converts to work as laborers, herders, and builders with little compensation. When small numbers of the boldest or most desperate people fled, soldiers returned them forcibly. Once back, they faced beatings and reductions in food as punishment. The missionaries justified such treatment as the only way they had to bring such barbarous and ignorant people to Christianity. Seventy-five years later, when the west coast became part of the United States, the Native population in California had fallen by at least 75 percent.

RELIGIOUS AND POLITICAL VISIONS

Tribal groups in the path of the expanding U.S. frontier also dealt with missionaries, but their experiences varied widely from those of the coastal peoples. In fact, their own shamans often incorporated Christian ideas and occasionally even Anglo-American practices into their teachings. Other prophets such as Neolin, who preached as early as 1760, called for their listeners to abandon trade with the whites and return to using traditional skills, tools, and goods. Forty years later, the situation had changed dramatically for many tribes. They had been on the losing side in the Revolution, thousands of pioneers poured onto their lands, and alcohol and disease ate at the heart of many villages. Traditional teachings seemed powerless either to turn back the clock or to offer protection from the ongoing difficulties people faced. Healers failed to end epidemics, political leaders signed away tribal lands, and military action brought only more death and destruction. In this circumstance Protestant missionaries offered their help to groups that had given up their tribal beliefs and to those so thoroughly defeated that they saw acceptance of the white man's way as the only road to survival.

Indian prophets responded to the situation too, leading movements of religious and cultural reawakening at the beginning of the nineteenth century. Just before the turn of the century, a Seneca girl reported visions in which the spirits called for a rejection of the religious ideas of the Quakers, then active along the U.S.-Canada border. In New York the Mohawks heard calls for abstinence from alcohol and for a return to the white dog sacrifice, which had long been abandoned. Then in 1799 a little-regarded Seneca shaman named Caneodiyo or Handsome Lake offered new teachings. Apparently he suffered from serious depression, and at one point his family thought that he had died. As they began to prepare his corpse for burial, he revived from what had been a deep trance or coma. He told of his experiences in the spirit world and offered what he called the four words—witchcraft, alcohol, love magic, and abortion and sterility—that formed the basis of his message. He preached that these evils had to be cleansed from Iroquois society if it were to survive. Handsome Lake had other visions that also became part of his teachings. Adapting some ideas gained from Christian missionary teachings, he suggested that the world faced destruction, and called for personal repentance of individual and group sins.

His teachings included distinctly Seneca ideas as well. Tribal ceremonies needed careful observance. At the same time, Handsome Lake urged leaders of the secret medicine societies to open their rites, and he made anti-alcohol efforts central in his preaching. Traditional mourning periods often lasted for months, which he thought placed too much emphasis on death. A pacifist, he urged his listeners to renounce warfare as an option for dealing with the whites. During his years as a shaman he encouraged the Iroquois people to combine the best elements of their culture with those of their neighbors. He stressed that agriculture, pacifism, and individual family actions had to be combined with clan and village practices if the Senecas hoped to survive.

His followers brought his ideas together as the Code of Handsome Lake or the Long House Religion, and some have followed these beliefs down to the present.

At about the same time, a Shawnee prophet began preaching a new message in Ohio and Indiana. A local shaman whose heavy drinking and excessive talking earned him the title of "Rattle" or "Noise Maker" from other villagers, he soon became the leader of a multitribal religious and cultural revival. In 1805 he fell into a trance, and his family thought that he had died. When he awoke, he claimed to have visited the spirit world, where the Master of Life instructed him what to say when he returned to earth. Changing his name to Tenskwatawa or Open Door, he quit using alcohol and began to travel from village to village with his new teachings. He encouraged his listeners to end their contacts with all whites, to stop the fur trade, and, in particular, to cease drinking liquor. At this point his message focused on bringing stability to family and village life, yet he also denounced the American pioneers as causing most Indian suffering. When other shamans questioned his teachings, he accused them of ignorance or even witchcraft.

Villagers from nearby tribes responded to the new prophet's teachings, sending groups to hear his ideas first hand. Within a year his influence grew, and he took part in the ceremonial burning of witches in several Delaware villages. When Indiana Territorial Governor William Henry Harrison heard about the Shawnee's spiritual claims, he scoffed. "If he really is a prophet," Harrison challenged, ask him to "cause the sun to stand still—the moon to alter its course—the rivers to cease to flow—or the dead to rise from their graves. If he does these things, you may then believe that he has been sent from God." Unwittingly, the governor boosted Tenskwatawa's credibility, because the shaman had learned about an upcoming eclipse of the sun. Using that knowledge, he responded to Harrison by telling villagers who doubted his teachings that the Master of Life would soon blot out the sun as a sign that the prophet spoke the truth. On 6 June 1808 the eclipse took place, and Tenskwatawa's followers carried the news and his claims from village to village, thereby increasing his prestige and gaining new converts.

The prophet's success in persuading his converts to join his village led him to accept an invitation to relocate the community to northwestern Indiana. There he established a new settlement on Tippecanoe Creek that came to be called Prophetstown. Some area tribes objected, but Tenskwatawa claimed that the Master of Life had commanded him to move and that mere mortals had no right to interfere. From this village runners fanned out spreading his teachings and recruiting others. When threatened by food shortages, he sent his brother Tecumseh north to seek help from William Claus in Canada. Tecumseh told Claus that the Indians wanted no part of any quarrel between the British and the Americans. Still, the villagers refused to accept the pioneers as close neighbors, and the warrior told his host that the Shawnees and their allies expected to drive the intruders from tribal lands. Tecumseh also promised that if the United States and Britain did go to war, the Ohio Valley tribes would join the British against the frontiersmen. Not satisfied with having sent a delegation to Canada, the prophet led another to visit Governor Harrison. While there, he pledged to remain at peace and succeeded in getting the governor to feed several hundred Indians for more than two weeks.

That support failed to help the villagers make it through the 1808–1809 winter unscathed. Food shortages left many malnourished, and disease swept through Prophetstown. Chiefs and shamans who considered Tenskwatawa's plan to unite the tribes as a threat to their status accused him of having poisoned those who died. As some of the tribes struggled with these internal divisions, Governor Harrison renewed his efforts to browbeat those in Ohio and Indiana into surrendering more land. At Fort Wayne in October 1809, he persuaded tribal leaders of the Miami, Delaware, and Potawatomi to sign another treaty of cession. In that agreement Little Turtle, Beaver, and Five Medals sold three million acres of Ohio and Indiana land for just a few pennies an acre. Their action infuriated both Tenskwatawa and his brother Tecumseh. The two threatened to kill other chiefs who dared sign any new treaties that surrendered more territory to the Americans. Tecumseh said that the land belonged to all Indians and that no one tribe or group had the right to sell it. At this point the leaders' attention shifted from cultural and religious issues to politics, economics, and possible military actions, as Tecumseh worked feverishly to unite all of the tribes beyond the Appalachians against the United States.

Farther south, the groups in the Creek confederation had not succeeded in settling their disputes either with the Georgia pioneers or among their own political elite. Treaty signings with Benjamin Hawkins, the government negotiator there, divided these villagers as well. By the early nineteenth century, the Muscogees tended to retain more of their religious and cultural practices than did many other tribes. They rejected missionary efforts, saying that they knew God without the Bible, and still used traditional practices such as the Black Drink Ritual and the Green Corn Ceremony. However, the villagers lacked unity both in their individual towns and within the confederation. Many leaders accepted the need for peace and accommodation with the white settlers. During the 1790s, Alexander McGillivray had urged the acceptance of livestock and a more sedentary life. While some followed that path, others wanted to direct the cultural changes rather than just accept everything from white society. Nativist leader Hillis Hadjo, or Josiah Francis, was one who took this approach.

Some Creeks traveled north to Prophetstown to hear Tenskwatawa's teachings, and during the winter of 1811–12 others flocked to hear Tecumseh when he visited the Southern tribes looking for allies against the Americans. His message showed Indian frustration and anger. "War now. War forever. War upon the living. War upon the dead," he raged. "Dig their very corpses from the grave, our country must give no rest to a white man's bones." This rallying cry brought the bitter internal divisions in Muscogee society to the fore, as the villagers debated whether or not to support the northern militants. As leaders in the Upper Creek villages who favored partial assimilation expanded their authority through the National Council, more traditional Creeks objected. The messianic teachings of the Shawnee Prophet attracted hundreds of followers, who came to be called the Red Sticks because of ceremonial staves they carried. Their disputes usually centered on religious and diplomatic issues, but often the militants objected to the growing property and greed of some tribal leaders. In response, they killed domesticated animals whenever they could, because livestock represented a clear acceptance of Anglo-American lifestyles. They also may well have objected to the animals because of the destruction they wrought on family cornfields.

When the traditionalists charged their opponents with witchcraft, they brought about division and violence. Several times they burned leaders whom they saw as too pro-American. Their opponents then used the authority of the Creek National Council and armed force to protect some of the accused while killing several Nativist leaders. In February 1813, Little Warrior led a group of Creeks sympathetic to Tecumseh's plans for intertribal unity on a raid in which they killed several white pioneers. This action brought his expulsion from the National Council and its decision in April of that year to execute him and his followers. With a contingent of between fifty and one hundred men, the council forces surrounded the dissidents and attacked their cabin. When the defenders ran out of ammunition, the attackers set the cabin afire, killing all but one of Little Warrior's group as they scrambled out of the burning building. This conflict tore the tribe apart, and during the War of 1812, Red Sticks fought their fellow tribesmen as well as the frontier armies sent against them, keeping the southeastern frontier in turmoil for years.

DIPLOMACY AND WARFARE

The teachings of Tenskwatawa and other prophets called for rejecting the goods and customs of the whites, but by themselves such teachings had only a modest impact. During the first decade of the nineteenth century, the map of the region beyond the Appalachians had changed drastically because of exploding pioneer settlement. In 1800 three territories—Northwest, Indiana, and Mississippi—joined two states there, Kentucky and Tennessee. A decade later, Ohio had become a state, and the Michigan, Illinois, and Louisiana territories encompassed nearly the entire area east of the Mississippi. These developments brought frontier settlers into frequent contact with tribal people. By 1810 the Shawnee Prophet's brother Tecumseh began calling for an alliance of all the tribes beyond the Appalachians to prevent further land cessions to the United States. News of his efforts terrified frontier settlers and upset government plans for signing more treaties of cession. The movement he led also split many tribes, with older established chiefs striving to keep peace and younger ones demanding warfare.

While villagers debated how to deal with the Americans, international issues brought the United States into the War of 1812 against the British. This conflict encouraged dissidents in many tribes to renew or continue their negotiations with the British in Canada and the Spanish along the Gulf Coast. Such groups as the Winnebago (Ho Chunk), Sauk, Mesquaki, Shawnee, and Delaware traveled regularly to Malden, just across the Canadian border from Detroit. There British officials encouraged tribal resistance to American advances and promised supplies and weapons. Despite the inconsistency of past British support, Indians saw few alternatives to asking them for help. In the South, Creeks, Choctaws, and Seminoles negotiated with local Spanish officials for assistance. As a result, well before the United States declared war in June 1812, raiding had begun in the West.

The incessant demands for land cessions angered tribal leaders regardless of what stance they took toward their expanding neighbor. However, the efforts of agents like Benjamin Hawkins among the southern tribes outraged militants everywhere. Frontier officers encouraged the adoption of American attitudes toward private property and the keeping of livestock, both issues that struck at the heart of village social networks. In addition, the whites' ideas about gender roles, particularly in farming, upset many. In most of the eastern tribes the women did the majority of the actual field work, tending and harvesting the crops, while the men performed other duties. Government officers denounced this division of labor, encouraging a change that put Indian women inside their lodges while the men conducted business, did the farming, and negotiated with the whites. These efforts disrupted village life and angered many who otherwise might have remained at peace. As a result, when actual war broke out, Indians felt that they had legitimate reasons to enter it, usually against the United States.

In the North most tribes divided, with some villages or bands siding with the British and the rest trying to avoid the conflict. Fighting began there well before any declaration of war. William Henry Harrison led an attack on Prophetstown in November 1811, as Tecumseh traveled across the South trying to recruit support for an anti-American confederation. Furious at his brother Tenskwatawa for having failed to avoid war, the Shawnee leader allied his followers with the British and persuaded large numbers of Ohio and Mississippi Valley warriors to fight against the pioneers in Michigan, Ohio, Indiana, and Ontario. They won some limited victories, but in the end American numbers turned the tide. In late 1813, Harrison led American forces into Canada north of Lake Erie. There the British commander Colonel Henry Proctor retreated until he reached the Thames River. When Harrison's troops attacked, the small British force fled, leaving Tecumseh and the Indians unsupported and outgunned. After suffering heavy losses, the warriors retreated. Tecumseh died in the fighting, whereupon many of his men lost heart and returned to their villages. In the upper Mississippi Valley, fighting continued into 1815, as Winnebago, Kickapoo, Sauk, and Mesquaki raids kept the frontier in turmoil for another year and a half, ending for the most part when the British stopped supplying munitions and weapons.

Fewer tribes opposed the American settlers in the South, because the Spanish there chose not to supply them as fully as the British had done in the North. Nevertheless, some Choctaws, Creeks, and Seminoles fought repeatedly, but to no avail. Most of the fighting grew out of the Red Stick War that resulted from the intense struggle among the Creeks over how they should deal with the Americans. The National Council denounced the minority Red Sticks as a threat to tribal survival and helped the pioneer armies from Georgia and Tennessee against their fellow tribesmen. Led by William Weatherford (Red Feather) and Peter McQueen, the dissidents attacked Fort Mims, a stockade that protected many of their tribal enemies and their mixed-race families. Some 250 defenders died in the fighting, as did fifty or more of the Red Stick attackers. During the winter of 1813–14, Andrew Jackson led a militia army south into Alabama, attacking Red Stick forces repeatedly. On 27 March 1814 his forces trapped the main Creek force at what is called Horseshoe Bend and destroyed some eight hundred of the outnumbered defenders. This reduced Creek resistance, but nearly two thousand of the Red Stick survivors fled southeastward into Florida, where they joined the Seminoles and their black allies there. Their frequent raids across the Spanish border into the United States kept the frontier situation confused until Andrew Jackson's 1817–18 invasion of Florida halted most of the violence.

ERODING TRIBAL IDENTITY AND LAND HOLDINGS

American victory in the War of 1812 ended military resistance as an option for most tribes east of the Mississippi. It also brought them face to face again with angry federal officials who considered the villagers to be defeated enemies. In some ways the situation resembled that of an earlier generation, when similar attitudes marked American approaches toward tribal people after the War for Independence. Village leaders faced new demands for negotiations in 1815 and 1816 and signed another round of treaties recognizing the supremacy of the United States, promising to remain at peace and agreeing to end their ties with foreign governments. Having lost the options of warfare and foreign alliances, at this point the Indians sought new ways to deal with the advancing frontier population. They could leave the United States and some did so, moving to Canada, Florida, or to the West. Few chose that option, however, because they wanted to keep what was left of their ancestral home-lands. Others, particularly in Illinois and Wisconsin, chose to avoid the pioneers whenever possible. This worked for another decade, but then the rush of frontier settlement flooded into the region, bringing new challenges with it.

The largest tribes remained in the Southeast, and they faced increasing pressures from citizens as well as from state and federal governments in the decade after the War of 1812 to change their way of life. In 1819, Congress established the Indian Civilization Fund, an annual appropriation of $10,000 to be spent in addition to existing treaty annuities for a program that focused on acculturation. Schools would teach the villagers to read, churches would bring them Protestant Christianity, and model farms would help them to become sedentary farmers. The program aimed at breaking down tribal communal landholding practices. If each family had its own farm, the theory ran, they would remain there, and would need less land than if they continued hunting and trading. They would become accustomed to wearing white man's clothing, speaking English, and being incorporated into the United States. In theory, this would make them appear less foreign and dangerous to the average citizen, thus promoting peace on the frontier. Supporters of the program reminded those who objected to spending good money on "the savages" that this would cost far less than war and was less dangerous too.

The federal acculturation program was nothing really new; it just focused more attention and cash on one of the existing programs. Missionaries, teachers, and a few government officials had visited and lived among some of the villagers for decades. During that time they all called for similar changes in village life. Personal private property, sedentary agriculture, altered gender roles, a greater use of English, and acceptance of Christianity all belonged to the message. These had a continuing effect on tribal life. As seen among the Creeks, white demands that they establish a national council caused a growth of central authority among the villagers. Now the leaders denounced those who refused to cooperate or who challenged their demands. Village shamans who urged the retention of traditional ceremonies found themselves opposing the changes that swept through tribal life. Wealthy leaders began to fence their land, in part to keep their domestic animals in, but also to claim the property as theirs. They acquired slaves who herded hundreds of cattle for them, often in the face of bitter opposition from some of their own people.

For groups still active in the fur trade, the government operated a series of "factories" or trading posts where the hunters could get reasonable quality goods at modest prices. Few Indians brought their pelts to the factories, however, because the law setting up the system prohibited the use of alcohol or credit in the trade. Still, this effort remained part of the machinery for dealing with the tribes until its 1822 closure. Even while many villagers welcomed the manufactured goods they obtained through trade, government leaders hoped that eventually the game animals would diminish, leaving the hunters with debts they could not pay. Then federal negotiators would suggest that the villagers pay their debts with land cessions. This process operated effectively prior to the War of 1812, as William Henry Harrison got eastern tribes to surrender about forty-five million acres between the Appalachians and the Mississippi. Clearly this provided one of the motivations for joining with the British in that conflict. The process continued after the war, as some villagers chose to retreat west beyond the Mississippi in order to escape their difficulties with the pioneers.

Others chose to adopt the parts of the acculturation program they considered useful. As early as 1804, Cherokee leaders welcomed the Reverend Gideon Blackburn, who came to build a Presbyterian school among them. Shortly after that, Chickasaw chiefs asked to have farmers and blacksmiths sent to their villages. They expected that these men would make and repair equipment and also teach young men the skills to do those things themselves. Such signs of tribal interest encouraged churches and missionary societies to support educational, vocational, and religious work among some groups. They cooperated with federal officials, who saw the mission groups as doing the work of "civilization" less expensively than others would. By 1823, one mission board called for support of its efforts because "the American Savage is capable of being both civilized and Christianized." Many village leaders in the South were the mixed-race offspring of British traders and Indian mothers, and often they saw the future differently from their full-blood relatives. They adopted slavery, large-scale agriculture, ranching, businesses, mills, and ferries, and sent their children north to secondary schools for their education. Such individuals hardly needed to be civilized. The issues that came to divide tribal groups went far beyond the leaders' parentage, however. Sometimes quarrels broke out between the traditionalists and those who chose to accept Anglo-American practices. At other times family, clan, and tribal political disputes divided tribal groups. Whatever the causes of such splits in village societies, the disunity weakened efforts to retain both tribal culture and lands.

VOLUNTARY REMOVAL

By the 1820s, the eastern tribes had few options left. They could try to acculturate, and hope that their pioneer neighbors would accept them or that the government might actually live up to its promises and protect their land titles. This rarely happened, and so as early as the late eighteenth century some village leaders had chosen to move away from their white neighbors. The Stockbridge and Munsee people of Wisconsin provide a good example of this. A combination of eastern Algonquian groups including Mahicans and Delawares, they lived originally in Massachusetts and New Jersey. By the 1780s, white settlers overran the mission settlement of Stockbridge, and the villagers accepted an invitation to live with the Oneida tribe in New York. Shortly after the War of 1812 ended, some of them chose to join groups of Delaware near the White River in Indiana. There hatreds resulting from wartime campaigning a few years earlier persuaded them to look farther west for a permanent home. In 1821 they negotiated a purchase of land along the Fox River in Wisconsin, and a year later they began moving. From 1822 until 1831 they cleared land, planted crops, and built several new villages in Wisconsin. Then, about the time they had finished the difficult work of settlement, white pioneers filtered into the area and federal negotiators persuaded the Indians to move to new land east of Lake Winnebago, where they remained until 1856, when they acquired a small reservation next to that of the Menominee tribe. During the 1820s and early 1830s, some of the Oneida and Brotherton Indians from New York also migrated to Wisconsin.

Other tribal groups began to consider moving away from the ever-present pioneers. From 1815 to 1830 at least a million people had settled beyond the Appalachians. This left the villagers there little land for hunting or agriculture, because the pioneers demanded all of the resources. Facing almost constant trouble with their neighbors, some chiefs decided that their only hope for peace lay in a voluntary move beyond the Mississippi. Earlier, during Thomas Jefferson's administration, federal officials had urged the eastern groups to abandon hunting and become sedentary farmers. The president persuaded Congress to let Indians exchange their eastern lands for areas in the new Louisiana Territory. Then he tried to pressure the Cherokee into relocating. Some village leaders among the Chickamaugas decided that the tribe should resettle, and so they moved to Arkansas. Others went west without selling their village sites, so that by 1811 at least two thousand Cherokees had left their homes. However, those who had become partially acculturated wanted to keep their lands and refused to negotiate any new cessions.

Two things happened in the decade after the War of 1812 that convinced federal officials of the need to step up their efforts at encouraging voluntary migration. First, the continuing flood of new settlers surged west, pouring into the new states of Indiana, Illinois, Alabama, Mississippi, and Louisiana. Their presence left only Florida in the South and Michigan and Wisconsin in the North for Indians trying to live in traditional ways. Pioneers in newly opened regions proved no more willing to live alongside Indians than had others on earlier frontiers. Village leaders recognized the growing pressures for them to acculturate or move. Some welcomed missionaries, teachers, and mechanics to their towns, but others urged their people to migrate. In 1817, Cherokee leaders Charles Hicks, George Lowry, and Going Snake signed a treaty that gave the United States nearly one-third of the remaining tribal lands. Under that agreement, they had the option of crossing the Mississippi, and by the 1830s at least six thousand of them had done so. Clearly, whether Indians liked it or not, by the 1820s they saw their freedom slipping away. They faced a rapidly growing white population and increasing demands that their lands and other resources be thrown open for the settlers.

When Secretary of War John Calhoun commissioned the Reverend Jedediah Morse to investigate conditions among the tribes east of the Mississippi, village chiefs cooperated, presenting two distinct views. For some, the onrushing pioneers brought disaster, and they sought some means of escape. Others such as the Cherokees, Creeks, and Choctaws had acculturated leaders, and many of these bilingual men had adopted white economic practices entirely. Their teen-aged sons went to secondary school in New England, while the fathers operated mills, ferries, ranches, and plantations. The Cherokees supported eighteen schools, often staffed by white missionary teachers. In the mid-1820s Sequoyah developed an easy-to-learn Cherokee syllabary that spread "through the nation like a fire among the leaves," bringing literacy in their own language to almost the entire tribe in less than a single decade. Clearly these people could not be labeled "naked savages." With educated leaders, growing economic strength, and widespread literacy, the tribe posed a major challenge to frontier politicians and land-hungry pioneers. When they realized that many Indians had no intention of moving west, state officials increased their clamor for some way to relocate the tribes. Their demands, and the desires of some federal officials to solve what they called the "Indian problem," led to calls for a formal removal program to do just that.

FORCED REMOVAL

Tribes and the government were on a collision course. Few Indians wanted to move from their ancestral homes, particularly when other tribes already occupied the lands farther west. At the same time, many voting citizens demanded that they leave. So from the mid-1820s through the mid-1840s, removal—at first voluntary, later forced—became national policy. Tribal groups devised a variety of tactics to deal with the crisis. Some signed treaties and moved despite their objections. Some stalled and hoped that they could avoid having to move. A few small groups hid or were overlooked and so retained some of their lands. Others enlisted white supporters and fought government actions through the courts. In two instances, the Sauks and Mesquakis in Illinois and the Seminoles in Florida, groups resisted,

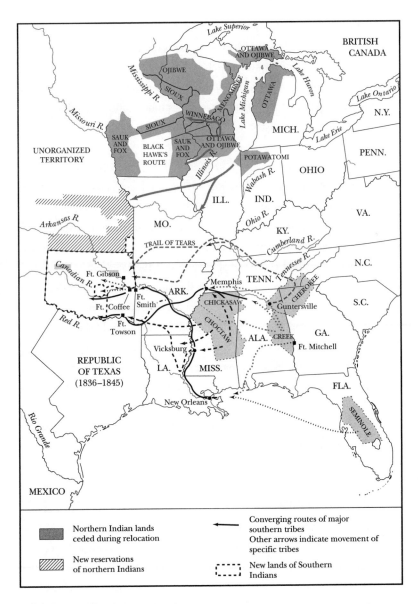

Indian Removal, 1820s–1840s

subsequently suffering through the Black Hawk War of 1832 and the Second Seminole War from 1835 into the early 1840s. Whichever tactics Indian groups tried, they faced increasingly hostile public opinion and impatient federal officers. As a result, the removal process, whether peaceful or violent, brought as much suffering and misery to many tribes as had the wars and intermittent raiding earlier in the century.

During the administrations of Presidents James Monroe and John Quincy Adams, federal negotiators fanned out across the frontier securing treaties by any means possible. Coercion, bribery, and threats of force all came into play, as the tribes and bands saw their lands shrink year by year. Bitter debates over how to deal with American demands pushed some tribal societies to the brink of civil war and made it all but impossible to halt the land losses. The nontraditional Cherokee leaders encouraged wider acculturation, hoping this would gain their acceptance by white neighbors. They established a national council and in 1827 wrote a constitution. This move brought immediate objections from some of the older and less acculturated chiefs. Led by White Path, they held an unofficial council to voice their displeasure with earlier laws that struck at traditional practices such as clan revenge, infanticide, matrilineal inheritance, and polygamy. At the same time, they denounced efforts to force Christian morality and practices on the tribe.

White Path and his fellow traditionalists had several goals. For one, they hoped to slow or even reverse the growing centralization within Cherokee society. The national council had reduced the number of chiefs by nearly two-thirds and also had cut back on the autonomy of the village councils. Cherokee shamans added to the confusion when they objected to what they feared was a movement to proclaim Christianity as the tribal religion. At that point the missionaries and Indian converts referred to the majority of the tribe that still practiced some of the tribal dances and other ceremonies as "backward," "ignorant," and "polluted." Clearly, the traditionalists felt threatened by such attacks on their cultural practices. They struggled to avoid the unwanted changes in their society, but the contest never went beyond angry debates. In May 1827, one of the missionaries reported that "the whole [Cherokee] Nation here is in the greatest turmoil. The greater part wants to have . . . the missions dissolved." Meeting into the middle of the summer, the two sides failed to settle their differences, but before the year ended the leaders wrote a national constitution patterned on that of the United States. This led directly to the decade-long removal crisis that overwhelmed the tribe. State authorities in Georgia reacted angrily to the new tribal constitution and in 1828 passed anti-Cherokee laws that abolished the new government, jailed chiefs if they tried to carry out their duties, and set up a state lottery to sell tribal land. That same year Andrew Jackson won the presidential election, bringing strongly held ideas about Indian affairs to Washington. Many of his Congressional supporters came from the South and the West, and in 1830 they passed the Indian Removal Act, which soon forced most eastern Indians west beyond the Mississippi River. Although divisions continued among the Cherokees, both sides rejected leaving their homeland. The acculturated tribal leaders hired William Wirt, the former U.S. Attorney General, to represent them in a suit against the state of Georgia. This resulted in the 1831 *Cherokee Nation v. Georgia* decision by Chief Justice John Marshall that described the Indians as "domestic, dependent nations." Although the Cherokees lost that case, the decision laid the foundation for the legal status of Indian tribes from that day to the present. It declared that they were not independent, but recognized that they had land claims and other rights. The next year, in *Worcester v. Georgia*, the Supreme Court found the tribes to be entirely beyond any state authority and subject only to the federal government.

During the middle 1830s the Cherokees often appeared divided and uncertain about how to deal with the United States. Nevertheless, most rejected the idea of leaving their native lands and moving west. As early as 1819, their national council had rejected any more land cessions, and their leaders, both the assimilated and the more traditional, saw no reason to change that stance. However, the Georgians' continuing assault on the tribe and the realization that the federal government had chosen not to protect them persuaded some to accept the need for removal. A small group that came to be called the Treaty Party formed around Major Ridge, his son John Ridge, and a nephew, Elias Boudinot, who edited and published the bilingual tribal newspaper the *Cherokee Phoenix*. Experienced, well educated, and economically successful, these men saw their less-acculturated tribal neighbors as having little chance to resist the greedy Georgia pioneers, so they supported removal. Angry at this defection, those opposed to removal impeached the Ridges and forced Boudinot to resign his editorial post. In this case the dispute divided the acculturated leaders rather than separating them from more traditional Cherokees.

Having been ousted from their positions of influence, the Treaty Party leaders decided that the tribe had no options. It had to accept removal or be destroyed. So in 1835 John Ridge led a delegation to Washington, but opponents blocked acceptance of the agreement Ridge had signed. In December 1835, American negotiators met the pro-removal leaders at New Echota and negotiated another treaty, one which called for the surrender of all tribal lands and prompt removal west. Despite pleas from the majority of Cherokees, the U.S. Senate ratified the treaty in 1836 and gave the tribe another two years to prepare for removal. This did little to change Cherokee thinking, and in early 1838 U.S. Army units began rounding up the unwilling Indians. As they waited in open stockades, many fell ill, whereupon Chief John Ross persuaded federal authorities to let the tribal government supervise the removal. By 1840 the Indians had walked and ridden west on what they called "The Trail of Tears" because of the suffering and fatalities experienced along the way. Removal pushed most eastern tribes west, as the tide of pioneer settlement continued to bring thousands of new inhabitants into the region between the Appalachians and the Mississippi River.

The Cherokees had attempted to use acculturation and legal maneuvers to ensure that they would retain their homelands, but to no avail. A few small groups tried to fade into the woods, hills, or swamps to avoid being pushed west, and at times they succeeded. Others simply refused to move and soon found themselves in a military struggle to retain their homelands. In the long run, that worked no better than acculturation or avoidance, but during the 1830s and early 1840s it spread terror across several frontier regions. By the removal era, bitter divisions frequently weakened village dwellers. The Sauk and Mesquaki of Illinois and Iowa offer a good example of how this led to unexpected conflict. These two tribes were closely related, often shared village sites, and frequently intermarried, yet their intratribal divisions helped bring about the 1832 Black Hawk War. American negotiations had planted the seeds for this episode in 1804 when William Henry Harrison persuaded a handful of Sauk leaders to sign a treaty that surrendered their lands east of the Mississippi. The agreement allowed the villagers to stay in Illinois until the government sold the land, and it took until 1829 for this to happen.

By that time the Sauk and Mesquaki leaders disagreed among themselves about removal. Some of the villagers had been living in Missouri and Iowa for several decades, while others returned to Illinois each spring to plant their corn crops. Black Hawk, an aging warrior, led the antiremoval group, while Keokuck persuaded a majority of both tribes that safety lay beyond the Mississsippi. When Black Hawk's followers, known as the British Band, returned to Illinois in April 1832, panic swept through the frontier settlements. Governor John Reynolds called out the state militia, and Gen. Henry Atkinson led a force of U.S. regulars after the Indians. Attempts by the Indians to parley failed, because the militia had no one to interpret. From May through August the Indians managed to avoid their pursuers, but the troops caught them trying to cross the Mississippi at the mouth of the Bad Axe River. When the fighting ended on 2 August, the British Band included only a few hundred survivors of the nearly two thousand people who had dared to "invade" Illinois that year. In Florida the longer Seminole War began in 1835. It ended with a similar result. Most of the tribe relocated west to Oklahoma, with only a few scattered remnants remaining in Florida.

By the 1840s, American officials were congratulating themselves on what they considered a successful conclusion to their handling of the Indian question. They had relocated the tribes, and virtually all federal lands lay available for pioneer purchase and occupation. For the Indians, removal had brought misery and bitter regrets. A traveler in frontier Wisconsin reported hearing an aging Ho Chunk (Winnebago) grieving. "A few short years and our nation will be unknown," he lamented. "Then, when the stranger . . . shall call out upon every hill, *where is the Winnebago?* Echo alone shall answer from the west— *where is the Winnebago?*" The refugees faced dissension and violence as they occupied new regions not always similar to their eastern homelands. At times western tribes attacked them, and the divisions and controversies existing at Removal continued to disrupt the village societies in their new homes. What neither the federal officials nor the Indians could have predicted—the growth of the United States from the Rocky Mountains to the Pacific coast during the 1840s— quickly destroyed any hope for long-term peace and harmony in the West. So, by midcentury Indians faced an aggressive and powerful United States, eager to occupy the West and to exploit its resources, often at Indian expense.

SUGGESTED READINGS

Dowd, Gregory Evans. *Spirited Resistance: The North American Indian Struggle for Unity, 1745–1815*. Baltimore, Md.: Johns Hopkins University Press, 1992.

Edmunds, R. David. *The Shawnee Prophet*. Lincoln: University of Nebraska Press, 1983.

————. *Tecumseh and the Quest for Indian Leadership*. Boston: Little, Brown & Co., 1984.

Green, Michael D. *The Politics of Indian Removal: Creek Government and Society in Crisis*. Lincoln: University of Nebraska Press, 1982.

Herring, Joseph B. *Kenekuck, the Kickapoo Prophet*. Lawrence: University Press of Kansas, 1988.

Horsman, Reginald. *Expansion and American Indian Policy, 1783–1812*. Reprint ed. Norman: University of Oklahoma Press, 1992.

Martin, Joel. *Sacred Revolt: The Muskogees' Struggle for a New World*. Boston: Beacon Press, 1991.

McLoughlin, William G. *Cherokee Renascence in the New Republic*. Princeton, N.J.: Princeton University Press, 1986.

Nichols, Roger L. *Black Hawk and the Warrior's Path*. Arlington Heights, Ill.: Harlan Davidson, 1992.

Prucha, Francis P. *The Sword of the Republic: The United States Army on the Frontier, 1783–1848*. Reprint ed. Bloomington: Indiana University Press, 1977.

Wallace, Anthony F. C. *The Death and Rebirth of the Seneca*. New York: Knopf, 1969.

The Indian Fort Sasquesahanok, 1720. A European depiction of an Atlantic coast village. Courtesy of the National Archives of Canada, C36345.

Return of the captives, 1760s. Peace agreements demanded that whites living as captives in the Indian villages had to be returned to colonial society. Courtesy of the Library of Congress.

Indian halting wagon train. Courtesy of the Library of Congress.

Monument to the largest group hanging in American history, at the end of the
Minnesota Sioux War, in Mankato. Courtesy of the Library of Congress.

Grass lodge used by the Kansa or Caddoan people at the eastern edge of the southern plains. Courtesy of the Library of Congress.

Teen-age Indian students at Carlisle Indian School in Pennsylvania, 1904.
Courtesy of the Library of Congress

ndian School

Indian children in their boarding-school uniforms at the Cantonment School, Oklahoma, 1890–1910 era. Courtesy of the Library of Congress.

Seminole family in traditional clothing, Florida, 1910. Courtesy of the Library of Congress.

Example of Pacific Northwest totem-pole art, 1910. Courtesy of the
National Archives of Canada, PA 41163.

New Mexico Pueblo leaders' 1923 protest against land-title changes. They hold canes given to them by President Lincoln as a promise of fair treatment. Courtesy of the Library of Congress.

American Indian Movement (AIM) protest poster, 1970s. Courtesy of the
Library of Congress, LC-USZ 62-3685.

Participants in the "Longest Walk," sponsored by the American Indian Movement in 1978. Courtesy of the Library of Congress, LC-U9-36364.

Chapter 5

THE STRUGGLE FOR THE WEST, 1840–1890

Regional and Tribal Varieties

 The western tribes differed widely. Along the Pacific Northwest coast, they lived in long cedar plank houses with elaborately carved totem poles nearby. They hunted whales and other sea mammals in large canoes capable of holding thirty or forty men. In the desert Southwest, Puebloan groups built multistory apartment buildings from rock or sun-dried adobe blocks. On the plains, hunters mounted on fast horses tracked the vast buffalo herds and lived in leather tepees. Still farther east along the Missouri River and between that stream and the Mississippi, agricultural villagers lived in large earthen lodges and hunted to complete their diets. At the beginning of the nineteenth century most of these people had mastered their physical environments. Their cultures flourished and they stood at the height of their social, military, and economic powers. Many possessed horses and almost all of the groups had firearms. These gave them both the mobility and the weaponry they needed for protection against enemies, whether Indian or white. So the large tribes of the plains—Lakota Sioux, Cheyenne, Arapaho, Pawnee, Comanche, and Kiowa—stood between the advancing Americans and the resources and wealth they sought. Yet the

Indians' very strength and success, as well as their lack of knowledge of the threat posed by the United States, led many into a near-fatal overconfidence.

Between the 1804 Louisiana Purchase and the 1848 Treaty of Guadalupe Hidalgo, the United States acquired the land stretching from the Mississippi River to the Pacific Ocean. This action brought the western tribes into increasing contact with American leaders who were determined to attach the new regions firmly to the United States. They cared no more for the claims of Indians there than for those of the eastern tribes then being forced west beyond the Mississippi. American exploration and gradual occupation of tribal homelands would change the country and its people forever. At first only small parties of explorers, fur traders, and trappers arrived, but within a few decades hordes of miners, farmers, and other settlers poured west, carrying with them disease, bigotry, and violence. This brought large, fiercely independent, and often mobile tribes into direct contact, competition, and conflict with pioneers who feared and despised the Native peoples. Indian efforts to retain their independence, cultural practices, and homelands included diplomacy, trade, religion, flight, and warfare, with only modest success. These actions stood at the center of their dealings with the United States for most of the nineteenth century.

EARLY MEETINGS

Many western tribes lacked experience with Americans, but that changed quickly. During early March 1804, a few Sauks stopped at St. Louis to visit the Spanish governor of upper Louisiana, Charles Delassus, whom they considered a friend. Years later Black Hawk, who was in the group, remembered learning that the United States would take over the region that same day, and that their "Spanish father" would leave. "We were sad," he said, "because we had always heard bad accounts of the Americans from Indians who had lived near them!" Later that summer, as the Lewis and Clark expedition worked its way slowly up the Missouri Valley, it only narrowly avoided disaster when encountering the Teton Lakota (Sioux). On 25 September 1804 the expedition halted in South Dakota to meet the Sioux, who came down to the river. When William Clark and a few men rowed to shore, the Indians there grabbed the bow cable of the boat and surrounded him. Thinking that the explorers were really traders, they threatened to drive them back downstream unless the Americans gave them more presents. When the leaders refused, the young men jostled Clark, who drew his sword, signaled his companions on the larger keelboat to prepare their weapons, and had a shouting match with the chiefs. The incident, though ending peacefully, offered an example of the conflicting goals and actions of the two sides. The Lakota wanted the American settlers to stay out of their country, and the explorers expressed the government's determination to enter it.

For the next generation the Lakota saw their goal of a free West nearly come true. Although modest numbers of traders, mountain men, and government explorers crisscrossed the region, the idea that the plains were desert and that the region beyond them lay outside the nation's borders kept all but the most hardy or foolish from venturing there. Yet the relative isolation most tribes enjoyed began to crumble after 1821, when Mexico achieved its independence. A brisk trade between the border merchants and Santa Fe developed, and in 1822, farther to the north, fur traders William Ashley and Andrew Henry sent the first of their hired trappers west to become mountain men. So, within just two or three years settlers began their penetration of the southern plains, the upper reaches of the Missouri River, and the northern Rockies. Almost overnight this brought them into frequent and often violent contact with tribes living in those regions. Still, the outsiders' numbers remained small for the next several decades, as few nontrappers or nontraders ventured west.

During that time the tribes of the Missouri Valley, the northern and central plains, and the Rockies played active roles in the fur and hide trade that dominated those regions. The hunters killed game and the women prepared pelts and hides for market. In a few villages white trappers and traders acquired Indian wives and became part of their communities. In many cases, however, the Native people considered the trappers interlopers, even thieves, who killed the beaver and other fur-bearers, took food from the Indian hunters' families, and left fewer pelts for the villagers to use in their own trade for manufactured goods. Even more disastrous, the whites brought diseases that raced through tribal camps, killing thousands. In the summer of 1837 traders carried smallpox to the people of the upper Missouri Valley and the northern Rockies, nearly destroying entire communities. Among the Mandans, one village of six hundred lost all but fifteen people in only three months. Terrified and angry, infected people fled, only to spread the contagion. In despair, Four Bears, a dying Mandan chief, reminded his listeners, "I do not fear Death my friends. You know it, but to die with my face rotten, [so] that even the Wolves will shrink in horror at seeing Me," that is too much. He urged the warriors to kill every white man they could find; but of the estimated 1,800 members of the tribe, only 138 survived the disaster, and they lacked the numbers to accept his challenge.

Although the Mandan example appears to be the most dramatic, the pox and other diseases swept across the West repeatedly in the nineteenth century, greatly weakening many tribes. The Blackfeet, for example, encountered smallpox while attacking a Shoshoni camp shortly before the opening of the nineteenth century. As they pushed their way into the enemy tents, one warrior recalled being "appalled with terror." "There was no one to fight," he stated; only "the dead and the dying" remained, "each a mass of corruption!" Two days later the pox began its march through the attackers' ranks, killing at least a third of that particular band. Other tribes reported similar terror and destruction when this disease first swept through their camps.

During the mid-1840s the situation in the West changed almost overnight. In 1845 the United States annexed Texas, and the next year negotiated a border settlement with Great Britain for the Oregon Country. Just two years later, American officials tore California and the Southwest from the grasp of a reluctant Mexico. Within just five years the nation had expanded to the Pacific, and this changed the Indians' circumstances immediately. Now, instead of having only occasional meetings with settlers, they encountered them repeatedly, as thousands of pioneers headed west to the fertile Oregon Country and California. When workers discovered gold at the Sutter's Mill site in 1848, tens of thousands of gold-maddened would-be miners raced to California. The less spectacular, but steadier, movement of pioneer farmers that began during the 1840s continued to lure settlers west as well. These miners, farmers, and townsfolk demanded territorial government and later statehood. By the time the removal program forcing most eastern tribes west of the Mississippi ended in the 1840s, pioneers had begun to arrive throughout much of the same area. This meant that the western tribes and those newly pushed there by the government could not escape increasing contacts with whites and their insistence that the land and its resources be taken from the Indians.

When tribal people encountered overland pioneers traveling to Oregon in the 1840s, they had no way of knowing that these people were only the advance party for the hundreds of thousands soon to follow. However, as they watched the wagon trains and livestock frighten the buffalo, destroy the grass along the Overland Trail route, and foul the water holes, the plains tribes objected. At first no major violence occurred, but Indian leaders complained about white incursions. At the same time, the pioneers asked for protection from the "Indian threat" they faced traveling west, and federal officials provided funds for mounted troops and for building forts along the trail. By 1849 the army had taken over the trading posts that became Fort Kearny in Nebraska, Fort Laramie in Wyoming, and Fort Hall in southern Idaho. Although small, often isolated, and too weak to protect westward-moving emigrants, these outposts became centers for the American invasion of Indian homelands. At each of them the western tribes met agents, soldiers, traders, and other whites, and almost from the start those encounters led to tension and occasional violence. Nevertheless, despite Hollywood's presentations, of the nearly quarter of a million pioneers who trekked west before 1860, fewer than four hundred died as the result of Indian raids, and most of the rest never encountered any hostile Indians.

NEGOTIATIONS AND CONFLICTS

Not anticipating major conflicts with the tribes, in 1849 Congress moved the Office of Indian Affairs from the War Department to the newly created Department of the Interior. In the Senate debate over this measure, Senator Jefferson Davis remarked that although "wars and rumors of wars came annually" in the past, by that time peace rather than war symbolized the normal relations between the United States and the tribes. This noble sentiment proved incorrect time and again over the next forty years, as Indians and whites clashed repeatedly. Hoping to protect the travelers crossing the northern plains, in 1851 the government hired former mountain man Thomas Fitzpatrick to negotiate a peace treaty with tribes from that region at Fort Laramie. Most of the groups responded, and in the treaty they agreed to stay at peace with each other, to allow the United States to build roads and forts through their country, and to make restitution for any later raids on pioneers moving west. In turn, the treaty called for the United States to protect the Indians from the pioneers and to pay them annuities for at least the next ten years. Once the Senate ratified this agreement, many felt that it had set a pattern for peaceful relations with the western tribes, but unfortunately, peace became a rare commodity.

Following the ratification of this agreement, the expected annuity payments drew thousands of Brulé, Oglala, and Miniconjou Lakotas to Fort Laramie each summer. Their camps along the major emigrant trails west led to violence almost from the start. In June 1853, while the Lakotas drifted in for their payments, one of the young men shot at a soldier operating the ferry across the Platte River. Rather than working to calm the situation, the post commander sent a young second lieutenant with twenty-three men to the Miniconjou village. There he seized the offender, and when fighting broke out, his men killed six of the Indians and then hurried back to the fort. The angry chiefs confronted Fitzpatrick when he arrived with the annuities, insisting that the fort be closed because "the soldiers of the Great Father . . . [had made] the ground bloody," but the authorities ignored their demand.

Having learning nothing from this rash behavior, the soldiers at Fort Laramie repeated it the next summer when hungry Indians killed and ate a cow that had strayed from one of the wagon trains. On 19 August 1854, Lt. John L. Grattan led thirty-one men with two artillery pieces to the camp of the Brulé chief Conquering Bear, where he insisted that the village leaders surrender the man who had killed the animal. When the band's leaders refused, Grattan ordered his men to begin firing. The chief died immediately, but mounted warriors killed all but one of the soldiers on the spot. Wounded, the lone survivor escaped to the fort but soon died there. The attack on their village so infuriated the Lakotas that they sacked the local trader's building and took many of his goods. Then they rode north to avoid other contacts with Americans. Although the soldiers were to blame for the so-called massacre, the War Department ordered U.S. forces west to punish the Indians. This led to Gen. William S. Harney's 1855 campaign, which culminated in a costly defeat for the Brulé at Ash Hollow.

These events on the plains are representative of the cycle of violence that occurred there for the next several decades. Often wild rumors, raids, retaliation, and flight became part of frontier life for Indians and whites alike. By the 1850s this was true in both the Pacific Northwest and California, as miners and farmers swarmed into those areas. Miners seemed particularly eager to exterminate nearby Indians. They formed local units of a group they called the California

Volunteer Militia, and marched from one mountain valley to another hunting their human prey. These actions reduced the tribal population from about 150,000 in 1848, when the United States acquired the area, to only 30,000 by 1861. While the miners diverted water and stole timber from them, the tribes suffered even more as farmers and ranchers took their land and drove them into the hills. Hoping to keep peace and gain control of most California land, the government sent negotiators to persuade the California Indians to accept reservations. These groups signed eighteen treaties setting aside about 7.5 million acres, but because Californians objected, the U.S. Senate refused to ratify the agreements. In 1853 Edward F. Beale became the Superintendent of Indian Affairs for California, and he managed to set up five small reservations that protected at least a remnant of the tribes there.

Farther north in Oregon, settlers treated the Indians nearly as badly as in California, so that by the mid-1850s raiding and warfare began there too. As they had on the plains, government negotiators sought to herd the tribes into out-of-the-way places and to keep them out of the settlers' path. Pioneers entering the Northwest heard lurid tales of the 1847 Cayuse War and the massacre of the Reverend Marcus Whitman and his family in that conflict, and they demanded that the local Indians be moved. In 1854–55, Washington Territorial Governor Isaac I. Stevens pressured many of the tribes to accept three treaties reducing their land base and opening much of the region for settlement. Tribal divisions and treaty provisions that forced groups with widely differing languages and customs to share reservations led to violence, and in 1855 war broke out. For the next three years the Yakima or Plateau Indian War brought many Native groups together against the whites. By late 1858 the hostilities had ended, but the disputes over land, the location of reservations, and constant white encroachments on the Indians' home territories kept relations between the tribes and the pioneers on edge for another generation.

As the tribes of the Far West lost their lands and much of their independence through warfare and population pressures, those farther east faced similar pressures. From Minnesota in the North to present-day Oklahoma in the South, tribal and village leaders heard a steady drumbeat of demands that they surrender some of their land and move either to smaller holdings or to new locations. In 1844, prior to the war with Mexico, frontier leaders began calling for the opening of parts of the Indian country in present-day Kansas, lands newly settled by eastern tribes. With the U.S. seizure of California and the Southwest in 1848, demands for railroad connections to the West Coast and for territorial government for the regions between the Missouri Valley and California brought renewed pressures on the tribes living in eastern Kansas and Nebraska. In 1854, as Congress created the new Kansas and Nebraska Territories, federal agents negotiated treaties with local groups such as the Kansa, Osage, and Pawnee, as well as with refugees like the Kickapoo, Miami, and Delaware, that stripped millions of acres from them. In Kansas, territorial officers openly speculated in Indian lands while squatters pushed their way into areas that still belonged to the tribes.

DIPLOMACY AND WARFARE

The years from 1860 to the 1880s brought repeated negotiations and clashes between Indians and other Americans as village leaders tried to protect their homelands. For groups living in the new territories, near mining camps or along the major western trails, each passing year brought more difficulties. The small army garrisons scattered across the West offered little help in halting incursions by pioneers, and when the regular troops headed east during the Civil War, sporadic violence broke out. In August 1862, conflict between the Dakota (Eastern Sioux) and the settlers began in Minnesota when the annuities owed to the Indians failed to arrive during a particularly hot, dry summer. Although the local agent and several traders there had plenty of supplies, they refused to issue any to the Dakotas before the actual payments from the government came. When Chief Little Crow asked for food, Andrew Myrick, one of the traders, said that if the Indians were "hungry let them eat grass or their own dung."

Outraged Dakotas stormed out of the meeting, and two days later four young Indian hunters arguing about their personal bravery killed two farm families. At that point Little Crow, who had worked for peaceful relations with the whites for years, decided he had little choice. His people could flee, they could fight, or they could remain and be destroyed. He decided to fight, and that summer more than a thousand settlers and perhaps an equal number of Indians died. The trader Myrick was among the first victims; the warriors left his corpse on the prairie, its mouth stuffed with grass. By autumn the Dakota had run out of ammunition and the war ended. The army confined 1,700 Indian prisoners to a stockade at Fort Snelling, in present-day Minneapolis-St. Paul. There military courts sentenced three hundred of the warriors to death, but President Abraham Lincoln pardoned most of them. Still, on 26 December at Mankato, Minnesota, the army executed thirty-nine of the men in the largest public hanging in American history. While this ended the fighting there, angry Dakotas fled westward, often joining relatives on the plains and spreading anti-American feelings.

Other plains tribes responded violently to American incursions and mistreatment as well. In Colorado prospectors found gold by the end of the 1850s. As thousands of miners trekked to Denver, they infuriated the Cheyenne and Arapaho of the central plains, and sporadic raiding kept tensions high for several years. In 1864, Colorado Governor John Evans demanded that all of the villagers return to their permanent camps. Those who refused to do so he considered hostile, although groups hunting on the plains had no way to hear about the governor's proclamation. In November, Southern Cheyenne leader Black Kettle camped near Fort Lyon on Sand Creek in southeastern Colorado, where he thought the local commander had promised him safety. There he and his followers fell victim to a brutal, unprovoked attack led by Col. John M. Chivington of the Colorado Volunteers. At

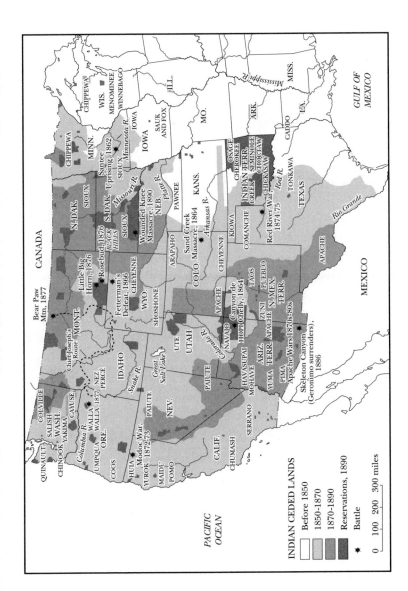

The Indian frontier and major conflicts

daybreak on 29 November 1864, some seven hundred militiamen stormed into the Indian camp and by day's end had killed more than seventy of the villagers, mostly women and children. In an orgy of violence, the Indians "were scalped. Their brains knocked out; the [militia]men used their knives, ripped open women, clubbed little children," a trader present at the scene testified later. Soldiers "knocked them in the head with their guns, beat their brains out, [and] muti-lated their bodies in every sense of the word." Their brutality, which earned the event the name "Sand Creek Massacre," outraged many Americans and led to a congressional investigation that denounced Colonel Chivington and his men. This incident stands as one of only a few white actions against Indians to be called a massacre. Usually that term was reserved for Indian victories.

The Civil War years brought little but violence to other Indian communities as well. In Indian Territory—present-day Oklahoma—the major southern tribes suffered badly after the 1861 withdrawal of federal troops. Because some of the tribes still identified with the south, their leaders joined with the Confederacy hoping for better treatment than they had received from the U.S. government. They organized four regiments of Indian troops numbering nearly five thousand men, and these units served throughout the Civil War. Not all of the members of each tribe backed the South, however, and Creek leader Opothle Yoholo led a mixed group of Creeks and others wishing to remain neutral north into Kansas. One of the Cherokee regiments followed and by the end of 1861 had defeated and scattered this group. For the rest of the war, Indian detachments raided Union forces, and as the Confederacy wore down, U.S. troops raided tribal communities. By 1865 more than ten thousand people in Indian Terri-tory were living in refugee camps, and all of the major tribal groups had seen their governments and economies destroyed. When the war ended that year, tribal support for the Confederacy gave the United States another excuse to demand land cessions, this time as repara-tions for wartime damages supposedly inflicted by the Indians.

Tribes in other areas suffered as well. As U.S. regular troops moved east to fight the Confederacy, hastily recruited regiments of volunteers replaced them in much of the West. Often comprised of pioneers or men from newly settled areas, these units had little respect for the Indians, as their actions at Sand Creek demonstrated. In the Southwest the frequent raiding between the citizens of New Mexico Territory and their Navajo neighbors led to demands that the tribe be punished. Responding in 1864, Gen. James H. Carleton ordered Christopher (Kit) Carson to invade the heart of Navajo country. Leading units of the California Volunteers, Carson destroyed livestock, orchards, and villages in a scorched-earth campaign that ultimately forced the Navajos to surrender. The victors then marched their prisoners on what became known as the "Long Walk" to a reservation at the Bosque Redondo in southeastern New Mexico. Sickness, infertile soil, and danger from raiding neighbors led the Navajo to ask for permission to return to their homeland. It became clear by 1868 that their relocation had failed to achieve its goals, and after four years of misery, they were granted permission to do so.

Once the Civil War ended, pioneers surged west again, plunging the plains into sporadic violence for another dozen years. Gold discoveries in Montana during the war had led suppliers of the camps to open the Bozeman or Powder River Trail north from the Platte River to the mines. This route cut directly through the heart of the best hunting territory of the Lakota or Teton Sioux, who raided travelers there repeatedly. Responding to the miners' calls for protection, the army built three forts to guard the route, but Lakota warriors under Oglala leader Red Cloud kept the troops penned up in their forts. On 21 December 1867 the Sioux lured the boastful Capt. William J. Fetterman and his eighty-man command into an ambush, killing them all. The Indians called their victory "The Battle of the Hundred Slain" and demanded that the United States remove the troops from the region.

Even before these events, many Americans had grown tired of reading about battles and warfare, and in 1867 the government established a peace commission to negotiate the movement of the tribes onto reservations throughout the plains. At Fort Laramie in the North and Medicine Lodge Creek in the South, the commissioners met Indians from the major tribes of each region. By this time many tribal leaders had come to accept the need for peace and moved grudgingly to the new reservations. Red Cloud's refusal to sign the treaty until the government agreed to abandon the forts on the Bozeman Trail led to one of the tribal people's few successes in getting the United States to back down. As the soldiers marched and rode south, Indians burned each of the three hated military posts to the ground. For the moment, that ended major problems on the northern plains, as the tribes began moving reluctantly toward their newly delineated reservations. Yet the 1868 Treaty of Fort Laramie included provisions that led to future conflict. It placed the Sioux reservation on the Missouri River, although tribal leaders wanted it farther west. By allowing the hunters to follow the buffalo herds off the reservation, it encouraged frequent movement, particularly by those who refused to accept land and become farmers.

When the peace commissioners traveled south from Fort Laramie to Medicine Lodge Creek in Kansas, the assembled tribes they met proved even less enthusiastic about accepting reservations and becoming farmers than those farther north had been. After listening to the American negotiators, the Kiowa chief White Bear, or Satanta, reminded his listeners that his people had not been at war and that they had no desire to settle on any particular part of their land. "I love to roam over the wide prairie," he said, "and when I do it I feel free and happy." The Comanche chief Ten Bears echoed these ideas. He chided the commissioners, claiming that American soldiers had begun hostilities against his people. Then he said, "I want to live and die as I was brought up. I love the open prairie, and I wish you would not insist on putting us on a reservation." At the same meeting Satank, or Sitting Bear, of the Kiowa expressed different ideas. He saw the new treaty as generous and ensuring peace. "You know what is best for us," he told the whites.

"Do for us what is best. Teach us the road to travel, and we will not depart from it forever." Such divisions among tribal leaders appeared frequently in treaty negotiations and help explain why lasting agreements and sustained peace remained so difficult to achieve.

Agreements with the United States often did not remove the existing points of conflict. For example, in the treaties signed at Medicine Lodge Creek in 1867, federal negotiators promised that the government would prohibit commercial buffalo hunting in areas claimed by the Southern Cheyennes, Kiowas, and Comanches, yet the slaughter continued. After complaining in vain, tribal leaders including Quanah Parker (Comanche), Lone Wolf (Kiowa), Stone Wolf (Cheyenne), and others agreed to a coordinated attack on the hunters at a camp called Adobe Walls in the Texas Panhandle. Their cooperation showed that the chiefs recognized clearly the threat the hide business posed, and they put aside their differences long enough to carry out the attack. What they failed to anticipate was that they had no weapons to counter the whites' long-range rifles, and despite repeated charges, they could not overrun their defenses. This June 1874 fight opened the Red River War, bringing several columns of cavalry into the region. By August the army considered many of the bands on the southern plains hostile, and a month later Col. Ranald Mackenzie led an attack at Palo Duro Canyon. Most of the Indians escaped, but the troops destroyed all of the food, camp items, and lodges and also captured over fourteen hundred horses. After taking the best mounts for his men, Mackenzie ordered the destruction of over one thousand of the animals. As a result of continued pursuit, frequent small-scale battles, and wretched late-autumn weather, most of the southern tribes drifted back to their assigned reservations. By 1875 the region largely had been pacified.

Tribes on the northern plains had been rather quiet following the 1867–68 treaty signings at Fort Laramie, but continuing white incursions angered the Indians. Work on the transcontinental railroad had begun earlier, in 1864, and within just a few years buffalo hunters had killed large numbers of bison to feed the construction crews. Still, aside from minor clashes, the people in that region remained at peace. In 1870, Red Cloud, Spotted Tail, and several other Sioux chiefs who had signed the Fort Laramie Treaty traveled to Washington hoping to get better treatment for Indians from the government. The reservation agent had told the leaders that they needed to change their way of life. Rather than living by hunting, now they had to become farmers, like the white men. Red Cloud, in particular, had other ideas. He had agreed to surrender much land to the United States, but not to become a farmer. Rather, he told federal officials, "the Great Spirit did not make us to work. The white man owes us a living for the lands he has taken from us." He insisted that their reservation should be near Fort Laramie, but got no new concession to do more than hunt there temporarily.

While Red Cloud tried persuasion, other Sioux leaders led their men on raids against nearby tribes and whites alike. Then in 1874 the government broke its promise to keep pioneers out of South Dakota's Black Hills, a region the Lakota people considered sacred. That summer Col. George Armstrong Custer led more than a thousand soldiers accompanied by prospectors and a host of newspaper correspondents north into the area. The newsmen reported that the region contained rich farmland, grazing land, and timberland, and one wrote that miners had found gold as well. This set off a rush of prospectors that the army had to keep out of the Indian lands. Despite the turning away of hundreds of gold-seekers, by the summer of 1875 at least eight hundred men were panning for gold there. Unable to keep the intruders out, federal officials moved to purchase the Black Hills that same year. They brought the subject up when Red Cloud and Spotted Tail visited Washington again and in September 1875 sent the Allison Commission west to the Red Cloud Agency to negotiate the sale. The commissioners got nowhere. Tribal leaders realized that the government wanted their land, and many of the Indians had no intention of selling it. Red Cloud asked sarcastically why the Great Father did not put wheels under the Indians so that he could move them whenever he chose? On the other hand, chiefs such as Spotted Bear demanded far more than the $6 million the negotiators offered. "Our Great Father has a big safe, and so do we," he said. "This hill [the Black Hills] is our safe." With that, he and others rejected both the $6 million and a substantial annuity in exchange for ceding the Black Hills.

When the talks broke down, the commissioners returned to Washington and many of the Lakota resumed their raiding across the northern plains. Some of the bands had attacked white travelers and railroad crews repeatedly over the preceding several years, and their actions created anger and frustration that led to frequent calls for unilateral action by the government. The commander of the U.S. Army, Gen. William T. Sherman, called upon Congress to abrogate the Treaty of 1868 "inasmuch as the Sioux have not lived in peace." His civilian counterparts went further. When they received the report of Inspector E. C. Watkins describing the actions of "certain wild and hostile bands" of Sioux and his recommendation that the army should "send troops against them in the winter . . . and *whip* them into subjection," they agreed. Together, Commissioner of Indian Affairs Edward Smith and Secretary of War William Belknap ordered the Sioux agents to tell their charges that they had to return to the reservation or be considered hostile. Some of the hunting bands had stayed out on the plains and so did not hear of the agents' demands. Others simply ignored the orders. Their inaction led directly to what became known as "Sitting Bull's War."

In the spring and summer of 1876, while many Americans celebrated the national centennial, army columns moved into the northern plains, hoping to force the tribes there onto reservations. The Indians who remained on the plains included large numbers of Lakota and Cheyenne who had no desire to give up their hunting lifestyle. In addition, almost all of the young men who had wintered on the reservation left to join their friends and relatives on the plains once spring arrived. As a result, that summer the Native people had plenty of

fighting men and defended their country skillfully. To end the violence, the army sent three columns of troops into the northern plains.
Coming from Montana, Dakota, and the southern plains, they hoped
to converge on the tribal people. Responding to this invasion of their
homeland, in mid-June Crazy Horse defeated Gen. George Crook's
forces at the Battle of the Rosebud.

Just one week later, on 25 June 1876, the most famous battle of
the Indian wars took place. The Battle of the Little Bighorn, fought
near the stream the Indians called the Greasy Grass, occurred when
Lt. Col. George Armstrong Custer led most of the Seventh Cavalry in
an attack on the summer encampment of the Sioux and Cheyenne.
Ignoring warnings from his Indian scouts about the size of the camp,
Custer divided his force of 650–700 men into three units and attacked.
A storm of shot and arrows killed all of those under his immediate
command. The disaster shocked the nation, and the army redoubled
its efforts to corral the plains peoples that fall and winter. Soldiers
tracked the scattered bands, defeating some and making it nearly
impossible for the rest to survive. By spring 1877, most of the Indians
had drifted back onto their reservations. Sitting Bull fled to Canada
with his followers, but they were to return five years later.

MIGRATION OR FLIGHT

Many tribal groups lacked the size and mobility the plains people
had used in their struggles to defend their homelands, so they turned
to migration, even flight, to avoid the grasping pioneers and their
government. By 1800 the Kickapoo began migrating to the West from
Indiana and Illinois. Some went as far as northern Mexico, but most
halted in Missouri and Kansas. Despite several treaties giving them
land there in the early 1830s, many later fled, joining their relatives in
Mexico. Their migrations back and forth across the border brought
accusations that they committed depredations on frontier citizens,
and in 1874 U.S. troops pursued them into Mexico. Shortly after

that, some of them moved north to settle in Oklahoma. Facing repeated demands from agents there to assimilate, they returned to Mexico twenty years later. Since then Kickapoos have maintained residences in both countries.

Far to the northwest, many of the Nez Perce, who lived in Washington, Oregon, and Idaho, also chose flight rather than resettlement on a reservation away from their traditional homeland. In November 1876, while discussing the tribe's reluctance to move to an established reservation, Chief Joseph told negotiators, "We will not give up the land. We love the land; it is our home." Gen. Oliver O. Howard, one of the commissioners, threatened to use force if the chiefs refused to lead their people onto the reservation. In Washington, officials gave the tribe until 1 April 1877 to move onto the reservation, setting up a situation remarkably similar to that of a year earlier, which had set off the Sioux War and led to Custer's destruction. In June 1877, a small group of young men killed nineteen settlers, terrorizing the frontier. Fearing indiscriminate retaliation, the leaders decided to flee. Led by Chief Joseph, Looking Glass, and Ollokot, some eight hundred of the nonreservation Nez Perce fled south into the mountains. They outrode and outfought the army, traveling hundreds of miles while seeking shelter from other tribal peoples. Finally, realizing that no one wanted to help them, they set out for Canada, but this tactic failed. When the refugees got within fifty miles of the border in Montana, Gen. Nelson Miles intercepted them, and after some difficult fighting in an early autumn snowstorm, on 5 October 1877, Chief Joseph surrendered.

The other clear example of flight occurred in Arizona Territory during the Apache Wars there. The situation in the Southwest resembled that of the Lakota and Nez Perce. The Indians were ordered by the government to move to a reservation, but they refused. In this case, the destination was the San Carlos Reservation, where, the Apache complained, "there is no grass, there is no game." Years later another Apache cynically described San Carlos as "a good place for the

Apaches—a good place for them to die." In 1877, as American troops pursued the Nez Perce in the Northwest, Chief Victorio and his Warm Springs band left the Arizona reservation saying that "it is better to die fighting than to starve." After eluding pursuit for three years, the fugitives migrated south into Mexico, where Victorio died at the hands of Mexican forces. Several times during the mid-1880s, Geronimo and other Chiricahua Apache leaders led small groups of their people south of the border to escape what they saw as virtual imprisonment on the reservation. Using Apache scouts to help locate Geronimo's band in 1886, the army talked the weary fugitives into surrendering and returning to the United States. Once the captives were back in the country, federal officials ordered them shipped east to prison in Florida, and few, if any, ever got back to Arizona.

CULTURAL INITIATIVES

As they experienced continuing disruptions of their lives, many tribes looked to their cultural and religious rites for assurance. Existing tribal medicine societies continued to direct ceremonies such as the Green Corn Dance, the Sun Dance, and the Buffalo Dance. Modifications of these activities and new practices were introduced as well. Among the Vermillion band of the Kickapoo, the shaman Kenekuk offered a combination of traditional ceremonies and new ideas by the 1830s, when his group moved from Illinois to Kansas. His teachings included a rejection of alcohol, an end to the usage of the old clan medicine bundles, and a flat prohibition on selling any more tribal land to the whites. Surprisingly, while most of the tribe migrated into Mexico, the Vermillion band managed to retain their small Kansas landholdings.

In the Pacific Northwest a Wanapam shaman known as Smohalla came to the fore as pioneers flooded into the region. A hunchback with a large head and short legs, he experienced visions and presented teachings from the spirits he encountered while dreaming. Skilled at predicting earthquakes and the start of the annual salmon runs, as well as at locating good hunting spots, he led tribal resistance to accepting the whites' ways. During the wars of the Columbia Plateau in the 1850s he urged his followers to remain neutral. His teachings, named the Washani Creed, spoke to traditional practices and values. Indians should avoid the white man's farming techniques and instead should accept the natural forces around them. He claimed that "men who work [like the whites] cannot dream" and taught that visions bring knowledge from the spirit world. He also preached against signing treaties and selling tribal lands to the whites. Those who ignored this, he predicted, would be cheated and "be punished by God's anger." His so-called Dreamer Religion gathered adherents throughout the area, and despite persecution by local Indian agents, he remained a strong force for tribal rights in the region until his death in 1895.

The shamans already mentioned used dreams, traditional rites, and prophecies to protect their followers and to help them cope with pressures for assimilation. Wovoka, a Northern Paiute from western Nevada, brought about something rather different. His visions led to the Ghost Dance movement that swept across the northern plains in 1889–90 and brought death and destruction to the Lakota Sioux in the 1890 massacre at Wounded Knee. Sick with fever, in 1889 he experienced visions that became the basis for his teachings. He preached that by returning to their old ways, tribal people could bring back their ancestors as well as the buffalo. Urging his listeners to reject alcohol and live in peace, he gave them a new rite, the Ghost Dance. He promised that, if done properly, this ceremony would bring a return to the old days when Indians lived happily without any white neighbors. When the Lakota heard of Wovoka's preaching, they sent observers, who accepted the shaman's new ideas. Among other things, he promised that "when the time comes there will be no more sickness and everyone will be young again." His teachings found ready acceptance, and soon the sound of the new dance echoed across the Lakota reservation. When Sitting Bull seemed to encourage his followers to join the dancing, agency officials became frightened and called for his arrest. That effort turned violent, as his adherents tried to prevent Sitting Bull from being taken to jail. In the melee that followed, Indian police shot and killed the aging leader. Fearing that the government meant to kill them too, hundreds of Ghost Dancers under Chief Big Foot fled, only to be overtaken by the Seventh Cavalry, Custer's old command. Misunderstandings on both sides led the troops to fire into the camp, and by the time the fighting ended, nearly 250 Indians had died, most of them women and children.

LOSING FREEDOM

Although tribal leaders had used diplomacy, military action, migration, and cultural tactics to deflect the onrushing American pioneers, by 1890 these efforts had failed. That left the survivors facing reservation life and continuing pressures from federal agents to acculturate. Officials demanded that all of the tribes abandon their traditions and join the white American mainstream. Indians had encountered such insistence for generations, often deflecting or avoiding the most damaging results. However, once a group lost its independence and moved onto a reservation, its options shrank quickly. The government's long-standing policy of using the church, the school, and the plow now became central in its program of forcing Indians to become sedentary farmers. Farming proved particularly ill suited to many of the western reservations, where poor soil, lack of water, and great distances from any possible markets hampered even the most ambitious efforts. In addition, a series of harsh winters and devastating summer droughts in the 1880s and 1890s destroyed much of western agriculture. Ironically, the official policy demanding that Indians become farmers came at a time when white American homesteaders gave up farming and began streaming into cities and towns as the nation changed from one of small farmers to one of people living in an urban, industrial society. This meant that the tribes continued to remain outside of the mainstream because of reformers' misguided and out-of-date ideas about how to solve "The Indian Problem," because of Indians' physical isolation from the rest of society, and because of growing racial antagonism and discrimination throughout the West.

As it evolved in the last third of the nineteenth century, reformers and officials alike saw the reservation as a training ground where tribal people could gain the knowledge and skills they needed to become part of American society. Some reformers who had worked toward the abolition of slavery, such as Lydia Maria Child and Wendell Phillips, turned their attention to Indian affairs once the Civil War ended. Others had dealt with tribal groups through earlier church- or government-sponsored programs for decades. Whatever their background, these supposed reformers expected to destroy the tribal cultures and to recast Indians in the image of other Americans. By the late 1860s these people and their ideas became central, as the federal authorities sought to make the West safe for settlement, to end the sporadic fighting there, and to cut spending on Indian affairs. Few whites expected any objections from the reservation dwellers. Even fewer proved willing to listen to any complaints. This left tribal and band leaders few options. Their resistance to the advancing whites had failed, and they had little hope of protecting their people or their cultures.

A certainty that Indians might disappear entirely if the whites failed to step in with help and supervision lay at the center of efforts to shape Indian policy following the Civil War. The Peace Commission–led negotiations at Fort Laramie in Wyoming and Medicine Lodge Creek in Arkansas during 1867–68 demonstrated this. The treaties resulting from those meetings called on Native Americans to adopt farming, live in white-built homes, and send their children to school. To help achieve those goals, in 1869 newly elected President Ulysses S. Grant signed legislation creating the nonpartisan Board of Indian Commissioners, a group of unpaid volunteers, to oversee government-Indian relations. Then he accepted the suggestion that to deal honestly with the tribes, the government needed to appoint Christian gentlemen as agents for the reservations. In theory, such gentlemen would avoid the greed and self-interest demonstrated by so many of the political appointees then holding Indian Office positions. Westerners in particular dubbed what they saw as a misguided effort to save the Indians from extinction as Grant's "Quaker Policy," because it relied on religious groups for nominations to fill reservation jobs. Unfortunately for the tribes, the new appointees often lacked the experience, personal skills, and good sense to serve effectively. They came and went as often as their predecessors, usually having accomplished little except to confirm Indian fears that these religious bigots wanted to destroy tribal rites and customs.

As more pioneers moved west, pressure on the government to open more Indian lands for whites continued. This led to continuing efforts to shrink reservations and a sort of latter-day removal policy that saw tribes such as the Northern Cheyenne and the Ponca being pushed into present-day Oklahoma, or the scattered bands of Western Apaches having to move onto the hated San Carlos Reservation. Once there, the tribal people faced often dreary prospects. Rarely did Indians find themselves residing in their homeland or having access to valuable land, timber, or water. Instead, they encountered agents who struggled to impose federal mandates on them. Agency personnel rarely understood tribal languages, and virtually none of them could speak one. They made few efforts to get to know the band or tribal leaders. Implementing federal policy meant trying to force Indian men to cut their hair, wear white man's clothing, have only one wife, speak English, live in a regular house, and practice small-scale farming on often infertile land that lacked sufficient water.

The agents' actions, and Indian attitudes toward their own forced acculturation, combined to bring despair to most reservation dwellers. The Ghost Dance that swept through some Lakota camps offered a more public display of the levels of desperation that gripped some tribes. Often the agents reported little success in persuading Indians to become farmers. Indian leaders themselves had predicted just such results even before the government forced them to abandon their traditional lifestyles. During the treaty negotiations at Medicine Lodge Creek in 1867, the Kiowa leader White Bear or Satanta had objected to accepting assignment to a reservation. "I don't want to settle there," he told the commissioners, because "when we settle down, we grow pale and die." The Lakota chief Red Cloud expressed similar sentiments in his 1870 discussions with federal officials in Washington. He described the Sioux reservation and nearby hunting lands as "nothing but an island. When we first had this land we were strong," he said; "now we are melting like snow on the hillside." These statements certainly described the situation on many reservations. While westerners cheered as the Indian population plummeted, reformers and government officials alike wrung their hands in despair. They wanted to destroy tribal cultures but did not expect to kill the people. By the late nineteenth century, new efforts to transform reservation life became central to federal efforts at dealing with Indian peoples for the next fifty years.

SUGGESTED READINGS

Anderson, Gary. *Little Crow: Spokesperson for the Sioux*. St. Paul: Minnesota Historical Society Press, 1986.

Franks, Kenny. *Stand Watie*. Memphis, Tenn.: Memphis State University Press, 1975.

Fritz, Henry. *The Movement for Indian Assimilation, 1862–1890*. Philadelphia: University of Pennsylvania Press, 1965.

Hampton, Bruce. *Children of Grace: The Nez Perce War of 1877*. New York: Henry Holt, 1994.

Kelly, Lawrence. *Navajo Roundup*. Boulder, Colo.: Pruett Press, 1970.

Olson, James C. *Red Cloud and the Sioux Problem*. Lincoln: University of Nebraska Press, 1965.

Prucha, Francis P. *American Indian Policy in Crisis*. Norman: University of Oklahoma Press, 1976.

Thrapp, Dan. *The Conquest of Apacheria*. Norman: University of Oklahoma Press, 1967.

Trennert, Robert A. *Alternative to Extinction: Federal Indian Policy and the Beginnings of the Reservation System, 1846–1851*. Philadelphia: Temple University Press, 1975.

Utley, Robert M. *The Indian Frontier of the American West, 1846–1890*. Albuquerque: University of New Mexico Press, 1984.

West, Elliott. *The Contested Plains: Goldseekers and the Rush to Colorado*. Lawrence: University Press of Kansas, 1998.

Chapter 6

SURVIVAL AND ADAPTATION,
1890–1930

Changing Worlds

 For many Indian groups, forced relocation onto reservations proved at least as traumatic as crossing the Atlantic Ocean did for European immigrants during the nineteenth century. They confronted new surroundings, language, clothing, food, religion, and limitations on their personal freedom, while being forced to abandon many traditional practices and ideas. At times the tribes faced ssituations as dangerous as their earlier military conflicts with the U.S. government, including malnutrition, poor housing, and disease at their new locations. They also encountered westerners who feared or despised them, and newspaper editors who attacked them regularly in print. One Arizona newsman claimed that accurate portraits of Indians showed their "low brows, the flat heads, the sunken eyes [and] the large mis-shaped mouths." In 1876, when news of Custer's disaster at the Little Bighorn spread, a Laramie, Wyoming, editor demanded that "a bounty [be] placed on Indian scalps." Attitudes of this sort made tribal people's adjustment to their new situations difficult and forced them to focus all of their skills on surviving.

Even before the plains wars ended, some of the chiefs had objected to moving onto the new reservations. Lakota chief

Red Cloud stated, "I do not want my reservation on the Missouri; this is the fourth time I have said so. . . . Our people are dying off like sheep; the country does not suit them." His complaints, like those of many others, produced no response. By the late 1860s, federal policies focused on settling the tribes on specific reservations, away from the main immigrant trails and mining areas. Usually this meant shifting people south into Indian Territory—present-day Oklahoma—or north into Dakota. For those who followed the buffalo herds, such moves limited their food supply and came at a time when commercial hunting had begun to push the vast herds toward extinction. Grieving over what some called a war between the whites and the buffalo, people reported seeing hundreds of skinned animal corpses left on the ground to rot. The hide hunters killed so many at one time that Indians who traveled through the Judith Basin in Montana recalled, "The whole country there smelled of rotting meat. Even the flowers could not put down the bad smell." The Indians thought that to escape the slaughter, the buffalo fled, entering an opening in one of the mountains and leaving the plains peoples to plead for food rations from the government.

For some, moving to the new reservations meant abandoning the scenes of victories over their tribal enemies, being unable to use their accustomed locales for traditional rites, or seeing others invade and despoil their sacred places. The Lakota experienced this when they lost the Black Hills, as did the Chiricahua Apache when federal actions forced them out of their mountain homes in southeastern Arizona. The idea of leaving family grave sites caused much unhappiness and unwillingness to migrate. Many tribes from the North or West, such as the Nez Perce from Washington and the Northern Cheyenne from Montana, sickened and died in what they called the "Warm Land," or Oklahoma, and the Chiricahua Apache from Arizona had a similar experience after being imprisoned in Florida and then Alabama. The reservation system itself proved equally demoralizing. As a bureaucracy whose goal was to remake Indians in the image of other nineteenth-century Americans, it was staffed by employees who rarely had much sympathy for the people they oversaw. The agents acted on orders from the Commissioner of Indian Affairs and held little autonomy. Most considered Indians to be a doomed race and lacked any sensitivity toward or understanding of tribal cultures. As a result, the agents imposed their own ideas about how to prevent the extinction of Native Americans. To achieve that goal, they thought it essential to attack everything that identified Indians as different from the rest of society. As the system developed after the late 1860s, agents' actions brought them into direct conflict with traditional leaders such as chiefs, shamans, healers, and military men on the reservation, leading to decades of misery and bitterness, some of which remains even today.

ATTACKS ON TRIBAL CULTURES

Government officials and Indians alike faced continuing pressures from reform-minded individuals and groups. Usually affiliated with Protestant churches and missionary societies, these so-called friends of the Indian played important roles in shaping and implementing federal policies. Beginning with the creation of the nonpartisan Board of Indian Commissioners, established in 1869, the reformers quickly built networks of concerned citizens. By the early 1880s they helped found such groups as the Women's National Indian Association and the Indian Rights Association. In 1883 these people held the first annual Lake Mohonk Conference of the Friends of the Indian at a posh resort in New York State. That meeting attracted the major groups and prominent individuals then working toward what they considered better treatment for native Americans. Unfortunately for the Indians, the reformers shared the goals of federal policy. They wanted the reservation dwellers to relinquish their culture and to look, act, and speak like other Americans. Often the only disputes they had with the government focused on dishonest federal employees and the tactics used to bring about the goal of cultural transformation.

On the assumption that Indians needed to speak, read, and write English in order to survive, education quickly became a cornerstone of the reformers' efforts.

Some tribes had operated their own schools or had cooperated with church or mission-society groups for decades. The Cherokees developed an educational system of their own. With largely acculturated leaders dominating their national council, by 1868 they were running sixty-four schools, including male and female seminaries, providing secondary education. These offered their students academic but no vocational training. The tribe hired the teachers, supervised the course contents, and encouraged some teaching in the Cherokee language. Still, the curriculum produced little beyond basic literacy and provided almost no help in retaining tribal culture. Although they appeared to vary little from their government-run counterparts, the Cherokee schools hired their own people as teachers and thus avoided the harsh treatment inflicted on the students at the federal institutions.

Despite the Cherokee example that showed the tribes could educate their own children, the government turned its attention to Indian schools. At first, teachers moved to the reservations, but by the late 1870s the beginnings of a boarding-school system had developed. Capt. Richard H. Pratt convinced his superiors that it made more sense to educate Indian captives then incarcerated in Florida and Alabama than to keep them imprisoned. In November 1879 he opened what became the Carlisle Indian School to work with students from Dakota and Indian Territory. Using former army buildings in Pennsylvania as dormitories and classrooms, he dressed the students in cast-off army uniforms, cut their hair, and addressed them in English. Students marched to and from their activities in formation, faced inspections, and received whatever benefits came from a military-school experience. Pratt expected that his graduates would move into white society, and so began what he described as an "outing" system, in which he sent the older students to work in white homes, factories, and businesses. In theory, this equipped them to become integrated into the national economy. In fact, they often became low-wage laborers for the local citizens.

Pratt became a sort of one-man advertisement for off-reservation boarding-school education, and by 1885, although the government had established 86 day schools on the reservations, it had built another 114 boarding schools. The Indian Office also contracted with church groups to operate a few other schools, but these played only a small part in the evolving system because in 1894 the government ended its support of church-operated institutions. Whichever variety of school—government- or church-run, day or boarding—their faculties strove to separate the children from their families, either by taking them far from home or by disrupting the cultural bonds that held tribal societies together. To do this, the reformers sought to break down "the degrading communism of the tribal" people and to replace it with individualism. Essentially, the missionaries, teachers, and agents wanted each child to have a "desire for property of his own."

At first, agents encouraged parents to send their children to the boarding schools, but once the families realized that the children might remain away from the reservation for years, they objected. Some hid their sons and daughters, while others simply refused to cooperate. By 1891, Congress passed legislation that required all Indian children to attend classes either at home or at one of the boarding schools. When this failed, federal agents began to use the Indian police or even detachments of soldiers from nearby forts to round up potential students. Years later, one of the participants remembered that the "proceeding created quite an outcry. The men were sullen and muttering, the women loud in their lamentations, and the children almost out of their wits with fright." Even these tactics failed to produce enough students, and soon agency personnel cut off the weekly food rations to uncooperative families.

Once located, the children boarded trains headed to distant towns, often in the East. To begin the cultural change, the school staff supervised the bathing of each newcomer and the exchanging of Indian blankets and moccasins for manufactured clothing. At Carlisle, each boy was issued two suits while the girls got dresses. All of them received underwear and boots as well. Then the school officials attacked the new students' long hair, as local barbers helped with the cutting. One young boy remembered crying because we "were all 'bald-headed.' None of us slept well that night; we felt so queer." In fact, for children from tribes such as the Lakota, who prized long hair, losing their braids proved one of their most traumatic school experiences. Having changed their charges' appearance, the teachers then turned to giving each child a new, non-Indian name. Occasionally the children chose their own names from a list on the chalkboard, before being able to read and having no idea how the names sounded or what they meant. At other times the school personnel assigned the students new names. The teachers had no idea how to pronounce the tribal names, so English names made their jobs easier. In addition, federal officials thought that giving Indians surnames would help them fit into the legal system and protect their property years later.

Despite being lonely, frightened, and homesick much of the time, some students found certain aspects of living away from home interesting, even fun at times. They enjoyed playing and marching in school bands, and also trying out their new clothes. Luther Standing Bear, a young Lakota, remembered that at first some of the boys had no idea whether they should button their pants in the front or the rear. He commented that his first pair of boots were too large, but he liked "the noise they made" when they squeaked as he walked. Along with other boys in his group, he spent much of the first night after getting the clothing walking the floor. Some of them even went to bed still wearing their new clothes. For a few children, school presented challenges to be overcome. Years later Charles Eastman reported that when he went east to school, his father told him, "Remember, my boy, it is the same as if I sent you on your first war-path. I shall expect you to conquer." Despite the hardships and the educators' efforts to stamp out all things Indian in them, some of the children came to terms with their alien surroundings, making lifelong friends there and creating their own "underground" society under the noses of the school employees.

Although few agents and teachers found much that was positive in the cultures they encountered, some federal officials disagreed. When Francis E. Leupp became Commissioner of Indian Affairs shortly after 1900, he recognized the tribal societies as having strong communal traditions. Because of that, he thought that efforts to acculturate the Indians should move less rapidly than school leaders considered necessary. He suggested that the students might learn more effectively if their classes were moved outside when pleasant weather made this possible. His efforts to dismantle the boarding-school system faded when he left office. Others accepted his critique of the schools, but for different reasons. By the early twentieth century, some reformers had become discouraged when many graduates "returned to the blanket" upon going back home, because they had no chance to practice their newly acquired skills on the reservation. Refusing to accept this situation as simply a lack of opportunity, whites explained it as the result of low-level intellectual capabilities. For example, an official at the Hampton Institute, a Virginia school that taught both blacks and Indians, described the tribal groups as belonging to one of the childlike races. "We should teach them to labor," he wrote, "in order that they may be brought to manhood." Many of the skills the schools imparted had little use once the young people returned home, but Indians benefited in some unexpected ways. Being forced to speak English allowed them to make friends with young people from other tribes, and by the end of the nineteenth century a new generation of articulate, poised tribal members wanted to use their acquired skills to help their people. Thomas Wildcat Alford, a Shawnee student from Carlisle, remembered leaving school ready "to use the club of white man's wisdom against him in defense of our customs . . . as given to us by our people."

The effort to destroy Indian communities went far beyond education. Various Christian churches had sent missionaries to work among the tribal people for generations, and once the government began to develop the reservations, the religious groups wanted to continue their efforts there. Following the Civil War, Baptists, Episcopalians, Presbyterians, Quakers, and Roman Catholics all sent clergy and lay representatives to do just that. Indians had mixed responses to the missionaries. Some wanted nothing to do with them and raised the same defenses that tribal leaders had used for generations. Watching the often bitter denominational fights over both doctrine and jurisdiction, they wanted no part of learning how to "quarrel about God." Others chided the whites for acting hypocritically by not practicing what they taught. After all, it was the supposedly Christian Americans who brought liquor into the villages and who corrupted the young women. More than one chief or shaman suggested that the churchmen get their own society to act according to the beliefs being presented before pushing them onto the Indians.

Some of their objections stemmed from zealous missionary efforts to stamp out traditional sacred dances and other ceremonies. When they witnessed the self-torture used as a central part of the Sun Dance, whites denounced the rite as a relic of barbarism and as something that needed to be halted. In the Pacific Northwest, the giveaway or potlatch ceremonies horrified local white observers. Some families and even individuals nearly bankrupted themselves by these ritual demonstrations of generosity and a willingness to impress other clans and villages. By the 1880s the reformers had persuaded federal authorities to outlaw both the potlatch and the Sun Dance. Yet some missionaries identified with their charges, serving them honestly and faithfully for years. They recorded meetings with the agents, wrote letters to Washington, translated the speeches of visiting officials, and denounced corrupt and incompetent federal employees. For example, the Sioux called Bishop Henry Whipple "Straight Tongue" because of his efforts to help them and his obvious honesty. Yet, to accept the missionaries' teachings meant abandoning or modifying their own beliefs. For some, the Christian God seemed more powerful than the spirits of their Native religious systems, but acceptance of the new religion came slowly and often without full understanding of its central doctrines.

COOPERATION AND RESISTANCE

Many reservation agents saw the need to reduce the chiefs' authority and strengthen their own in order to enforce the regulations so many Indians hated. Prior to being pushed onto reservations, villagers had used various sanctions such as ridicule, social pressure, and custom to direct people's actions. As the chiefs and shamans lost influence, other controls became necessary. By the early 1870s a few agents began recruiting men to serve as Indian police, not only to help keep the peace but also to enforce the demands of federal officers. On the San Carlos Apache reservation in Arizona, agent John Clum organized a tribal police force within days of his arrival. He told tribal leaders that he wanted "to appoint some Indians as police-men" who would help him keep order among the groups sharing that reservation. Clum publicized his recruitment efforts shamelessly, and soon the Commissioner of Indian Affairs, Ezra Hayt, learned of them. In 1877, Hayt asked for money to recruit reservation police, and a year later Congress appropriated the funds. Such forces were "to be employed in maintaining order and prohibiting illegal traffic in liquor" on the reservations. Initially, up to 480 officers and men could be hired. The authorities considered this program so successful that in 1879 Congress doubled the size of the force. By 1890, fifty-nine reservations had their own police.

Young Indians enlisted in the police force for many reasons. For some, it helped break the monotony and alleviate the lack of employment opportunities available to them. Others used police duty as a way to avoid the backbreaking labor needed to start farms. Particularly in societies with strong warrior traditions, having a uniform and firearms made reservation life bearable. However, those looking for excitement or adventure soon found that police duties included mostly routine and minor tasks. They served at the pleasure of the local agent, and so became a sort of enforcement arm for his office. In that capacity their work entailed such tasks as carrying messages, helping with the monthly ration handouts, and building roads. They helped keep intruders off Indian lands, investigated horse thefts, tracked down children who fled their schools, and kept order by arresting drunks or others who angered or refused to cooperate with the agent.

Not all agency police performed effectively, and their actions had the potential to shatter local communities. In order to get and keep their jobs, the officers had to serve as models of acculturation. They cut their hair, wore white man's clothing, and followed orders not to participate in outlawed tribal ceremonies. In fact, their orders required that they report instances of traditional rites being carried out, but often they avoided doing this. Their efforts at enforcing antiliquor laws, breaking up family fights, and arresting people earned them little popularity. In fact, one agent reported that "the police are looked upon as a common foe, and the multitude are bitterly opposed to them." This became clear in the incident that led to Sitting Bull's death. In December 1890 Standing Rock agent James McLaughlin feared that the Lakota leader was about to flee the reservation and join the Ghost Dancers, so he asked the police to arrest Sitting Bull. Lieutenant Bull-head, who led the police detachment, told the chief that he needed to visit the agent and then could return to his home. When Sitting Bull resisted, the police tried to pull him outside and get him on his horse for the ride to the agency headquarters. As soon as the chief's followers realized that he was being arrested, they rushed to protect him, and one of them shot Lieutenant Bullhead. At that, the other officers shot Sitting Bull, and pandemonium broke out. When the firing ended, Sitting Bull and seven of his supporters lay dead. Four of the policemen were killed immediately and two more died soon after the fight.

In early 1883 the government established a system of courts for Indian offenses as another tool for bringing reservation dwellers into the general society. Headed by respected leaders, the new courts could be used to enforce regulations against holding traditional ceremonies, as well as to deal with other minor offenses. They focused their attention on polygamy, shamans' anti-Christian activities, the use of alcohol, and other actions the agents wanted to end. These courts relied on the reservation police to enforce the agents' rulings and to gather and present evidence. Men who served as judges also had to practice white cultural norms: cutting their hair, avoiding liquor, and having only one wife. Although the decisions handed down in these tribal courts needed the agents' approval, often the judges used their positions as a way to protect tribal customs. For example, when the Cheyenne judge Wooden Leg heard of old men who had multiple wives living separately on different parts of the reservation, he "just listened, said nothing, and did nothing." Quanah Parker, a Comanche leader, managed to ignore all of the rules and still retain his judgeship for a time. He wore his hair long, kept all of his wives, and later worked toward the legalization of peyote in Oklahoma. When he refused to give up his polygamous ways, he lost his court office, but in the meantime he personified resistance to the crushing federal policies.

In 1866, Congress created the Indian Scouting Service, assuming that this would help army units in the West and undermine tribal identification at the same time. However well this worked for the military, it failed to break down traditional cultural patterns, particularly among groups with strong warrior ethics. Often members of such groups as the Pawnee or the Apache scouts enlisted in order to live up to tribal ideals of warfare as the way to gain honor and status in their society. The scouts got uniforms, horses, and weapons—all things they lacked outside of military service. At the same time, they helped their own people by using their alliances with the United States against their tribal enemies. Chief Plenty Coups of the Crow described how tribal leaders decided to help the whites, because "we had always fought the three tribes, Sioux, Cheyenne, and Arapaho, anyway, and might as well" continue to do that. He remembered that his people helped the Americans against their enemies "because we plainly saw that this course [of action] was the only one which might save our beautiful country for us." Whatever military experiences they had, the scouts used to retain aspects of their own culture.

Hoping to protect their people, some leaders simply defied federal authorities by moving off assigned reservations. In 1877, when the Northern Cheyenne heard that they might be sent to live on the Southern Cheyenne reservation in Oklahoma, they objected. "Our people did not like this talk," one chief remembered; "all of us wanted to stay in this country near the Black Hills." Nevertheless, for three months that summer the more than nine hundred Indians trekked south, and on 5 August 1877 they reached their destination. In agreeing to make this trip, they had understood that if the reservation proved unsuitable, they could return and live with the Lakotas. In just a few days the newcomers learned that the agent lacked enough food for them, and that the infertile soil and poor hunting meant that they might face starvation. Even worse, after only a few months they started to die from fevers and malaria. Chief Little Wolf told the agent that his people had come south to visit, and that they had been promised that if they did not like the new country, they could return north. The agent told them that they had to remain in Oklahoma.

After the Northern Cheyenne suffered through the winter, they faced a summer worse than the last. By August 1878, some of the chiefs had decided to return north regardless of what the agent or the soldiers said. Their agent urged them to remain for another year, but Little Wolf replied, "We cannot stay another year, we want to go now." After more meetings, some of the chiefs chose to flee. They told the agent of their plans, but apparently he did not believe them. In September, Little Wolf and Dull Knife led some 297 people away from the reservation. They moved north quickly, but army units followed with orders to force them to return. On 13 September the soldiers attacked, but had to retreat after the fight. From then on, the small band moved through Kansas and then Nebraska, often only hours ahead of pursuing army units or civilian vigilante groups. By October, the group had split. Those wanting to return to their traditional homeland in the Tongue River country left with Little Wolf. The rest traveled toward Fort Robinson, when the cavalry caught up to them. In January 1879, orders came from Washington that the Cheyenne had to return south. They refused, and the local commander ordered them locked in unheated barracks without food for five days. At the end of that time they still refused and then broke out of the barracks, only to be pursued and, in most cases, killed by the soldiers. Little Wolf managed to surrender his band without more fighting and described the end of the trek with some bitterness: "Dull Knife took one-half of the band and surrendered near Fort Robinson. . . . They gave up their guns, and then the whites killed them all."

The Ponca people of Nebraska also tried to ignore reservation assignments, but with less-disastrous results. They too, after bitter objections, had moved south from their homeland to Oklahoma with an army "escort." In 1878 the government offered a new reservation, but the Poncas had to walk the 150 miles to get there. Lacking implements and food, many fell ill and died. As the last son of Chief Standing Bear lay dying, he made his father promise to bury him in their Nebraska homeland. So, in January 1879, a party of sixty-six Poncas headed north to carry out the promise. When they reached the Omaha Reservation, troops arrested them, under orders to return them to Indian Territory. This time a different result lay ahead. General George Crook gave the story of Standing Bear's action to an Omaha newspaperman named Henry Tibbles, and he in turn recruited a sympathetic lawyer who pleaded the Indians' case. At the end of a widely publicized trial, the federal district court judge ruled in *Standing Bear v. Crook* that the Poncas were a people and that they could act independently from the wishes of the federal government. Unfortunately, the decision failed to bring any immediate changes in Indian policy implementation.

FACING ALLOTMENT

Reformers and bureaucrats almost all supported the work of the schools and churches and service as police, scouts, or judges, but these efforts paled when compared to the allotment policy as a way to destroy tribalism. The idea of giving individuals or families their own land for farms had been around for decades, but in the 1880s it became the central component in the government's program to acculturate the tribal people. Speakers at the Lake Mohonk Conferences, members of the nonpartisan Board of Indian Commissioners, and popular authors such as Helen Hunt Jackson all joined their voices with those of missionaries, educators, and politicians to support this idea, which grew out of the realization that the reservations kept Indians isolated from the rest of society. Allotment seemed one of the most effective means to dismantle the reservations. Government officials and reformers alike objected to communal landholding as somehow un-American and suspect as socialistic. One reformer echoed missionary ideas from an earlier generation when he denounced the reservations as "hopelessly wrong," calling for actions to make Indians "more intelligently selfish" by persuading them to accept land as personal property.

A policy of cutting the reservations into small family farms attracted support from promoters, business groups, and pioneers. Local politicians objected to large reservations, because they viewed them as blocking economic development and discouraging population growth. One governor complained about the "enormous tracts occupied by tribes" which he thought could bring prosperity to the region once the Indians' land base was reduced to a reasonable size. Miners, farmers, timbermen, and others joined the chorus, as they sought ways to exploit resources that lay on tribal lands. Local boosters used newspapers effectively to claim that taking Indian lands would be "the impetus of the development" of their particular region. Throughout much of the West, they or their local representatives sent a steady stream of petitions, complaints, and requests to Washington asking that reservation lands be opened for use by white Americans. This combination of support persuaded Congress to take action, and in 1887 it passed the General Allotment or Dawes Act.

This legislation incorporated the reformers' ideas and at the same time met the desires of western business interests seeking access to tribal lands and resources. It called upon the president to order the survey and division of reservations into family farms with allotments or land parcels of 160 acres for heads of families, 80 acres for single adults, and smaller portions for minor children. Each person or family had to select their own land, but if they chose not to do that, the local agent designated a plot for them. Agents conducted a reservation-wide census, prepared tribal rolls, and, using those rolls, made the land assignments. When an Indian accepted his plot, the federal government held title to it for the next twenty-five years, ostensibly to protect him from losing the land until he learned about its value. As individual families gave up tribal practices and became self-supporting farmers, they could become American citizens, and by doing so, they would ensure that the government plan to dismantle the tribes had succeeded. Once all tribal members received their allotments, the government could declare the unassigned acreage as "surplus" land, which could then be offered for sale to the nearby whites. In passing this legislation, Congress overlooked one significant detail that has haunted tribes ever since. The law made no provision for any population growth. Children born after the allotments were recorded and the surplus lands sold had no chance to receive any allotment, but at the time no one raised this as an issue.

Both during the debate over severalty and after passage of the 1887 act, some people urged caution or raised questions about the future. For example, during the debates over the bill Senator Henry Teller predicted that in less than a single lifetime the allotment policy would cost Indians much of their reservation land. "The real aim of this bill," he noted, "is to get at the Indian lands and open them up for settlement." He said that the great variety among the tribes made chances for success unlikely, and that the reformers should work at getting the Indians acculturated before giving them their own land. Even Senator Henry Dawes, whose name became tied to the bill, lost his enthusiasm prior to its passage. When President Grover Cleveland signed the bill into law, Dawes foresaw trouble ahead and commented about "the hunger and thirst of the white man for the Indians' land." By 1881, Ohio Senator George Pendleton joined those predicting problems when he said that the Indians needed "to change their modes of life or they will be exterminated." Yet, beyond raising that note of concern, he offered little constructive advice. Less than twenty years later, one of the reformers described severalty as "a mighty pulverizing engine for breaking up the tribal mass."

On the reservations themselves Indians had few choices because those who objected had little chance to say so. When the leaders learned of the coming legislation, they complained, but the Commissioner of Indian Affairs ordered the agents to prevent their representatives from traveling east to oppose the policy. So, even though many on the reservations wanted no part of allotment, their voices were seldom heard. Within a few years, survey crews had completed their work and the agents began to allot land to each family or individual. The process varied widely, but usually occurred in one of three patterns. In some places, individuals chose their family plots and moved onto them. In others they ignored the agents' orders and so received land assigned to them by those officials; for example, at Cheyenne River in Dakota one man remembered that "they allotted land to us and wherever our land was, was our homestead." Occasionally tribal groups chose their lands all in the same place and then continued living communally.

Once allotment went into effect, many reform groups thought that what they called "the Indian Problem" had been solved, and so they turned their attention to other issues. However, Native Americans, the government, and white settlers all saw frequent changes in the policy and its implementation. The program aimed at making the

Indians farmers, but often their land was poorly suited to agriculture, and many reservations lay in areas that suffered droughts regularly. After trying and failing to harvest more than scanty crops, many Indians sought other ways to use their land, and in 1891 Congress authorized them to lease it to nearby whites. This assured the landowners at least a modest income from their allotments, without their having to work as farmers at all, and struck at the heart of the reformers' assertions that the family farm would lead Indians to accept American values. Congress continued to modify the program and, in the 1906 Burke Act, permitted officials to withhold citizenship from some Indians to protect them from being swindled out of the land. Whatever actions the government took, swindlers and land thieves stayed ahead of them, so that the tribal land base that stood at about 138 million acres when allotment began shrank to a mere third of that within the next four decades.

CHANGING RESERVATIONS

On the reservations themselves, a new generation of younger, often boarding-school-educated leaders joined village chiefs in exercising authority. Like the older, more traditional chiefs, they sought to protect their people and customs. Frequently this meant using the new reservation situations in ways that differed from what their elders might have done or the bureaucrats might have expected. Even where Indian police and judges lacked much support, their actions tended to bring varied bands together, if only to decry what fellow tribesmen did. At Cheyenne River in Dakota, police and band officials from all parts of the reservation met periodically, tying disparate groups together. Within a couple of decades, members of the Blackfeet, Mineconjou, San Arc, and Two Kettle bands of Lakota began to drop some of their strong band identification as they came to live and work together. By 1903, leaders of the separate bands agreed to organize a twelve-man tribal business council, with representatives from each area on the reservation. This council had the authority to approve tribal financial dealings and to fend off land grabs by area politicians, and gradually the elected councilmen came to replace traditional band leaders in dealing with federal officials.

Other examples abound of people ignoring, avoiding, or twisting to their advantage policies set for them by outsiders. Residents of the Round Valley Reservation in California faced Methodist missionaries determined to assimilate them quickly. At first, the Pomo people there looked at Round Valley as a seasonal refuge where they received government food and clothing. But they and other bands living there also saw the reservation as a refuge or homeland, much the same as the people at Cheyenne River had done. Statements from several band leaders all expressed similar ideas. James Sherwood, the Pomo leader, said, "We want land, plow, garden, and work." "We want our own farms," another stated, while a third echoed these sentiments, adding, "We want to do something for ourselves." Despite such statements, the Indians had no desire to abandon their band or tribal identity. They saw their agent Henry Sheldon as a tyrant and opposed him repeatedly, refusing to work for the wages he offered. This proved so successful that at one point he complained they would laugh at him when he offered wages lower than they demanded. They stole grain as well as other goods from the agency storage. When the agent tried to prevent them from attending rites at two sweat lodges they had established, workers simply broke or damaged the reservation equipment, stopping work until Sheldon got it repaired. In these ways they directed activities despite what the agent and missionaries wanted.

Not all western tribes became farmers. Among the Nez Perce in Idaho, many preferred to raise cattle, and by 1890 tribal members owned at least seven thousand head. However, they lacked the capital to fence their lands, and by then at least as many cattle from the herds of nearby ranchers were also fattening on Indian grass. For tribal members who tried farming or lacked interest in cattle raising, land leases became common. This brought ever larger numbers of non–Nez

Perce animals onto the reservation and caused increasing tensions between the Indians and their neighbors. Farther east, in Utah, the Northern Utes faced similar pressures to surrender or lease their land to the nearby ranchers. There a few tribal members who became ranchers gained influence because they worked with agency officials and even white ranchers some of the time. William Wash, one of the Indian ranchers, often served as a spokesman when land-use issues arose. For example, in 1913 Ute stock owners opposed any further leasing of tribal land to white ranchers, and he presented their arguments. "The Indian has always held it [the land]," he said; "they do not want to lease it at all." Wash and his ranching neighbors represented the changing face of their part of Indian country at the turn of the century.

Wherever they lived, Native Americans faced wrenching economic and social change. Men from the hunting cultures of the plains groups had few outlets for their interests and often fewer chances to gain satisfaction or prestige in traditional ways. If they rejected agriculture, most could not acquire cattle for ranching. If they considered service as Indian police or scouts, they faced ridicule or ostracism for serving the government rather than their own people. Many accepted part-time or day-labor jobs such as herding for nearby ranchers, hauling hay, or repairing fences. Women turned their attention to gardening and, under the direct scrutiny of the field matron service, to home-making. A few managed to escape the boredom and poverty of the reservations by traveling with one of the Wild West shows then operating. William Cody (Buffalo Bill) and Gordon Lillie (Pawnee Bill) hired men and women to show several aspects of Indian life. Dressed in buckskins and wearing feathered headdresses, the men roped cattle, raced horses, and attacked stagecoaches to the delight of eastern and foreign audiences. The women practiced Native crafts, set up tepees, and demonstrated clothing, jewelry, and hairstyles. During most of the 1880s the Buffalo Bill show included eighty to one hundred Indians each season. In 1885 even Sitting Bull traveled with Cody's show for a time, receiving a trained horse from the entertainer.

Other Native Americans got jobs entertaining crowds attracted by
the advertising for medicine-show outfits that crossed the East selling
patent medicines and a little excitement. Begun in 1881, the Kickapoo Medicine Company, the largest of these groups, operated thirty
outfits. Each of these included a purported doctor with a name like
Yellowstone Joe or Nevada Ned dressed in western garb, a scout, and
anywhere from twenty to thirty Indians, including men, women, and
children. The tribal people wore Indian costumes, danced, and
drummed for interested audiences who saw them as exotic. Few
medicine shows tried their magic in the West, fearing that the
pioneers might kill everyone in the group, but they crisscrossed much
of the East. After the entertainment had attracted a large crowd, the
doctor gave his sales pitch for the cure-all medicine Kickapoo Sagwa.
A phony drink made of colored water with a few spices and a little
alcohol to give it some zip, the elixir appears to have sold well and
probably did little harm to its users. The medicine or Wild West shows
got Indians off the reservations and out from under the eyes and rules
of their local agents. Reformers and government officials both objected
to Native American's traveling with these groups, and although the
Standing Bear v. Crook decision of 1879 allowed Indians freedom of
movement, reformers tried to end such activities. Commissioner of
Indian Affairs Thomas Jefferson Morgan called on agents to "discourage"
reservation residents from accepting these jobs, but the directive had
only a modest impact.

Even while several thousand Native Americans managed to escape
the dreary life of the reservation, the vast majority could not. At many
agencies, tribal shamans continued to practice the ceremonies that
officials had declared illegal. Prophets urged their adherents to remember traditional rites and beliefs. In the Northwest, Smohalla visited
many tribes preaching active rejection of the white man's ideas and
practices. When responding to demands that Indians give up hunting
and turn to farming, he retorted, "You ask me to plow the ground.
Shall I take a knife and tear my mother's bosom?" Ideas similar to that

circulated among many tribal groups as they continued to resist agency rules and pressures for acculturation. The Ghost Dance of 1898–90 received the most attention, but Indian people all across the West sought help for their new circumstances.

Of all the cultural and religious responses to the forces of change in Indian country, the Peyote Cult or religion became the most widespread and long-lasting. Tribal people in the Southwest had used peyote fruit or buttons (gathered from a cactus that grows there and in northern Mexico) in ceremonies for generations, perhaps even centuries. It produced mild hallucinogenic dreams or visions and, for some people, vomiting and headaches as well. In some ways it resembled the so-called black drink that Muscogean groups in the Southeast had used generations earlier to cleanse themselves as a part of worship. Most scholars think that the Comanches brought peyote back from their raids into northern Mexico and introduced it to other groups on the southern plains. Apparently early reservation users tried the buttons as a way to escape their wretched conditions, but by the late nineteenth century a set of religious ideas and practices had developed around the drug. Quanah Parker, the outspoken Comanche leader, urged its acceptance in Oklahoma. Gradually the ceremonies came to include singing, prayers, drumming, meditation, and the use of peyote as a sacrament in the combined Indian and Christian practices that evolved. Unlike the Sun Dance or the potlatch ceremonies, which took place in public and drew plenty of attention, the peyote rites could be conducted in homes, sweat lodges, or other settings away from the prying eyes of agents or reservation police. So the practice spread, offering religious solace as well as a sense of rebellion against the pressures to assimilate.

The new "Peyote Road" attracted unwanted attention from reformers and federal officials alike. Even though the teachings stressed hard work, monogamy, and the avoidance of alcohol, reformers complained that Indians were wasting time at the ceremonies when they should be working. They also feared the "demoralizing effects of all-night seances" and the possibility that using this new substance might "make the Indian contented with his present attainments [and] seriously interfere with his progress." Both federal and state authorities tried to end peyote use but without success. In 1898, Oklahoma Territory banned the substance, and the U.S. Department of Agriculture used federal agents at the Mexican border to intercept and destroy shipments of the buttons into the country. Facing continued attacks, adherents of the new beliefs organized in 1918 as the Native American Church in Oklahoma. Since then the group has spread slowly despite opposition from some Indian traditionalists because it includes some elements of Christianity in its ceremonies. In spite of the objections raised by reformers, government officers, and some shamans and other tribal leaders, the Native American Church has provided Indians with focus and support for much of the past century.

NEW CHALLENGES

In many ways the reservation groups avoided having to comply with directives from Washington and the meddling of teachers, missionaries, and agency employees, but some things could not be ignored. In 1917 the United States entered World War I, and that action had major long-range effects on Native American life. For several decades before that conflict, army officers serving in the West had suggested creating all-Indian units in the military, similar to the segregated all-black regiments already in operation at the time. Despite the existence of companies of Indian scouts for years, and even a few all-Indian companies during the 1890s, most American planners rejected this idea. While considering how to use Native Americans in the military, they heard sharp criticism of the idea from the pan-tribal Society of American Indians, still in its infancy. That group opposed segregated units, arguing that "much of the popular clamor for a spectacular Indian regiment or battalion arises from the showman's brand of Indian as seen in the circus." Nevertheless, some all-Indian National Guard units from Oklahoma preferred their uniqueness. The SAI's argument aside, Indians from almost all tribes participated in the war effort.

When America entered the war, the Selective Service Act of May 1917 applied to all citizens, and since allotment had given individuals who took the land citizenship for at least a full generation by that time, most Indian men became eligible for the draft. Nevertheless, enlistments exceeded the numbers drafted during the war. To the dismay of missionaries and educators, armed service seemed to call for the very skills and ideas they had worked to suppress. Military officials claimed that Indian soldiers had superior abilities with weapons and as trackers, and many became snipers. As the war neared its end, the Commissioner of Indian Affairs, Cato Sells, bragged that three-quarters of the Native Americans then in service had enlisted. In Europe some local commanders used men from the reservations as messengers and radiomen, having them speak in their own languages to confuse and frustrate the Germans. The figures vary, but it seems likely that as many as sixteen thousand men left the reservations for military service.

Not all groups cooperated wholeheartedly. The Six Nations Iroquois living in New York, for example, issued their own declaration of war against the central powers, claiming that they had never surrendered their tribal independence, and so they joined the war effort as separate nations. Despite calls such as that by Gertrude Bonnin, editor of *American Indian Magazine*, to "stand by the flag, red men, it is your flag," in scattered places young Indians objected to the draft. In western Utah and eastern Nevada, some Gosiutes refused to register for the draft and threatened violence. After an investigation of local issues, it became clear that much of the resistance came because the men thought they had not become citizens and so were exempt from the draft. In early 1918 a sheriff's posse supported by a platoon of soldiers took the last of the protesters off to the county jail, ending the impasse. Some Oklahoma Indians organized the Green Corn Rebellion, and while much of their protest stemmed from economic changes in agriculture, they denounced both the war and conscription. At one meeting, some two hundred people listened while Ellen Perryman attacked the war. "To hell with the Government and the Allies," she said. "The Indians are not going to the slaughter fields of France." Certainly not all Native Americans loved the country that had mistreated them for so long.

The war changed many things for Native Americans on reservations. Because of Indians' participation in the conflict, in 1924 Congress passed legislation giving American citizenship to any Native individuals not yet possessing it. Of at least equal importance, many of the men who did not go off to the military and some of the women from the reservations got war-related jobs away from home. No sooner had the U.S. entered the war than the government called on farmers and ranchers to increase food production. Commissioner Sells saw the Indians' participation in war programs as just another way to hasten them along the path to acculturation and as a new chance to pressure the tribes to become part of the national economy. He sent officials to lecture about the latest farming techniques, give advice on soil conservation, and offer small cash prizes for increased crop production. Patriotism swept across some reservations as tribal people there worked to increase their crops. In Montana, Blackfeet leader Medicine Owl assured the agent that "we will plant more corn to feed your soldiers and we will raise more goats and sheep [so] that your soldiers may be clothed." The acres in production jumped sharply, as some groups put land being rested back into production and others tried to raise two crops in a single year. By the time the government and the farmers got their efforts under way, the war came to a close; and by 1919 surplus crops brought lower prices, and the use of marginal land and the increased leasing of acreages to white farmers and ranchers hurt the economic base of many reservation groups.

Even before the conflict began, other trends began to break down tribal isolation as well. By the first decade of the twentieth century, hundreds of boarding-school graduates had moved into the cities, traveled to distant places, and gone to college or beyond. Indian physicians, lawyers, journalists, and writers left the reservations and shifted their focus from one of retaining tribal culture to bringing tribal people together. Their efforts produced a pan-Indian movement as they worked at simultaneously improving the lives of all Native Americans and bringing their ideas to the general public. In 1911 an impressive group of educated, literate, and articulate young people met to organize the Society of American Indians. Founded and led by such people as Carlos Montezuma, Thomas Sloan, Henry Roe Cloud, Charles Eastman, and Gertrude Bonnin, they wanted to break down barriers between and among the tribes, and to show them which issues they faced in common. In 1916 they began to publish the *American Indian Magazine*, but deep splits within the leadership soon weakened the group. They argued bitterly over peyote use and about how much to cooperate with federal officials. Carlos Montezuma focused his anger on the Bureau of Indian Affairs, and when the others objected, he left the organization and began publishing his own journal. He denounced federal policies because, as he wrote, "when you kill racial pride, you kill the Man." U.S. entry into World War I and continuing tensions within the leadership doomed the Society of American Indians, and by 1923 it had collapsed. During its short life it demonstrated the difficulties Native Americans have had in moving beyond their own tribal issues, but at the same time it laid the groundwork for later multitribal organizations.

The postwar era saw increased quarreling among reformers over how to treat Native Americans. The thousands of Indian bureaucrats opposed most changes as threats to their jobs. Missionary groups, educators, and social conservatives denounced any move to slow or stop programs aimed at crushing tribal cultures. They received plenty of support from the popular *Saturday Evening Post*, which attacked proposals to change Indian policies. Church publications such as *Missionary Review* labeled Native Americans as "pagan worshipers" and called for increased missionary efforts. Traditional ceremonies and dances drew the most criticism, being seen as backward cults that included "horrible, sadistic, and obscene" practices. After inspecting some of the New Mexico pueblos in 1926, the Commissioner of Indian Affairs denounced the residents as "half animals" and ordered the arrest of some pueblo leaders, because their actions violated religious-crimes regulations. Strong anticommunist feelings led to personal attacks on those who defended tribal freedom of religion as "anti-American, and subversive . . . agents of Moscow."

Other reformers began to oppose the forcible destruction of the reservations and all things Indian. Groups such as the General Federation of Women's Clubs focused much of their attention on improving reservation conditions. The author Hamlin Garland wrote positively about tribal cultures and urged that the government stop outsiders from "regulating the amusements and daily lives of the natives." In 1923 John Collier, a social worker, helped organize the American Indian Defense Association, which differed from earlier reform groups in that it supported religious freedom and cultural pluralism for Native Americans. Collier and other like- minded reformers drew public attention to scandals over oil leases to business as well as to squatters who threatened tribal lands in New Mexico. Increasing public attention persuaded federal authorities to examine reservation conditions, and in 1926 the Secretary of the Interior hired the Institute of Government Research in Baltimore to review Indian policies and their results. Lewis Meriam headed the team of investigators that fanned out across the country. Two years later, in 1928, they published their findings as The Problem of Indian Administration, usually known as the Meriam Report. A scathing attack on almost all aspects of federal programs, it called for changes and improvements in such things as education, housing, diet, and public health, bringing national attention to long-ignored problems facing reservation dwellers. Before serious reforms began, the economic collapse of 1929 and the Great Depression that followed brought the economy and the government to a standstill.

Any implementation of the Meriam team's findings had to wait for the New Deal a couple of years later.

SUGGESTED READINGS

Adams, David Wallace. *Education for Extinction: American Indians and the Boarding School Experience, 1875–1928*. Lawrence: University Press of Kansas, 1995.

Dunlay, Thomas. *Wolves for the Blue Soldiers: Indian Scouts and Auxiliaries with the United States Army, 1860–90*. Lincoln: University of Nebraska Press, 1982.

Hagan, William T. *Indian Police and Judges: Experiments in Acculturation and Control*. New Haven, Conn.: Yale University Press, 1966.

Hagan, William T. *Quanah Parker, Comanche Chief*. Norman: University of Oklahoma Press, 1993.

Hertzberg, Hazel W. *The Search for Indian Identity: Modern Pan-Indian Movements*. Syracuse, N.Y.: Syracuse University Press, 1971.

Hoxie, Frederick E. *The Final Promise: The Campaign to Assimilate the Indians, 1880–1920*. Cambridge, England: Cambridge University Press, 1995.

Iverson, Peter. *"We Are Still Here": American Indians in the Twentieth Century*. Wheeling, Ill.: Harlan Davidson, 1998.

McDonnell, Janet A. *The Dispossession of the American Indian, 1887–1934*. Bloomington: Indiana University Press, 1994.

Moses, L. G. *Wild West Shows and the Images of the American Indians, 1883–1933*. Albuquerque: University of New Mexico Press, 1996.

Prucha, Francis Paul. *American Indian Policy in Crisis: Christian Reformers and the Indian, 1865–1900*. Norman: University of Oklahoma Press, 1976.

Chapter 7

FROM RESERVATIONS TO ACTIVISM, *1930–1973*

The New Deal Era and Beyond

 When Franklin D. Roosevelt swept into office as president in 1933, his administration tried to institute changes that would lift the nation out of the Depression, and Indian affairs received their share of attention or more. While much of the economy neared collapse, conditions on many reservations fell below the minimum standards found anywhere else in the country. The 1928 *Meriam Report* had presented the state of health, education, and economic life in Indian country in chilling detail. The isolated reservations had become rural poverty pockets. Per capita income stood at between $100 and $200 per year, contrasted to the national average of $1,350. The authors of the report called on the government to drop its central goal of demanding that all tribal people become Americanized. They urged that most of the boarding schools be closed and that the children be taught near their homes. More money needed to be made available for education, in particular for feeding the schoolchildren, whose diet rarely included either fruit or vegetables and cost the government only eleven cents per child each day.

General health and living conditions proved even more dismal than the schools themselves. Poor housing and inadequate diet on the reservations lowered people's resistance to diseases of all kinds. Measles, pneumonia, and tuberculosis swept through tribal communities. For example, the tuberculosis rate in Arizona stood at seventeen times the national average, while pneumonia killed the Yakimas in Washington at a rate twenty times that of the rest of the population. Trachoma, a serious eye disease, caused widespread vision problems, and the available treatments often resulted in blindness. Mortality rates among Indians soared well beyond those of other groups and of the population in general. Even worse, the infant mortality rate of 190.7 per one thousand live births far exceeded those of blacks (114.1 per thousand), or whites (70.8). The investigators charged that the differences stemmed from the miserly congressional appropriations for Indian health care. The total healthcare budget stood at $756,000, which provided workers with only about fifty cents per person to cover treatment costs each year. While the figures brought no national outcry, they gave such a realistic description of reservation conditions that it became possible for reformers to demand and get large increases in federal funding once the New Deal began its work.

John Collier, a vocal proponent of Indian rights during the 1920s, became the new administration's Commissioner of Indian Affairs. He accepted the idea of cultural pluralism, and worked to end all efforts at breaking down what was left of tribal cultural ideas and practices. When he chose not to abolish the BIA, Alice Lee Jemison, a young Seneca woman from New York, complained that "we are weary unto death of the propaganda for a continuance of the bureau to 'protect' the Indian." Yet, under his leadership it hired more Native Americans than ever before and gave them increased authority. Collier encouraged the use of tribal languages as well as social and religious ceremonies, a clear change from the earlier persecution of traditionalists who had tried to retain elements of their cultures. His orders overturned a century of efforts by religious and other reformers who had sought to destroy such "heathen" practices. Indian students at federal boarding schools no longer had to attend Christian worship services either. These actions opened a debate over what Indian policy should attempt, and many tribal people objected to the commissioner's ideas and actions. Christian Indians agreed with shocked missionaries who attacked Collier's actions as "Christ-mocking, communist-aiding, subversive." Although he sought to help the tribes and to give them more direct control over their affairs in ways that had not been tried, Collier failed to discard the old view that the bureaucrats knew what was best for Indians. So, while he appeared to be moving in a new direction, his approach proved as top-down and authoritarian as the methods of reformers of preceding generations.

At the same time, Collier wanted to help tribal groups recover from the earlier efforts to destroy their culture and the discrimination they had encountered. He hoped to encourage Indians "to develop their own life in their own patterns . . . as noble elements in our common life." One step taken to achieve this goal was to allow religious freedom on the reservations. This meant that people could revive long-outlawed traditional rites such as the Sun Dance and other ceremonies. Rather than forcing Indian men to cut their hair, the new openness encouraged them to wear it long if they chose. In tribal communities, religion and health care often merged, as shamans conducted both healing and religious ceremonies. For years agents, physicians, and missionaries had criticized the Indian Shaker Church in the Pacific Northwest and the Native American Church on the southern plains as pagan and dangerous. One observer denounced those who favored legalizing tribal ceremonies as "idiotic, exceedingly stupid, and ignorant." Yet, during the 1930s, as they came to realize that most Indian religions encouraged family stability and abstinence from alcohol, some health-care workers and bureaucrats changed their minds. As a result, these pan-tribal groups came to be seen as helping to improve reservation life, and Native healers were recognized as having legitimate places in their communities.

Tribal languages, arts, and crafts all received encouragement, a complete reversal of more than a century of efforts to destroy or replace them. The BIA hired linguists to record tribal languages. Then, moving beyond the mere preservation and study of those languages, they turned to producing bilingual materials that could be used in Indian schools. These stunning changes led to widespread criticism of Collier and the BIA reformers as communists, atheists, or worse. Nevertheless, the spirit of change then sweeping through the upper levels of the BIA continued. As Native medical practices and religious ceremonies became accepted and encouraged, so did many forms of tribal art and crafts. Building on established programs at the Museum of New Mexico in Santa Fe, Collier encouraged tribal cultural expressions, which led to an upsurge of interest in such activities. Potters, weavers, basket-makers, silversmiths, and carvers began producing what became a flood of cultural and artistic materials. A few people revived totem-pole carving in the Northwest, while Navajo weavers and Pueblo potters used both traditional patterns and techniques as well as new ones. In 1933 the BIA supported small demonstrations and exhibitions of weaving, pottery-making, and other crafts at the Chicago World's Fair. Two years later, Congress established the Indian Arts and Crafts Board to help Indians promote and market their products.

Having stopped active federal programs aimed at destroying tribal cultures, Collier and his allies worked to protect the changes they had brought about by getting Congress to pass new legislation. In 1933 the New Deal's Civilian Conservation Corps (CCC) included an Indian Division that offered work for young men. Living temporarily at seventy-two CCC camps scattered across the West, these workers labored on a wide variety of projects that included building water reservoirs, digging and enlarging wells, reforesting overgrazed land, marking trails, clearing forest underbrush, fencing land, and assisting with anti-erosion projects. The CCC camps provided temporary housing and gave the workers a modest salary plus food, usually for six months at a time, and without this program some reservation dwellers would have had none of those things. Yet, while the conservation efforts of federal programs did protect and even improve some tribal lands, other actions hurt reservation social and economic practices and sparked bitter criticism. Because thousands of tons of topsoil blew away during the 1930s Dust Bowl years, federal employees came to view some Indian ranching and grazing practices as wasteful and harmful to the environment

This led to the erecting of fences to keep animals away from already overgrazed lands—a worthy goal, but one that disrupted some tribal stock-raising practices. The Navajo Stock Reduction Plan probably caused more Indian dissatisfaction with Collier's direction of the BIA than any other single action he took. BIA officials on the scene saw the range as having been nearly destroyed by the Navajos' large sheep and goat herds, which numbered about 800,000 animals, and sought to persuade the Indians to sell or slaughter enough of them to allow the grazing lands to recover. However, the Indians felt that continued drought, not their animals, had harmed the range. More important, they saw their livestock as a measure of their wealth and community standing, so they resisted federal efforts to kill their animals. They also objected to how the program actually worked. Those with large herds could simply cull the weakest and least-desirable animals. Poorer Navajos, however, often had to surrender their prize sheep, and they objected bitterly. Still, a decade later, nearly half of the animals had been sold or slaughtered. As Commissioner of Indian Affairs, Collier became the Indians' favorite target. According to one of the tribal elders, all had gone well until the commissioner had come along "and stomped his big foot on our sheep, goats, and horses—and crushed them before our eyes." On some parts of the reservation, bitterness over the stock-reduction plan and its implementation remains to the present day.

The central thrust of the Indian New Deal came with the 1934 passage of the Wheeler-Howard or Indian Reorganization Act. At first, this legislation incorporated all of Collier's hopes to refashion national policies for dealing with Native Americans. As the bill moved through Congress, its contents changed considerably, yet when enacted it shifted the course of federal policy substantially. At least in theory, cultural pluralism and encouragement of tribal rites and ideas replaced forced assimilation as central goals, yet federal officials sought these goals without bothering to ask what the tribes wanted. One of the most important provisions of the IRA was that it officially ended the nineteenth-century allotment program. Then it provided funds for tribes to repurchase some of the lands lost because of that policy, and within the first three years Native Americans added more than two million acres to their existing landholdings. The new law met long-standing demands that the government hire Indians for many jobs on the reservations and instituted the practice of preferential hiring within the BIA and related offices.

Collier's efforts to reconstitute tribal governments proved important in bringing long-term changes to the reservations. Like so many other reform efforts, it failed to consider Indian traditions and wishes. The original legislation ignored the Alaskan Native groups and exempted several tribes in Oklahoma as well. The Oklahoma Indian Welfare Act made some of the 1934 IRA provisions available to the later groups. To establish new governments, tribes had to vote within one year in favor of taking that step. Hoping to explain what was happening and to allay suspicions, Collier traveled west to ten separate locales in Indian country. To his surprise, not all reservation groups supported the idea of tribal government, and many openly opposed it. The Iroquois tribes in New York attacked the effort, and many of the Plains Indians were against it as well. Yet during the next several years the voters in 174 groups approved going ahead, and another 78, including the Navajo, the largest of the tribes, voted against new governments. Eager federal officials counted abstentions as votes in favor, and this tactic may have changed the results in some close races. In several places the effort to create new tribal governments further divided already badly split reservation groups. Partially assimilated and Christian groups opposed the effort as communistic and as steps backward and away from Americanization. At the same time, others complained about moves to reduce or destroy the roles and status of traditional clan and tribal leaders. Most of this opposition caught the bureaucrats by surprise and worsened existing divisions within tribal communities. Despite the confusion, debate, and rancor, most present-day tribal governments got their start under the IRA.

WORLD WAR II

Despite the New Deal programs, Indians and other Americans did not escape the Great Depression until World War II revived the national economy. Native Americans had left their homes for jobs in nearby cities prior to the war, that conflict accelerated the movement, as thousands of reservation dwellers sought employment and another 25,000 left to serve in the military. In 1940 Congress passed a Selective Service act, which brought back the old arguments about whether to place Indian young men in their own units or to integrate them. John Collier suggested that as many as 42,000 men from the reservations might be eligible for the draft. Not surprisingly, given his ideas about tribalism, he recommended that all-Indian units be established. Tribal members split on the issue, but Navajo Tribal Chairman J. C. Morgan supported it, because he thought that segregated units were a way to get young men with weak reading skills into the army. He feared that if they served in regular companies, many of the young Indian men might encounter discrimination, because they had little off-reservation experience. Writing about the issue, Morgan noted that the "Navajo will cheerfully accept any assignment . . . but it would seem wise to consider the advantages of maintaining the Navajo as an indigenous regiment." Selective Service officials ignored such ideas, and Native Americans served alongside other Americans throughout the war.

Most tribal members supported the war effort wholeheartedly, but some groups and individuals objected to the draft. Utah Paiutes and Mississippi Choctaws claimed that they lacked citizenship. In the summer of 1941 a Choctaw elder wrote that "Choctaw Indians never vote or pay poll tax. The white friends here say we are not allowed to vote. . . . If we are not citizens, will it be right for [us to fight]?" Religious scruples kept some from cooperating. Five Hopi tradition-alists refused to register on religious grounds, claiming that tribal teachings predicted a major war. Those beliefs warned that the tribes-men were "to show their bows and arrows to no one" at that time. The judge rejected their defense and sentenced them to a year and a day in federal prison. At Taos Pueblo in New Mexico the men considered their long hair to have religious significance, but they too had to serve. In one incident, John Collier intervened to get a twenty-six-year-old rain priest from the Zuni tribe the same treatment other clergymen received. Among the Tohono O'odham in Arizona, an aged leader urged the men not to register, so the authorities arrested him and another villager for advocating the same thing.

The German-American Bund and some communists tried to encour-age noncompliance with the draft, but their activities seem to have had little result. Among the Six Nations Iroquois Confederacy in New York, long-standing issues brought some resistance. These groups questioned the authority of the U.S. government to order their men into a war. The Iroquois had long claimed to be independent sovereign nations within both the United States and Canada, and the Mohawks, Senecas, and Tuscaroras all referred to earlier treaties to claim that they lacked citizenship. The Saint Regis Mohawk tribal leaders stated that "under our treaties with the United States of America, we are a dis-tinct race, nation and people owning and occupying and governing the lands of our ancestors and under the protection of the federal government in reciprocation for our friendship." John Collier urged them to register as aliens and then take their claims to court, which they did. In 1941 the U.S. Second Circuit Court of Appeals ruled against their claims in *Ex parte Green*. At the same time, federal officials suggested that a small delegation from these tribes come to Washington, where they could announce their own tribal declarations of war against the Axis Powers, and this seems to have lessened some of the opposition.

These scattered objections included only a tiny minority of Native Americans, and most supported the war as enthusiastically as the rest of the population. Within six months after the declaration of war, about 7,500 Indians had entered the military. By the conflict's end, 25,000 men and women had served in the armed forces. Of these, over 21,000 were in the army, many of them as volunteers. They helped invade the beaches of Normandy on D-Day, raise the flag on Iwo Jima in the Pacific, and pursue the Germans across North Africa. Some units used Native Americans as radiomen, because they could send messages in their tribal languages. In the Pacific, the Navajo Code Talkers used a special coded version of their language that even other Navajos could not understand. When the Japanese invaded the western Aleutian Islands, tribal people in Alaska served in what they called Eskimo territorial guard companies on the mainland. Clearly, Indians fought wherever American military forces operated during the war. Native American women served either as nurses or as WACs or WAVEs, doing support work for combat units.

Wartime service gave many young people much more experience with other Americans than they had had before. They traveled far from home, often overseas. They gained respect for their actions and a sense of accomplishment and personal worth from their wartime duties. Four decades later, in 1997, the Navajo Code Talkers marched in President Bill Clinton's second inaugural parade, and in 2001 they received citations from President George W. Bush only six months after he had taken office. Rituals that long predated the present century received renewed attention and use, as reservation communities welcomed the veterans home. Among the Lakotas and the Kiowas on the plains, returning servicemen were accorded traditional honors of war, and their presence helped to revive the nearly extinct warrior societies on those and other reservations. The veterans may have enjoyed this attention, but they also faced the traumas that resulted from modern war. Alcoholism, an inability to settle back into former patterns, and dissatisfaction with treatment on or near the reservations plagued some for years.

Those who had remained at home during the conflict had new experiences, too. Thousands left reservation communities to work in wartime industry or agriculture. Some of them held regular, full-time jobs for the first time. They enjoyed the benefits of steady wages but also faced discrimination, poor housing, and loneliness away from home. They could not always leave their work to attend traditional ceremonies or celebrations on the reservation. Used to being surrounded by friends and family, or certainly near them most of their lives, they found city life isolating and stressful. Those who stayed on the reservations faced the same kinds of shortages and rationing as other Americans, but their long-term poverty before the war made such experiences less difficult than for some others.

Expecting to find changes when they returned home after the war, Indian men faced disappointment. Unemployment, poor housing, mediocre medical care, and discrimination still existed. Not only had few changes taken place, but the strong feelings of American nationalism that had developed became a major threat to tribal survival in the next two decades. As early as 1943, opponents of John Collier's programs began a renewed attack on him, on the Indian Reorganization Act, and on tribalism itself. Congressional hearings that year led to calls to abolish the BIA and to begin the process of getting the government "out of the Indian business." The thinking was that when Indians proved themselves fully capable of dealing with the rest of American society during the war, they showed that they deserved to be treated equally. This meant reducing expenditures for tribal programs and ending government programs that fostered collectivism and paternalism toward the tribes. Religious groups such as the National Council of Churches called for an end to efforts that encouraged Indians to "return to the blanket" by practicing their "pagan" rites and dances. Popular magazines such as *Reader's Digest* published articles demanding that Native Americans be given the same freedom enjoyed by other citizens.

INDIAN CLAIMS COMMISSION

Such ideas sounded good. Native Americans deserved equal treatment. The government erred by continuing its supervision of their tribal funds and reservation facilities; however, groundwork was laid for a fundamental change leading toward the cessation of government responsibilities toward the tribes, responsibilities that had existed for generations. In 1945 repeated criticisms persuaded Collier to resign. One observer described the mid-1940s attitudes as showing a renewed anti-Indian bias that wanted the tribes turned loose from federal programs "even if it means starvation for large numbers" of people. To achieve the goal of giving the tribes their freedom and cutting federal expenses, in 1946 Congress established the Indian Claims Commission (ICC), a body that was to examine past dealings between the federal government and the tribes over land cessions, treaty payments, and other long-standing issues. Once past claims and injustices had been settled, the government hoped to end its financial responsibilities toward Native groups.

Although it was supposed to do its work in just five years, the Claims Commission actually operated for more than thirty. Some 176 tribal groups filed 370 separate claims to the commissioners, far more than Congressional supporters of the program had anticipated. Each case went through several stages, with Indians, scholars, and lawyers all participating in the process. Reservation-based oral accounts had less influence than the paper evidence presented by researchers and the government, and it often took years for any particular group to work its way through the process from entering its claim to receiving any compensation. Tribes that had received less than the going market price for land taken during the nineteenth century had to provide evidence showing the land's value at the time the government took possession of it. The commissioners eventually would rule on how much more the Indians should have gotten and how much interest should be credited to their account. Some groups received millions, but not all won their cases. In the case of the Lakota Sioux, the tribe became eligible for more than $17 million as payment for having lost the Black Hills in South Dakota. The Lakotas rejected the settlement, however, demanding that their lands be returned, but the government refused. Others also objected to getting cash rather than land, but few followed the Lakotas' example and turned down the federal dollars. When the claims process ended in 1978, the government had awarded around $818 million, settling just 285 of the 850 claims brought before it.

TERMINATION

If it had worked as its congressional backers expected it to, the ICC would have ended the issue of Indian claims against the government. Instead, its operations took longer and cost more than anticipated, and drew tribal attention to past federal misdeeds related to a variety of issues. While righting past wrongs, the Commission had a more sinister goal as well. It represented the first step in the broad-based effort to end federal responsibilities toward the tribes, and led directly to the Termination policy. By 1947, anti-Indian members of Congress had begun working toward abolition of the BIA and its programs. That year the Senate Civil Service Committee called for an end to federal services for some tribes, and demanded that the BIA prepare a list of reservations where people could operate without further federal assistance. The next year the Hoover Commission, examining governmental efficiency, recommended that all special programs for Indians be halted. By the early 1950s, western senators such as Arthur Watkins of Utah, Frank Church of Idaho, and Henry Jackson of Washington all supported the idea. With this broad base of support, what became Termination soon arrived.

The movement's supporters rejected cultural pluralism. Like the nineteenth-century reformers, they demanded that Native Americans shed their differences and become part of the general society. Commissioner Dillon Myer, a pro-termination man, went so far as to close some reservation day schools, enlarge the boarding schools, and urge teachers and other staff members there to do whatever they could to assimilate their students. At least for a time, such orders appeared to roll the clock back fifty or even seventy-five years to the early reservation era. What contemporary observers overlooked was the fact that those who supported cutting the tribes loose from the federal government expected that business interests would be able to renew their exploitation of reservation natural resources, as they had done prior to the Collier era. Strangely enough, the supporters' actions resulted in reducing federal appropriations for their home districts and states. Actual Termination began with the 1953 passage of House Concurrent Resolution 108, which stated that Indians would be "subject to the same laws and entitled to the same privileges" as other citizens. Then it announced that Congress wanted to end existing wardship status for particular groups, and listed tribes and bands in nine states that would lose federal services.

A few weeks later, President Dwight D. Eisenhower signed Public Law 280, setting the new policy into motion. Not surprisingly, no senior federal official had bothered to consult with any tribal members before Termination went into effect. As a result, when Native Americans did learn about it, they had little specific information at hand. The first opposition came from the National Congress of American Indians. A relatively new group founded in 1944, it tried to mobilize tribes against the policy and linked tribal leaders across the country in attacking it. One Blackfeet spokesman described trying to plan for the tribe's future while facing Termination as being like trying to cook "a meal in your tipi when someone is standing outside trying to burn the tipi down." Some acculturated Indians cheered the policy, hoping that it would lead to the closing of the reservations and the incorporating of their populations into the general society. But few tribal people agreed. Years later, historian John Wunder described the process as the "most successful legal attack on Indian rights and sovereignty" since the nation's founding fathers had signed the Constitution.

Particular tribes such as the Menominees of Wisconsin and the Klamaths of Oregon suffered greatly after Termination. Both groups owned substantial timber reserves on their reservations, and federal officials thought that both had an economic base solid enough to cope with the changes. This view proved overly optimistic. In Wisconsin the Menominee reservation became the state's poorest county. The tribal hospital could not meet state health standards and had to close. Because the tribe lacked a strong tax base, it could not provide many needed social services. Within a couple of years, the corporation that had been formed to manage tribal assets resorted to selling off prime vacation spots on the former reservation to wealthy people from the Chicago area. The tribal sawmill had to lay off many workers because the timber business could not support the payroll. In Oregon the Klamaths divided into two groups: one wanted to continue tribal forest management, and the other wanted to sell tribal timberlands and divide tribal assets on a per capita basis. Eventually both the Menominees and the Klamaths managed to be reconstituted as tribes, but only after much strife, suffering, and loss of resources. Dozens of other tribes and bands also experienced Termination. Nevertheless, only about 13,000 out of nearly 400,000 Indians belonged to those groups, and their landholdings constituted just over three percent of tribal lands at the time. Still, the uncertainties over Termination, the erasing of long-accepted treaty rights, and the intratribal bitterness that resulted all made "Termination" a dirty word.

RELOCATION

If the Claims Commission was to pay off past federal debts to Native Americans, and Termination was to end other governmental responsibilities, then the planners needed something else to bring Indians into the general society. In 1948 they began a trial program offering to help Navajo people relocate to Denver, Los Angeles, and Salt Lake City. By the 1950s this led the Commissioner of Indian Affairs, Dillon Myer, to establish a Branch of Placement and Relocation within the BIA. Through this office he hoped to lure tribal members into the cities and away from the reservations, where they lacked any chance for well-paying jobs. Individual Indians had been moving into town since the 1920s, and for many groups the program represented only a formal effort to accomplish what had been happening for decades. At first, some reservation dwellers viewed the relocation plans as just another federal plot to undermine tribal life and a part of the hated Termination policy. Certainly, if successful, this effort would weaken reservation societies, tribal ties, language, and religion; so their fears had a solid basis. Still, given the isolation and lack of economic opportunity among many Native American groups, the new policy made some sense.

As it evolved over the next decade, the program established relocation centers in cities near large concentrations of Native Americans and in other selected urban centers. Places as widely separated as Minneapolis, Chicago, Tulsa, Los Angeles, Dallas, Cleveland, and Albuquerque had such offices. The BIA printed attractive posters showing young families moving to these and other cities and by 1960 had assisted about 33,000 Indians in leaving their reservation homes. At first, about all the bureaucrats did was to give one-way bus tickets to town, and at times they purposely sent people to cities far from their particular reservations, hoping to discourage them from returning home. Some of the urban newcomers lacked job skills and experience, and finding work was not easy. So many gave up on city life that in 1956 Congress provided funding for job training and placement services as well. This cut unemployment, but failed to help with the many social problems facing Native Americans in the large cities.

As a program, relocation lasted just about a decade and had only a modest impact. Individual and family movement far outstripped the federal efforts, as two-thirds of those leaving reservations at the time did so without government assistance. The migration into the cities that had begun during and after World War I accelerated sharply by 1960, and according to the 1970 census, some 44 percent of Native Americans lived off the reservation. That figure continued to climb, and by the year 2000 about two-thirds of American Indians in the United States resided in cities or towns. The experiences of those moving into urban areas varied widely. One Chicago dweller remembered that he worried about his children because of heavy traffic, "but I think that they got a better education here [than] they would back home." For him, the reservation had little attraction. "What is there back home?" he asked. "When I go back I see no jobs, nothing to do, everyone drinks." A middle-aged woman had the opposite reaction. "I wish we had never left home," she said. "This will never be home to me. It's dirty and noisy and . . . crowded."

Despite government expectations that the city dwellers would become fully assimilated, the program failed. Leaving their reservations surely weakened tribal identity for many, yet the city experiences had effects similar to those of the boarding- school era. Coming from close-knit communities, Indians sought each other out when they came to town. In many places they organized their own cultural or neighborhood centers. Rarely did many people from a single reservation or tribe come to the same place at the same time, so the centers served to bring individuals from many groups together. Soon they recognized that they shared customs and ideas more often than they differed, and this caused a gradual shift from tribal self-identification to a more general awareness of themselves as Indian people with interests and needs different from those of other city groups. By the middle of the 1960s, these growing pan-Indian feelings gave rise to new Native American organizations that either came into being or first became active during the social unrest of that decade.

Migration changed the lives of those who moved to the cities, and it had mixed effects on those who chose not to leave their tribal homes. On some reservations the young, educated, and independent people left, and those who remained were mostly the old, the very young, the sickly, and the unskilled. Where that was true, social and economic problems worsened as the communities became poverty pockets with few skilled people and a shortage of money for needed social programs such as public health, housing assistance, and education. However, that was by no means the whole story. Often urban workers returned to the reservations for family occasions, tribal ceremonies, powwows, or just to visit. When they did so, they brought much-needed money with them. Others who acquired education and job skills in the cities came home to help the tribes improve life there. Still, for some groups the situation remained grim for the next several decades.

MILITANCY AND CHANGE

By the 1960s, demands for many kinds of reform swept through American society, and this movement soon came to include Indians as well. Having benefited from improved education and their urban experiences, a new generation of Native Americans stood ready to speak out for changes in their lives and in their treatment by the government. Until that time, most tribal leaders or spokespersons for pan-tribal groups such as the National Congress of American Indians had protested occasionally, but not as stridently as they came to do in this decade. The "new urban Indians" had gained experience in organizing and working together at the cultural centers that had been established earlier in many cities. The regional powwow circuit that operated on the plains expanded as both reservation dwellers and urban Indians looked for entertainment that offered them a sense of cultural identity and pride. At the same time, the Native American Church reached out to members living far beyond its original confines in Oklahoma. Young and articulate Native people had the skills and organizational experience to work toward new goals.

In 1961, at the American Indian Chicago Conference held at the University of Chicago, new ideas emerged for how to deal with the government and the rest of society. When established chiefs and other tribal leaders seemed too cautious, younger and more outspoken attendees denounced them as "Uncle Tomahawks" and "Apples" (red on the outside but white within). Dissatisfied with the conference discussions, the young militants left town, headed to Santa Fe, and convened their own meeting. There they founded the National Indian Youth Council, proclaimed a "Declaration of Indian Purpose," and then demanded what they called "self- determination." Their newspaper, *Americans Before Columbus*, served to spread their ideas. Clyde Warrior, an Oklahoma Ponca from a traditional family, became one of the new protesters' outspoken leaders. "We are not free," he objected. Those living on reservations have their "choices and decisions made by federal administrators, bureaucrats," and the subservient tribal governments. Others living elsewhere had their "lives controlled by local power elites." Words like his struck a responsive chord among many tribal people, who increasingly turned to nontraditional public confrontation to attract public support for their demands.

As early as the mid-1950s, tribal fishermen in the Northwest had begun challenging Washington state laws limiting their salmon fishing on the Columbia and other rivers there. The 1854–55 treaties between the United States and the northwestern tribes had assured the Indians they could continue to fish at their "usual and accustomed grounds and stations." Both commercial and sport fishermen had opposed this for decades, and the state government passed regulations that essentially cut off tribal people from their fishing rights. Several groups sued the state, trying to end the regulations but lost. Feeling that the ruling ignored their treaty rights, the Makah tribal council asked the National Indian Youth Council to help them demonstrate. This led to a series of "fish- ins," which brought local Indians into direct conflict with police, sheriffs, and state game officials, as the protesters demanded their rights to take salmon from the local rivers, and arrests followed quickly. The dispute attracted increasing media attention when one local official denounced the Indians bitterly. "We had the power and force to exterminate these people from the face of the earth" years ago, he said. "Perhaps we should have!"

Such statements and the continuing violence soon grabbed national headlines, bringing the participation of entertainer and civil-rights advocate Dick Gregory and movie stars Marlon Brando and Jane Fonda, whose presence attracted even more nationwide media attention. By 1970, continued Indian demands finally persuaded the Department of the Interior that it had to support Indian treaty rights. So the federal government and the tribes moved into federal court against the state of Washington. After a bitter legal fight between the state and the fishing industry on one side and the federal government and the tribal groups on the other, the judge ruled in favor of the Indians. The mid-nineteenth-century treaties, he said, had protected existing tribal fishing rights rather than granting the tribes any rights to the fish. In his 1974 *United States v. Washington* ruling, Judge George Boldt awarded one-half of the annual salmon catch to Indian fishermen. The decision raised a firestorm of protest from whites, who rejected the tribes' rights to any of the fish. White thugs bombed Indian fishing vessels, and frequent violence erupted before tempers cooled. The state of Washington appealed the ruling, but in 1979 the Supreme Court upheld Boldt's decision.

The growing militancy among many younger Indians led to clear divisions among tribal peoples. Often the older, established leaders who participated in the National Congress of American Indians balked at public demonstrations. They saw themselves as differing from other minority groups seeking full integration into the national society. Instead, they wished to retain a separate identity. The Indian wanted more than equality, one spokesman explained. "He is fighting to retain his superior rights as guaranteed to him by treaties and agreements as the original inhabitants."This attitude widened the gap between established reservation officials and the growing numbers of younger militants, who saw the turbulence of the civil-rights era as a chance to help all Native Americans, but particularly those who now lived in the cities.

As their actions and rhetoric became increasingly more strident, militants demonstrated at national meetings of the National Congress of American Indians as well as against the federal, state, and local governments. They sought to achieve what came to be called "self-determination," a goal they shared with many more conservative reservation-dwelling people. By this they meant that they wanted to control and manage the programs that directly affected their lives. To gain more attention, they turned to direct action. An early example occurred in 1964 at Alcatraz Island in San Francisco Bay. Just the year before, the federal government had closed its prison there and declared the island to be "surplus property."Then officials learned that a small group of Sioux Indians had moved onto the island and claimed the right to settle it under the terms of the 1868 Treaty of Fort Laramie. That agreement had promised the Lakotas the right to use vacant federal property. U.S. marshals removed the small group quickly, but the Sioux then took their case into federal court. In 1968 they lost, and a year later they began a second occupation of Alcatraz. In November 1969, a small group calling itself American Indians United landed on the island with the intention of establishing an Indian cultural center. Again federal officers removed them. About ten days later, seventy-eight more people, calling themselves Indians of All Nations, moved onto the island. Within just few weeks the occupiers numbered more than three hundred people and represented about fifty tribes. Although led by militants, the group reached out to more conservative Indians by defending tribal traditions and promising that the cultural center they expected to build would help retain the beliefs and languages of reservation groups.

The occupation became an immediate media success. At first, network TV news gave daily reports of activities on the island. Indian leaders used this newfound access to national media effectively. Proclaiming that they were "attacking the whole system [of federal tribal relations]," they claimed Alcatraz by "right of discovery," set up a local government, opened a school, started a police force, began publishing a newspaper, and established a "Bureau of Caucasian Affairs." When their actions drew so much attention that some harbor cruise boats visited the island, they began charging tourists $5 for landing. At one point they shot an arrow at a boat of sightseers, and they also fired homemade rockets at Coast Guard vessels checking on them. While gathering plenty of national attention, the militants failed to gain their primary objective—title to the island and permission to build a cultural center there.

Nevertheless, the occupiers' actions got the full attention of the White House. One administration aide denounced the invasion as "confrontation politics" by "an irresponsible, but P[ublic] R[elations] conscious group." Another labeled it as "superb showmanship." Several administration staffers proposed launching a commando operation with U.S. Navy Seals, a combined land and sea invasion with the Coast Guard and the Navy, and even a dawn invasion using tranquilizer guns against the occupiers. Leonard Garment, the official responsible for managing the affair, stopped these ideas cold. He cautioned that "Alcatraz could become the biggest political side show of 1971" if a single Indian or federal marshal died. So, the government avoided doing anything aggressive. Instead, it cut off water and electricity to the island and waited for public interest to fade. On Alcatraz, differences over goals and tactics split the occupiers, and the college students who had led the occupation returned to their classes the next fall. When the daughter of Richard Oakes, one of the leaders, died after falling down a stairway in the former prison, the militants began to drift away. As a result, in June 1971, when federal marshals returned to the island, the remaining occupiers agreed to leave.

For much of the late 1960s and early 1970s, the militancy that had led to the Alcatraz incident spread across the country, causing repeated demonstrations and occupations. In New York State, Mohawk tribal members had enjoyed the right to cross the border into Canada and return without question under the terms of the 1794 Jay's Treaty. When Canadian agents at toll booths on the Cornwall Bridge now tried to make Mohawk travelers pay, the Indians objected, and in 1968 and 1969 tribal members blockaded the bridge several times. After the second incident, the Canadian government accepted their right to use the bridge without interference. In 1968 Minneapolis Indian leaders such as Clyde and Vernon Bellecourt, George Mitchell, and Dennis Banks formed the American Indian Movement (AIM).

Established to gain equal treatment for Native Americans in that city, the group expanded quickly. After its participation in the Alcatraz events, it became the most widely recognized militant Native American organization. Its actions encouraged protests from one end of the country to another over the next couple of years. Indians seized Fort Snelling near Minneapolis and Fort Lewis in Washington, occupied a lighthouse on Lake Superior, and marched in Lassen National Park in California. On 4 July 1971, Lakota (Sioux) members demonstrated against the loss of the Black Hills to the United States over a century earlier by climbing atop the heads at Mount Rushmore in South Dakota. Others demonstrated at a Boy Scout program in Topeka, Kansas, objecting to the Scouts' use of Indian dances for public entertainment. At Plymouth, Massachusetts, on Thanksgiving Day 1972, they painted Plymouth Rock red and boarded the replica of the *May-flower* there. Other groups tried to occupy BIA offices from California east to Pennsylvania while they denounced the agency for "bossing

Indians around." Most of these protests sought to focus public interest on the social and economic needs of Native Americans and to call attention to the "many, many broken treaties and promises" that marked the federal government's past dealings with the tribes.

That complaint led to the 1972 Trail of Broken Treaties, which brought militants east to Washington, D.C. In the autumn of that year, Vernon Bellecourt, one of the AIM leaders, agreed to coordinate the effort, which had support from nine pan-tribal groups. In the first phase, automobile caravans started out from Seattle, San Francisco, and Los Angeles. As the convoy traveled toward the capital, people from reservations and cities along the route would join in, so that by the time the group reached Washington, hundreds of protesters representing dozens of tribes were on hand to present the Nixon administration with their demands. They reached the District of Columbia just one week before the presidential election, making national leaders nervous. When only a few low-level BIA officials appeared, the hundreds of militants sitting in the BIA building's auditorium seized the site. Some rampaged through the offices breaking windows and furniture, burning correspondence, and seizing tribal records. After barricading the doors, they proclaimed the building the Native American Embassy. Earlier they had smuggled cans of gasoline and rifles inside, and so they would not be dislodged easily.

The occupiers' actions presented the administration with few choices less than a week before the election. By doing nothing, officials would appear weak and indecisive, but "any use of police power to evict [the Indians] would have been a holocaust," according to one Nixon advisor. Restraint had worked at Alcatraz, but that event did not unfold at the end of a reelection campaign; White House advisors decided to present a strong face to the public by denouncing the illegal trashing of the BIA building and records. Any potential use of violent action they deferred until after the election. Instead, they reviewed the protesters' list of complaints, which included unjust and broken treaties, issues of religious freedom (e.g., the use of peyote and eagle feathers in Native rites), calls for the restoration of tribal lands, and demands that more funds be spent for Indian health care and education. The protesters outraged President Nixon, who saw their actions as a repudiation of his efforts to help the tribes. One staff member said that "the President took the occupation very hard." Whatever he thought privately, his aides soon negotiated a settlement. The militants received $66,000 to pay for their return to their homes, and officials promised to study the demands that had been made.

Reactions to the Trail of Broken Treaties illustrate the divisions within and between Indian groups. Alaska Inuit leader Joseph Upicksoun called the entire event a "fiasco," while Hopi Clarence Hamilton labeled it the "Trail of Destruction." Speaking for the National Tribal Chairmen's Association, Webster Two Hawk attacked the people who occupied the BIA headquarters as "irresponsible, self-styled revolutionaries," and urged the government to prosecute all of the participants. Navajo tribal chairman Peter MacDonald testified that the demonstrators' actions resulted from the "rage and frustration" Indian people felt, and he pointed out that Native Americans had many real complaints over their treatment by the government and the rest of American society. At the same time, many of the militants returned home to cheers and enthusiastic welcomes in their communities because they had dared to attack the BIA and to show the entire nation their frustration and anger.

Although the caravan to Washington had achieved its central goals of delivering complaints and focusing public attention on Indian grievances, the protest seemed to die out as the caravan members drove home. They soon learned that the federal task force appointed to consider their grievances had rejected all twenty of them. As protests continued, two AIM leaders, Dennis Banks and Russell Means, went to the Pine Ridge Reservation in South Dakota to help traditional Lakotas defeat Richard Wilson, the tribal chairman there. His opponents accused Wilson of having a personal "goon squad" to intimidate his rivals and keep himself in office. This had resulted in a virtual civil war on the reservation, with Wilson's opponents charging that his thugs had beaten dozens and murdered at least sixty people there. A Lakota named Wesley Bad Bull Heart was killed by a non-Indian just off the reservation. When local officials charged the accused killer with manslaughter rather than murder, Indians protested what they saw as clear evidence of unequal law enforcement. Showing their frustration and anger, they attacked and set fire to the courthouse in Custer, South Dakota. Local unrest continued as violence between AIM protesters and local police broke out in Custer City and Rapid City as well.

In the middle of this situation, Richard Wilson's "enforcers" attacked AIM leader Russell Means, and the next day, 27 February 1973, AIM supporters began an armed take-over of the nearby town of Wounded Knee. They chose this community because of the symbolic importance of the 1890 massacre of Big Foot and his followers there by the U.S. cavalry, and the public awareness of that event resulting from Dee Brown's best-selling book *Bury My Heart at Wounded Knee*, which had just been published. As one observer later said, "Wounded Knee received more attention in its first week than the entire previous decade of Indian activism." About two hundred armed activists, including AIM members and anti-Wilson traditionalists from Pine Ridge, occupied the village. They brought explosives, rifles, and shotguns to defend themselves, and within hours the BIA police and Wilson's police surrounded them. FBI agents, federal marshals, and U.S. troops joined the siege for the next several months, and on the night of 26 April 1973 the two sides fired six to eight thousand rounds at each other. It's a "miracle that no one has been killed," one federal observer noted. "Some morning we will wake up to see 8 to 10 people dead" here. While a few officials demanded that the government isolate the village, cut off all supplies, and move in with force, moderates directed federal actions. "We could end the siege in a day if the marshals attacked," one conceded, but "we don't need an Indian massacre on our hands." When the incident ended, the casualties numbered only three: two occupiers died, and one FBI agent was wounded and paralyzed.

The standoff brought an immediate flood of TV, radio, and print journalists to the scene, and at least for the first several weeks national newscasts offered a positive or at least neutral account of the situation. Civil-rights leaders, black activists, and supporters from other tribes trekked to South Dakota to endorse the occupation. In March 1973, traditional leaders at the scene announced the formation of the Oglala Sioux Nation, declaring their independence from the United States. While being interviewed for network news, Russell Means stated the occupiers' determination to shoot anyone who crossed their border. They demanded that the existing tribal government at Pine Ridge be abolished, and that they be free to return to their traditional forms of tribal organization, as they claimed the Sioux treaty of 1868 promised. By early May, federal and Indian negotiators reached an agreement. The government promised to discuss the 1868 treaty, to investigate Wilson's administration of the reservation, and to prosecute any people accused of wrongdoing. In return, the Wounded Knee leaders promised to lay down their arms and to accept possible federal arrests. When the standoff ended, the FBI arrested nearly 250 individuals.

The tensions and violence at Pine Ridge continued for several more years, but AIM had lost most of the public support it enjoyed when the occupation began. By the time the surrender came, few reporters remained to describe the event. Public interest had waned, and to some degree had turned against the demonstrators. For much of the rest of the decade the militants seemed to lose their cohesion. Federal officials visited Pine Ridge as promised, but when the talks concluded, they told their listeners that the treaty system had lapsed in 1871 and that the government had to accept the existing tribal governments. Clearly, Indian militancy remained, but it proved less focused than earlier. In 1975 two FBI agents were murdered at Pine Ridge, and the government quickly charged AIM activist Leonard Peltier in the case. On the basis of what many considered shaky evidence, Peltier received two life terms for the murders. By that time the public had lost all interest, riots in the cities had ended, the Vietnam War was over, and the entire population seemed eager for calm. No matter the reasons that might have brought it to an end, violent militancy had changed the public image of Indian societies forever. Whatever else one could say, American Indians now faced the future with a new confidence and with substantially increased popular interest.

SUGGESTED READINGS

Bernstein, Alison. *American Indians and World War II: Toward a New Era in Indian Affairs.* Norman: University of Oklahoma Press, 1990.

Deloria, Vine, Jr. *Custer Died for Your Sins: An Indian Manifesto.* New York: Macmillan, 1969.

Fixico, Donald L. *Termination and Relocation: Federal Indian Policy, 1945–1960.* Albuquerque: University of New Mexico Press, 1986.

Iverson, Peter. *"We Are Still Here": American Indians in the Twentieth Century.* Wheeling, Ill.: Harlan Davidson, 1998.

Josephy, Alvin M., Jr. *Now That the Buffalo's Gone: A Study of Today's American Indians.* Norman: University of Oklahoma Press, 1984.

Kelly, Lawrence C. *The Assault on Indian Assimilation: John Collier and the Origins of Indian Policy Reform.* Albuquerque: University of New Mexico Press, 1983.

Olson, James S., and Raymond Wilson. *Native Americans in the Twentieth Century.* Urbana and Chicago: University of Illinois Press, 1984.

Parman, Donald L. *Indians and the American West in the Twentieth Century.* Bloomington: Indiana University Press, 1994.

Smith, Paul Chaat, and Robert Allen Warrior. *Like a Hurricane: The Indian Movement from Alcatraz to Wounded Knee.* New York: The New Press, 1996.

Chapter 8

TRADITION, CHANGE, AND CHALLENGE SINCE *1970*

Jealousy and Backlash

 By the early 1970s most Americans had lost patience with the turbulence of the preceding decade. They longed for an end to the riots, demonstrations, and strident demands that bombarded them through television newscasts and the daily paper. Native American militancy gradually receded, but new federal laws and court decisions broadened the authority of tribal governments at a time when many citizens objected to further changes in their society. The 1975 passage of the Indian Self-Determination and Educational Assistance Act set into law the independence that tribal leaders and militants had sought for years. They now came to deal with federal officials on a government-to-government basis. The passage of this Act reinforced the perceptions of some whites that over the years fumbling bureaucrats and fuzzy-minded liberals had given the tribes too many benefits and too much authority. A broad anti-Indian backlash occurred in many parts of the country and continued intermittently for several decades.

Occasionally western officials expressed anger and frustration when nearby reservation dwellers seemed to have reached near equality with the rest of the citizenry. For example, in

August 1979 a commissioner from Sanders County, Montana, fired off a letter to the Senate Select Committee on Indian Affairs. As others had suggested, he called on the Senators to abolish the reservations because the government had "been taking care of RED MEN long enough." This assertion grew from a belief that the tribes received special treatment and enjoyed more privileges than their neighbors. When Self-Determination empowered tribes to regulate economic activity on their reservations, businessmen joined their complaints with those of the local politicians. In January 1986 the Mobil Oil Corporation deleted a Colorado company from its list of approved subcontractors for work on the Navajo Reservation when it learned that the company's president had rejected tribal labor regulations that required hiring Navajo workers if they possessed the necessary skills. After calling the Indians "members of the vanquished and inferior race," this company president told tribal officials that he did not "recognize the legal existence of the so-called Navajo Preference in Employment Act of 1985 or any other part of the so-called Navajo Tribal Code."

Disputes over fishing and hunting rights listed in nineteenth-century treaties, the enforcement of state game laws, and the demands of local sportsmen all focused attention on what whites perceived as "special treatment" for Indians. In 1974 Wisconsin state game wardens arrested several Anishinabe (Ojibwa) men for spearfishing out of season. The tribe sued, claiming that the treaties guaranteed its members fishing rights regardless of state regulations. After nearly a decade, a 1983 federal court decision upheld the Indians' right to spearfish when they chose. Sport fishermen and northern Wisconsin resort owners reacted angrily, because they feared that the Anishinabe spearing of walleyed pike would harm both local fishing and the economy tied to it. Hundreds of protesters lined the stream and lake banks to jeer, throw stones, and issue threats against the Indians while they fished. Pickup trucks sported bumper stickers reading "Save a Walleye, Spear a Pregnant Squaw," as the spearing continued. Anti-Indian groups, including one called Protect Americans' Rights and Resources in Wisconsin, sued to overturn the 1983 decision, and the state offered to pay the Lac du Flambeau tribe $35.6 million if it would give up all but ceremonial rights to the spearfishing. When the tribe refused, the suit continued, and in 1991 the federal judge fashioned an agreement under which the Indians and the state agreed on how many fish Native Americans could harvest each spring. The tribe filed a countersuit against a group known as Stop Treaty Abuse (STA). In 1992 the court ruled in favor of the tribe and cut off the filing of more injunctions from the fishermen's groups. Although it did not end the dispute entirely, this decision indicated clearly that the federal government would uphold treaty fishing rights.

Similar protests erupted elsewhere, and during the late 1970s an antisovereignty movement developed. A national umbrella organization, the Citizens' Equal Rights Alliance (CERA), coordinated the activities of at least fifty member groups operating in thirty-three states and supposedly including at least a half-million members. In 1978 it published a manifesto entitled "200 Million Custers," which was given widespread distribution. The most outspoken and active of these groups included All Citizens Equal and Flathead Residents Earning Equality in Montana, the Committee for Equality in North Dakota, and Totally Equal Americans in Minnesota. In addition to leading local protests and circulating anti-Indian materials, these groups flooded BIA offices with up to six hundred protest letters a week. Frequently they worked to clog state and federal court dockets with nuisance suits, including twenty actions by ranchers against the Salish and Kootenai tribes over disputed water rights.

Bitter anti-Indian feelings developed in Washington and Montana as well. Usually these stemmed from disputes over fishing and hunting issues or other land-use questions. One angrily worded manifesto attacked tribal efforts to limit or control hunting and fishing by other sportsmen. "Uncle Sam is giving America back to the Indians," its authors raged. To these protesters it seemed as if federal bureaucrats were running a "nationwide, sinister juggernaut, exacting from Americans sacrifices of property, money, rights, and identity," and turning these over to the tribes. In Montana, non-Indians living on the Flathead Reservation became outraged when the Indians enforced new regulations on them. After being arrested by tribal officers for hunting without a permit on his own land, one bitter resident defended himself saying that "no Indian government is going to tell me what I can do on my own land or anywhere else. I don't recognize that government's authority at all." In 1981, Crow tribesmen blocked a highway bridge across the Big Horn River to keep non-Indians from coming onto their reservation to fish. CERA officers rallied public support, filed lawsuits, and even proposed legislation to reduce the authority of tribal governments.

When challenged that their actions had a racist base, many of the protesters rejected the charge. "Now don't you make us out to be racists and extremists," Del Palmer, one of the most outspoken, said. Almost immediately thereafter, however, he complained that "the time's coming that we're going to have . . . Indian this and Indian that in government. What would happen if our next governor was an Indian? We'd all be down the drain." Whether they believed it or simply thought that the voters demanded such rhetoric, elected Montana officials seemed to echo that line of reasoning. One state legislator disagreed that white racism played any role in the disputes. At the same time, he chided Flathead attorney Pat Smith, saying, "Pat, your problem is, you don't think like a white man." William Covey, who helped found the Citizens' Equal Rights Alliance in 1988, claimed that racists could be found on both sides. "If an Indian admits that he is a racist, that's O.K.," he said. But "if a non-Indian says he's a racist, that's terrible." Responding to such ideas, most Indian leaders remained calm, and one observer noted the controversy existed because "lots of whites are just plain jealous."

There can be little doubt that growing Indian local sovereignty kept people in many parts of the country angry because of what appeared to be favoritism toward Native Americans and because of the increasing impact tribal courts and regulations had on people living on or near the reservations. For example, the Chemehuevi, who live just beyond the Colorado River along Lake Havasu in eastern California, encountered anguished cries from whites residing on their land when the tribe raised the rental fees. The modest rents lagged far below those charged by neighboring property owners, but the new rates angered many of the leaseholders who had enjoyed the previously low charges. In the early 1990s the Seneca tribe in New York State encountered similar difficulties. A century earlier, in 1892, tribal leaders had leased the land on which the town of Salamanca now stood. The original agreement called for an annual payment of $17,000, which may have been a reasonable sum when it was signed one hundred years ago. However, by the 1990s the situation had changed drastically. Some Indian activists suggested that the town-dwellers might be evicted, and reporters from New York City poured in to record the dispute. Few angry whites considered destroying their homes or other property, but when the dispute ended, the city fathers agreed to a new lease in the amount of $60 million per annum. Disputes like these two meant that the public could not escape some notice of the changing status and power of tribal governments.

LEGISLATION AND COURT ACTIONS

More isolated than most Indian groups, the Alaska Native people received little attention until 1959, when that territory gained statehood. Within just a few years the Alaska Federated Natives organized several regional associations to protect their land and resource claims. Their demands led to the 1971 passage of the Alaska Native Claims Settlement, which upheld their rights to forty-four million acres of land and paid the groups some $962 million for other claims they held. That action came about as a result of new legislation and court decisions that focused on the concept of self-determination and related issues. Presidents Kennedy, Johnson, and Nixon all took an interest in Indian affairs. Johnson gave an address entitled "The Forgotten American," wherein he called for an end to Termination. He then set up the National Council on Indian Opportunity and charged it with recommending new directions for federal-tribal cooperation. Continuing studies of reservation conditions produced reports on Indian health and educational opportunities that suggested important policy changes. The Indian Education Act of 1972 and the 1975 Indian Self-Determination and Educational Assistance Act provided new funding and greater attention to Indian needs and ideas than had been the case earlier.

Asking for and obtaining some local sovereignty brought unexpected and occasionally harmful results for tribal groups. The Navajo found, to their surprise, that the Indian Civil Rights Act of 1968 might be used against them. Apparently that is just what some of its Congressional supporters expected. That year a public quarrel between the white tribal attorney and one member of the tribal council occurred. When the council banned the attorney from the reservation, he sued to be allowed to return and won under the terms of the new 1968 legislation. Ten years later, in *Oliphant v. Squamish Indians*, the court ruled that tribal governments could not try nonmembers for criminal actions on the reservation. That same year, however, the *Santa Clara v. Martinez* decision gave tribes the right to determine their own membership criteria. Following traditional practices in that case, the Pueblo government decided that only children of Santa Clara Pueblo men were tribal members. When the Pueblo refused to accept the Martinez children as tribal members because their father was a Navajo, the family sued. Although traditionalists and women's-rights supporters expressed shock and dismay, the decision strengthened tribal courts in dealing with internal reservation matters. It also gave reservation governments immunity from suits filed against them under the 1968 Indian Civil Rights Act.

Indian religious practices continued to come under federal and state scrutiny despite the American Indian Religious Freedom Act. Peyote use drew objections throughout the twentieth century. As early as 1940, the Navajo tribal council legislated against its use or possession on the reservation. Years later the Native American Church sued the tribe, but in 1959 the court ruled that tribal leaders had the authority to block even the religious use of peyote. A few years later, the result differed when authorities arrested John Woody and other Navajos for peyote use in California. In its 1964 *People v. Woody* decision, the state supreme court overturned the convictions, ruling that California could not interfere with those who included the drug in a religious ceremony. Nevertheless, a 1990 decision showed how easily Indian religious freedom could be challenged. Two members of the Native American Church who worked as drug and alcohol counselors for the state of Oregon lost their jobs for taking part in a peyote ceremony at church. In *Employment Division of Oregon v. Smith* the U.S. Supreme Court ruled that the state could prohibit the religious role of peyote because it had the right to regulate drug use. This decision remained in force until 1993, when the Religious Restoration Act became law. Some disputes focused on the use of feathers from eagles and other protected birds, and in 1986 the U.S. Supreme Court ruled that tribal religious ceremonial needs for feathers did not entitle Indians to possess them outside the usual set of federal regulations. The issue of tribal rights to bird parts and feathers from protected species for religious ceremonies remains an unsettled and contentious one.

RESOURCES AND ECONOMIC ISSUES

Since World War II, employment and economic self-sufficiency have remained elusive for many Native Americans living on reservations. Most tribes held lands with little value and few resources, but some enjoyed better circumstances. Tribal lands contained at least 3 percent of the oil and natural gas then located in the United States. In addition, Indians owned at least 10 percent of the known coal deposits in the country, amounting to between 100 and 200 billion tons. Other reservations had uranium deposits, forest lands, or water resources that might prove valuable to corporations and bring income and jobs to tribal groups. Unfortunately, when corporations negotiated drilling or mining leases, reservation leaders lacked the expertise to obtain fair payments. For example, the Peabody Coal Company persuaded the Navajo and Hopi tribes of the Southwest to sign contracts that paid them only 17.5 cents per ton of coal the company mined on their land. That miserly fee came at a time when coal prices rose sharply, so that the tribes got less than a two percent royalty for their fossil fuel.

Responsibility for negotiating reasonable contracts lay with the BIA, and clearly that agency's officials were not up to the task. Often the office staff understood little more than their Indian charges, and long-standing federal legislation allowed the contracts to operate for years before any changes could be made. In 1976 the Department of the Interior raised its leasing rates to 17 percent, roughly eight times higher than negotiated previously. Because they realized how bad the leases were, tribal leaders began to protest. On some reservations reformers and younger leaders attacked those who had signed the existing contracts, gaining leadership roles for themselves. Hoping to redo the leases and gain more funds for tribal needs, in 1974 some reservation officials formed a federation of tribes with natural resource holdings. A year later other leaders broadened the group, founding the Council of Energy Resource Tribes (CERT). During its history, this organization included at least twenty-five tribes. It worked to gather information on resource production and uses as well as to make the data available to interested tribes. In early 1977, CERT chairman Peter MacDonald tried to turn the organization into a resource cartel like that of the Arab oil-producing nations, but the move failed. Still, MacDonald's effort brought new attention to reservation difficulties, and for a time some tribes increased oil production as well.

Although many Indians seemed to welcome resource development because of the new jobs it brought to their reservations, some objected. At Black Mesa in Arizona and on tribal lands in eastern Montana, serious questions arose about the environmental costs of large-scale mining. Even some ranchers in eastern Wyoming joined their tribal neighbors in trying to head off large-scale strip mining by the Peabody Coal Company on grazing lands that had been in their families for generations. For those who had worked as uranium miners during the 1950s and 1960s, questions over resource development became intensely personal. By the late 1970s, lung cancer swept through the ranks of former Navajo miners who had worked at Kerr-McGee mines in Arizona and New Mexico years earlier. "No one ever told us of the danger," one tribal council member remarked. The mines paid well and brought the only jobs that Indians there ever had, yet "now the people are dying."

In the Black Hills and in nearby Montana and Wyoming, uranium mining left ruined landscapes and dangerous radioactive waste at open pit sites. By 1979 the Department of the Interior described contamination there as unsafe for animals. Meanwhile, Indian activists complained that the Black Hills were "not just another mine site," but rather "a spiritual center" for tribal people. Farther south in Arizona, Stewart Udall, former Secretary of the Interior, worked to obtain compensation for the families of miners who had died from cancer after working in the uranium mines. He visited Navajo communities, gathered information about the illnesses and deaths, and filed four suits on behalf of miners and people in Utah who lived downwind from the atomic test sites. By 1990 the courts had ruled against him in three of the suits. Still, his efforts paid off because that year Congress set up a compensation plan that would give $100,000 to miners who contracted cancer or to the families of those who died from it, and half that much to the so-called down-winders as well. The issue continues into the new century. In August 2001 officials in the George W. Bush administration halted payments to all but the actual miners or their families, eliminated the down-winders from coverage, and called for further study of the medical links between mining and atomic tests and increased risks of cancer.

Timber and other rights also continued to disturb relations between the tribes and their neighbors. In Wisconsin the Mole Lake Anishinabe (Ojibwa) retained their treaty right not only to spearfish, as discussed earlier, but also to cut timber freely. By 1990, they had authorization to begin cutting in the Northern Highland–American Legion State Forest in the north-central part of the state. They planned to sell the timber to nearby sawmills but also hoped to build tribally operated mills. At the time, the five other Anishinabe bands there had not yet decided whether to exercise their timber-cutting rights. Other reservation groups' property claims antagonized or frightened their neighbors. For example, during the late 1980s in Tacoma, Washington, the Puyallup tribe held rights to more than three hundred acres of downtown property worth several hundred million dollars. In 1988 the fourteen hundred mostly poor tribal members voted to drop their claims in return for a promised $162 million in cash and land, with an additional promise of jobs. On the East Coast, the Penobscot and Passamaquoddy Indians sued for the return of two-thirds of the state of Maine because the land had been acquired illegally. This brought quick action from Congress, and in 1980 President Jimmy Carter signed the Maine Indian Settlement Law, paying the tribes $81.3 million as compensation for their former lands.

Issues related to water supplies and to lands lost to flooding behind government dams continue to raise serious questions. Nearly all disputes dealing with tribal water rights are based on tribal claims that resulted from the Supreme Court's 1908 *Winters v. United States* decision. There the court found that whenever the federal government had established a reservation, that action also set aside enough water to allow the Indians to carry out their economic activities. It also guaranteed that the tribes would not lose their water rights if they did not immediately use them. The Tohono O'odham of southern Arizona received an annual allotment of Colorado River water from the Central Arizona Project in 1977 in exchange for dropping their suit against non-Indian water users. During the 1980s more than fifty suits over tribal water rights clogged the courts, but in each new decision the reservation groups won. In 1989 the Shoshone and Arapaho people of Wyoming received a large grant of water. The water-rights issues remain unclear, and claims from Indians and their neighbors are so contentious that at present dozens of cases continue to work their way through the courts or various other forms of arbitration.

EDUCATION

As tribal groups gained increasing control over local affairs, they turned their attention increasingly to educational matters. When Native Americans moved to the cities, many encountered the negative stereotypes of Indians that appeared regularly in public-school curricula. The growing sense of Indianness and awareness of Red Power led to complaints about the negative classroom materials. Partly in response to this dissatisfaction, in 1964 Rupert Costo and Jeannette Henry Costo founded the American Indian Historical Society. Seeking to bring knowledge about their past to tribal members, they published *Textbooks and the American Indian*, which demonstrated the one-sided and inaccurate treatment public-school textbooks gave when discussing Native Americans as part of the nation's history. Not long after this work appeared, a broader examination of over one hundred U.S. history textbooks supported their charges. In fact, this study reported that "the notion of the blood-curdling, perilous, massacring savage is common" in existing texts. To remedy that perception, within just a few years the Newberry Library of Chicago sponsored academic meetings in Washington, Chicago, and Los Angeles that brought university and college instructors together to develop strategies for incorporating historically accurate Native American materials into existing courses. Such efforts persuaded national textbook publishers to make numerous deletions and corrections and to insert accurate material into their products.

Creating an Indian Historical Society and putting pressure on textbook publishers certainly brought results. Yet many tribes and individuals continued to need help or changes closer to home. Although federal programs sent increasing funds to local school districts, Indians rarely saw evidence that the money reached their children's schools. They began to question local administrators, and when that seemed to have no effect, they elected tribal members to the school boards. In the West, large tribal populations made this easier than in much of the country, and by the mid-1970s at least seventy-eight school districts on or near reservations had Native American majorities on their boards. Others conducted sit-ins such as that carried out by Navajo parents in Ship Rock, New Mexico. Although these actions brought some response, the Navajo tribal government decided to establish its own school, and in 1966 opened the Rough Rock Demonstration School. Founded with the idea that it should provide students with a solid base of tribal language and culture, Rough Rock offered bilingual classes and sought to develop tribally based instructional materials. Tribal leaders and school officials controlled all aspects of the curriculum, going so far as to exclude non-Indian faculty at the school from any role in setting administrative policies.

Other tribes followed suit, as Indian-operated schools opened from the Midwest to the Pacific. In New Mexico several used bilingual instruction and tribally based classroom material. Tribes in Montana operated the Rocky Boy School, providing their students with Anishinabe and Cree history, language, and literature. Working with preschool children, the Viejas Indian School in Alpine, California, offered help similar to what Head Start gave other American students. It also operated after-school programs for older students. In the Midwest, heavy concentrations of Native Americans resulted in efforts to begin similar institutions in the cities there. Anishinabe and Dakota students had schools in both Minneapolis and St. Paul, and local Native Americans opened one in Milwaukee, Wisconsin, as well. All of these institutions tried to develop and incorporate teaching materials based on tribal culture, history, and language. Their success in doing so varied. Among some groups the students had little motivation because their parents did not use the tribal language at home. Other groups had few people who possessed both language and teaching skills. In fact, some tribal elders complained that having to compete with the elements of TV-spread American popular culture made retaining their languages and cultures difficult at best.

In trying to overcome such problems during the late 1960s, some tribes decided to found their own colleges. They hoped that such institutions would provide skilled workers and trained leaders to help run reservation affairs. The Navajos led this movement, and in 1968 founded Navajo Community College in Many Farms, Arizona. Classes began a few months later. In 1971 Congress passed the Navajo Community College Act. The tribal Board of Regents strove to ensure that Navajo history, culture, and language had a central place in the course offerings. In 1997 the school was renamed Diné (Navajo) College. The founding and early success of this institution encouraged other tribes and groups to open colleges, often—but not always—located on their reservations. The Tribally Controlled Community College Assistance Act of 1978 provided federal encouragement and funding that enabled many groups to establish schools on their reservations. As of 2001, thirty-two tribal colleges were operating in twelve states. These included all of the states westward from Michigan to Washington along the Canadian border, Kansas and Nebraska in the Midwest, and California, Arizona, and New Mexico in the Southwest. Almost all of these institutions are community colleges offering the first two years of college academic classes as well as technical and vocational courses. Usually underfunded, they often lack good facilities or adequate equipment but all have strong support from the tribal communities and are sources of intense local pride.

Many Indian students left the reservations or urban enclaves to attend other colleges and universities. Their presence at such schools led to the growth of American Indian Studies programs at many institutions. In 1968, Native students at the University of Minnesota asked for classes in their own languages, including courses on Indians' roles in the state's history. Surprisingly, although this effort came at the time the American Indian Movement began in Minneapolis, the push to establish such courses remained peaceful. News of their success at Minnesota brought calls for similar offerings at schools across the country, and by the mid-1980s well over a hundred colleges and universities had incorporated them. The programs vary widely, from institutions that offer only an undergraduate minor to others that now award the Ph.D. These academic innovations have brought a new sense of urgency to many efforts designed to help the tribes. Critical language programs not only offer courses in tribal languages, but also gather oral versions of ceremonies, poetry, history, and religious beliefs. Some work to produce dictionaries, grammars, children's stories, and other items that will help keep tribal languages from disappearing.

TRIBAL ACKNOWLEDGMENT

As federal willingness to grant self-determination and limited local sovereignty to tribes continued, groups that wanted to be recognized as Indians came forward to press their claims. From the passage of the 1934 Indian Reorganization Act through the late 1970s, nearly thirty tribes had achieved that goal. Some persuaded an interested congressional representative to introduce legislation to help them. A few benefited from executive actions granting them tribal status. Once that happened, their members became eligible for BIA programs and access to the Indian Health Service. A few groups received other benefits too. In 1980, for example, the Houlton Band of Maliseets in Maine, numbering about 350 people, gained tribal recognition. This enabled them to share in the Maine Indian Land Claim settlement and brought the band about $1 million. With those funds they purchased some land and reestablished a formal presence in the state. Their success brought them legal status as Indians and the opportunity to take part in existing federal programs.

Even before the Maliseets won their struggle, however, observers both within and outside the federal government had called for some established framework that could be used to settle claims related to Indian identity, because many groups clamored for recognition as legitimate tribes. As a result, in 1978 Congress approved legislation establishing the Federal Acknowledgment Project. Its name has changed slightly since then, but the process it began continues to the present. In some ways the procedure resembles that of the Indian Claims Commission which operated right after World War II. Tribes must apply and go through a series of hearings, where they present the evidence gathered in support of their application. Many of the petitioning groups consist of people who claim to be the descendants of tribes or bands assumed to have disappeared generations or even centuries ago. Perhaps their ancestors purposely hid in the forests or mountains as they tried to survive. Some became so thoroughly acculturated that their neighbors had no idea they were Indians. Others represent substantial race-mixing with nearby whites or blacks over many generations. For whatever reasons, at some time in the past they ceased to be recognized as "real" Indians.

As ethnic awareness permeated American society by the last quarter of the twentieth century, Native Americans wanted to have their ethnic identity made public, and at the same time they looked forward to receiving the benefits that tribal status would give them. The Acknowledgment Project then faced the task of sorting through the claims from what officials expected would be a few dozen groups. The BIA staff members set up a list of requirements they thought would make the task of deciding which people qualified for federal recognition a relatively easy one. They were wrong. What began as an open process became one that demanded increasing amounts of data, often nearly impossible for the applicants to obtain. When the program started, the bureaucrats had no clear idea of how many groups might apply. During the first ten years of its operation, however, 111 separate applications reached their desks. This number continued to grow, and by 2001 more than 200 applications awaited action. Not only did the increasing numbers of applications clog the process, but representatives from long-recognized tribes became increasingly worried about the recognition of new tribes. They reasoned that federal funds for Indian-related programs would remain stable, and if the number of new tribes grew, the existing ones would lose some of their funding. Members of recognized tribes had come to fill most positions at the BIA, and some of these bureaucrats reflected the biases of their home communities.

Despite such difficulties, as of 2002 the program continues to operate. To prove their Indian heritage, applicants must submit documentation demonstrating that they have always been considered Indians, have lived in a particular place continually, are descended from a historically known group, have had some tribal government or authority over the members, and possess some criteria for group membership. These requirements call for just the sort of materials the applicants have the most difficulty producing. Because their ancestors tried to fade into the countryside to avoid conflict with their white neighbors, now they themselves have great difficulty in securing the required documents. Once considerable intermarriage with either local blacks or whites occurred, small tribes often lost their spoken language, and the descendants of such unions came to be seen merely as neighbors rather than as tribal members. Certainly the need to produce evidence that some type of tribal government existed and functioned for generations became a major stumbling block for many of the petitioners. As a result, by 2001 only half of the twenty-some groups that went through the process had achieved recognition. Almost thirty years after the project was initiated, critics have begun to denounce the entire process.

GAMBLING AND CASINOS

By the opening of the twenty-first century, tribal leaders faced a variety of contentious issues that often put them at odds with their non-Indian neighbors. As it had in the past, gaming or casino gambling drew much public attention and debate. Tribal cultures have included small-scale gambling for centuries, so when some groups opened their bingo halls to the public, few Indians gave it much thought. Reservation gambling facilities as they exist today started in 1979, when the Seminole tribe in Florida began awarding $10,000 prizes at their newly opened bingo hall. At the time, Florida law limited bingo payments to only $100, and state officials therefore moved to close the tribal games. The Seminoles sued, and the federal court ruled that the state had no jurisdiction over the size of bingo payouts. The tribe opened several new bingo halls and soon had nearly ten thousand players pouring millions of dollars into their treasury. Within the next decade, other reservation groups began opening various gambling facilities as leaders saw the potential for income and employment for their people.

During the 1980s California authorities tried to close existing Indian gaming facilities and to prevent the development of any new ones, but they failed. In 1987 one band sued the state, and the resulting *California v. Cabazon Band of Mission Indians* decision declared that California had no authority over reservation activities. The next year Congress passed the Indian Gaming Regulatory Act, which established a National Indian Gaming Commission to oversee tribal gaming issues and operations. The legislation made funds available through the BIA as loans to help tribes build facilities ranging from modest bingo halls to multimillion-dollar resorts. Within less than a decade over one hundred tribes had opened some kind of gambling facilities in twenty-four states, and by the end of the 1990s tribal gross revenues from these operations exceeded $5 billion. Granted, 40 percent of the earnings came from only eight tribes, but Indian leaders recognized the immense popularity of gambling and began referring to it as "the new buffalo" for their people.

The federal legislation set up three classes of gambling that tribes might offer, but nearly all of the resulting disputes focus on what they call Class III gambling. This includes modern, sophisticated games such as slot machines, blackjack tables, and other Las Vegas–style games. States that allow any gambling had few choices but to accept Indian practices if such operations remained on tribal land. In California the governor objected and refused to negotiate compacts between the state and the tribes, but the federal court decision there forced state authorities to sign gaming agreements. In 1998 at least 65 percent of California voters supported Proposition 5, which allowed Indian gaming in that state. Casino operators in Nevada objected to the spread of Indian competition in their customer-rich neighboring state but had little recourse. On the East Coast, Donald Trump tried unsuccessfully to use the federal courts to shut down tribal competition to his Atlantic City operations.

The most spectacular success came to the Mashantucket Pequots in Connecticut. In 1983 they received federal acknowledgment as a tribe and since then have enlarged their membership from fewer than one hundred people to about three hundred in 2001. By the 1990s they had added some fifteen hundred acres to their tiny reservation, and in 1992 they opened Foxwoods Casino there. Within easy driving distance for nearly fifty million people, their gaming operation became an instant multimillion-dollar success. At first, Connecticut governor Lowell Weicker rejected their efforts to install slot-machine gambling at the casino. When tribal leaders offered to donate $1 million each year from their profits to help support assistance programs for economically depressed small towns, he withdrew his objections. Within just a couple of years Foxwoods generated hundreds of millions of dollars, which the tribe used to build a resort complex, a museum, and a historical research facility. It has subsidized national multitribal meetings, given money to help build the National Museum of the

American Indian in Washington, D.C., and stands as the showcase for successful Indian gaming operations.

A few isolated groups have realized only small profits and several have actually closed their gaming facilities because they lost money, but other issues continue to make commercial gambling on reservations contentious. In 1990 at the St. Regis Akwesash settlement in New York, the Mohawks fought bitterly over building casinos. Elected leaders opposed reservation-based gambling while Warrior Society members backed it. Before the dispute ended, two people were murdered and the casino building burned. Twice since then reservation voters have rejected building a new casino, and the tribal members remain sharply divided over the matter. In New Mexico, members of the Mescalero Apache tribe sued to have the laws allowing reservation-based gambling declared unconstitutional. Next door in Arizona in 2001, the operators of dog- and horse-racing tracks brought suit hoping to prevent the governor from negotiating gambling contracts between the state and the tribes. The court ruled in their favor and sent the entire matter back to the legislature to be reworked. Although many tribal leaders see the right to offer casino gambling on their reservations as a sign of having achieved a degree of tribal sovereignty, issues surrounding gaming still generate heated debate. For example, in the 2002 general election, Arizona voters faced three separate gaming initiatives on their ballots.

REPATRIATION OF TRIBAL REMAINS

By the 1970s, Indian activists had stepped up demands for holdings in American museums, archaeology laboratories, and university research collections to be returned to the tribes. They objected to the display, storage, or study of funerary items, sacred objects, and skeletal remains that had been found on tribal burial grounds during the preceding two centuries. Archaeologists defended themselves, saying that they were trying to preserve tribal cultures. The activists responded by

········· Line of 20 inches annual rainfall

Larger Indian reservations, 1880–1890

charging that, to the scholars, the only real Indians were long-dead ones. Most of the argument focused on artifacts and remains gathered from Indian burial sites during the nineteenth century by amateur pot hunters and military officers. Thousands of such items reached the Smithsonian Institution or other museums and research centers, and only gradually was that trend reversed. Beginning with the 1906 Antiquities Act and moving through the Historic Sites Act of 1935 to the 1966 National Historic Preservation Act, the laws began to limit what might be collected, as well as where collecting might take place and under what circumstances. Once Congress passed the 1978 American Indian Religious Freedom Act, such discussions became central to the disposition of the more than half a million tribal skeletal remains and sacred objects of all sorts held by museums. By 1987, Robert McC. Adams, former secretary of the Smithsonian Institution, announced that curators, anthropologists, and archaeologists had "an obligation to return skeletal remains in our collections to tribal descendants."

Since then, two new laws have taken the requirements much further, changing the situation entirely. In 1989, legislation creating the Smithsonian Institution's National Museum of the American Indian called for the return of skeletal and funerary remains to the appropriate tribes and groups. The next year Congress passed the Native American Graves Protection and Repatriation Act, which directed that tribal artifacts and skeletal remains be identified and disposed of when held by U.S. agencies and other organizations that receive federal funds. The last clause effectively included nearly all of the museums, historical societies, and universities in the country and so had a greater effect than all of the earlier legislation put together. It called on museums and other repositories to examine the Indian items in their possession and then to notify tribes if the collections included material that might have come from their ancestors. For the first time in generations, perhaps ever, curators went through dusty storage bins and seldom-visited archives, taking inventories of what they had. The results of that effort astonished many in the museum world, because neither they nor their predecessors had ever conducted a thorough evaluation of their holdings.

Professional archaeologists and curators feared that the new laws might lead to what they considered unreasonable tribal demands for everything on museum shelves. In some places they fought the spirit of the law whenever possible. For example, the museum staff at the University of California at Berkeley denounced the new rules. Frank Norick, a researcher there, became outraged and complained that "science should not be sacrificed on the altar of religious beliefs!" Despite similar denunciations elsewhere, increased public awareness and continuing federal pressure brought much of the debate to a close. Within just a few years, the National Museum of Natural History had returned more than 18,500 cultural items and skeletal remains to tribes across the country, including groups of Hawaiian Islanders. Often, tribal elders held public ceremonies to rebury skeletons identified as belonging to their ancestors. Of equal importance, sacred objects such as pipes, wampum belts, religious masks, and medicine bundles have been sent back to tribal authorities as well. At present, tribal leaders and scholars have reached agreement on many issues that divided them bitterly only a decade or so ago. In fact, in some cases Indians have declined materials being returned because they lack the facilities, trained personnel, and funds to care for the items effectively. Debates over which materials need to be returned to tribal groups and what group should get a particular item continue.

RELIGIOUS SITES AND RIGHTS

Related directly to the return of medicine bundles and other religious materials, the disputes over the protection of particular Native groups' sacred sites continue to fuel debates and spark demonstrations into the twenty-first century. This issue first received public attention during the early 1950s when the Indian Claims Commission proposed to settle the government's quarrel with the Lakotas over the Black Hills. The ICC offered millions of dollars for the lands illegally taken from the tribe, but the Lakotas rejected the settlement, demanding that the land be returned. Since then, Native Americans have become increasingly outspoken about their religious sites and the need to return or preserve them for tribal use. During the 1980s, when the Peabody Coal Company began large-scale strip mining of coal in the Four Corners area of Arizona, New Mexico, Colorado, and Utah, some members of both the Hopi and Navajo tribes objected. Traditionalists opposed the mining because it destroyed the land itself. To them, "the Mesa, the air, the water, are Holy Elements" to be prayed to for the "well-being of each generation." Others complained that pollution from the operations hid the sacred San Francisco Peaks so that they could not view the mountains. In the 1983 *Wilson v. Block* decision the tribes lost a suit in which they tried to halt construction of a ski resort in the same mountain area.

In other places the results of similar disputes varied. The Chumash Indians of southern California won a delay in the construction of a proposed natural-gas terminal at Point Conception on the coast. At the end of the 1970s a consortium of power companies began planning for the facility. The Chumash enlisted help from nearby activists, and the resulting site occupation and demonstrations caused enough negative publicity to postpone the project. By 1980, falling utility prices made the plant economically unfeasible, so construction halted. The tribes lost their battles to protect particular sites in several other locales. During that decade the U.S. Forest Service decided to open a road in northern California, as it needed to improve access to timber and recreational areas nearby. However, their own expert testified that the road might destroy sites essential to holding ceremonies which "constitute the heart of the Northwest [Indian] religious beliefs and practices." When the tribes sued, the lower courts supported their religious claims. The U.S. Supreme Court ruled against them, however, finding that the American Indian Religious Freedom Act offered no protection in this case. Construction of the road took place.

Sometimes religious disputes divided reservation communities and instigated harsh feuds. In Arizona the Hopi villages split in 1989 when the tribal council approved a gravel pit for the tribally owned construction company to use as a source for highway material. The pit did not occupy a sacred site, but it lay near the area from which the Snake Society priests gathered live snakes for their annual ceremonies. The priests complained that the site was the "nesting place" of the snakes and that the council had reached its decision "without consulting us." They feared that "if we let go of any part of our religion, our Hopi way of life will be discontinued." With that level of anxiety, the tribal leaders sought a compromise to the dispute. Farther south, in Arizona, astronomers from universities in the United States, Italy, and Germany chose Mount Graham as the best place in the country for a new multi-mirror observatory. The first investigation of the site produced no objections. In fact, several Apache elders said that it had no religious significance for their people. Others in the tribe thought differently, however, and a bitter fight over construction of the observatory broke out, including federal court suits, Congressional actions, protests, violence, and sabotage. While construction continues, so do the protests.

TEAM MASCOTS

Throughout much of the twentieth century, high-school, college, university, and professional athletic teams across the country have used Indian names and symbols. Although some tribal groups may have objected earlier, in 1972 AIM leader Dennis Banks and others attacked the use of Indian mascots as racist and demeaning. Threatening suits against the owners of the Atlanta Braves and Cleveland Indians baseball teams for using Indian caricatures as mascots and for marketing team souvenirs, the activists focused national attention on the issue. College teams from across the country had such nicknames and mascots as Indians, Redmen, Illini, Seminoles, and Warriors. Professional teams in baseball, basketball, football, and hockey competed as Braves, Black Hawks, Chiefs, Indians, Redskins, and Warriors. Some thoughtful tribal leaders pointed out that except for the "Fighting Irish" of Notre Dame, few teams used other national, ethnic, or racial groups as their symbols. They denounced the use of tribal terms or supposed Indian attributes as acts of cultural thievery. Teams that had such mascots were guilty of stealing parts of tribal culture. Many Indians found the caricatures more objectionable than the mere use of the names. The Atlanta Braves celebrated each home run they hit by having "Chief Noc-a-homa" come out of his tepee and dance. At the University of Illinois, "Chief Illiniwek" amused crowds at football games, and fans of the Florida State University Seminoles and of the Atlanta Braves did the tomahawk chop to celebrate their teams' achievements.

When protesters objected to universities and professional teams promoting such images and actions, many fans and alumni reacted angrily. They considered such complaints attacks on tradition and good fun. After all, some said, teams used their mascots to recognize Indian bravery and courage, and many people laughed off the complaints. Native American students at Dartmouth, Illinois, and Stanford Universities took the issue more seriously, and campaigned to have the mascots dropped. At both Dartmouth and Stanford they succeeded, and the teams now play under new nicknames. The authorities at Illinois, however, refused to act. In fact, in 1989, when the protests reached their peak there, the university chancellor defended Chief Illiniwek as a "dignified, respected, [and] even [a] revered symbol" of the school's teams. The dispute there attracted so much attention that before it ended, the state legislature adopted a resolution supporting the university administration. Meanwhile, professional sports clubs proved even more resistant to dropping their team names and symbols. In March 2002 they could point to a *Sports Illustrated* survey claiming that even most Indians had few objections to teams using tribal names or mascots. So the debate continues.

MISHANDLING TRUST FUNDS

Many of the contentious issues that separate Indian groups from the rest of American society focus in some way or another on the question of tribal sovereignty. Laws, federal court decisions, and disputes between tribal governments and local or state authorities all play roles in the ongoing drama. The most contentious current dispute between the tribes and the federal government grew out of the mishandling of Indian trust funds since the 1887 passage of the Dawes Act. That legislation initiated a system for government supervision of Indian land leases and tribal funds which has operated ineffectively ever since. For several generations, reservation leaders asked agents and other officials about their money but got few answers. By the 1980s the growing ethnic awareness that resulted from the Red Power movement and from self-determination policies encouraged some Native Americans to demand an accounting. When federal officials refused, Elouise Cobell, a Montana Blackfeet, raised money for a federal court suit. The case went to trial in 1996, and the special investigator found that Department of the Interior employees had destroyed hundreds of cartons of records needed by the tribes and the court. In 1999, Judge Royce Lamberth found Secretary of the Interior Bruce Babbitt and Secretary of the Treasury Robert Rubin in contempt for refusing to cooperate with the investigation and fined each of them $625,000. He described the bureaucrats' handling of tribal funds as showing "a shocking pattern of deception," and ruled that the government must prepare quarterly statements accounting for its handling of tribal funds. When an appeals court upheld Lamberth's decision, the George W. Bush administration dropped further appeals. Ongoing investigations will provide the data for those who must determine the size of the multibillion-dollar final awards.

SOVEREIGNTY OR ASSIMILATION

A variety of issues continue to separate American Indians from the rest of society. Both radical and traditional leaders have sought to expand their tribal sovereignty, but for vastly different reasons. Unemployment, poverty, poor education, and health concerns all demonstrate that tribal members do not share equally in the national well-being. In some parts of the country, overt racism and discrimination still exist, but for the most part, in the major urban centers where most Native Americans now live, it is no longer a major issue. During the last several decades of the twentieth century, many Americans became more interested in their own ethnic and family backgrounds, and this seems to have fostered more widespread tolerance. For Indians, this means that American society is more ready than ever to welcome them as one more ethnic group in the national social mix. Ironically, this ethnic awakening that has swept through American society has engendered an almost opposite response among American Indians. Many appear to want increasing ties with their tribal groups, and this is particularly true for those living away from the reservations. Indian rodeos, the Indian Powwow circuit, language classes, and on-reservation religious and cultural ceremonies all have experienced increased attendance.

At the same time, some actions by tribal people have moved them directly into the American mainstream. On 22 November 2002 the space shuttle Endeavor carried John Herrington of the Chickasaw Nation, the first Indian astronaut, to the international space station. During the past several years, Indian actors and moviemakers have produced films such as *Smoke Signals* and *Skins*. Others participated in a Hollywood film depicting the Navajo Code Talkers of World War II and a 2002 television version of the Tony Hillerman novel *Skin Walkers*. If everything goes according to schedule, in late 2003 the National Museum of the American Indian will open its doors to the public in Washington, D.C. Despite these examples of successful Indian participation in national activities, the future directions tribal people will take remain unclear at best. What is certain is that in the twenty-first century, Indians will have far more to say about their lives and places in American society than has been the case in the past.

SUGGESTED READINGS

Ambler, Marjane. *Breaking the Iron Bonds: Indian Control of Energy Development.* Lawrence: University Press of Kansas, 1990.

Echo-Hawk, Roger. *Battlefields and Burial Grounds: The Indian Struggle to Protect Ancestral Graves in the U.S.* Minneapolis: Lerner Publications Company, 1994.

Eichstaedt, Peter H. *If You Poison Us: Uranium and Native Americans.* Santa Fe, N.M.: Red Crane Books, 1994.

Forbes, Jack. *Native Americans and Nixon: Presidential Politics and Minority Self-Determination.* Los Angeles: American Indian Studies Study Center (UCLA), 1981.

Horning, Rick. *One Nation under the Gun.* New York: Pantheon Books, 1991.

Iverson, Peter. *"We're Still Here:" American Indians in the Twentieth Century.* Wheeling, Ill.: Harlan Davidson, 1998.

Nagle, Joane. *American Indian Ethnic Renewal.* New York: Oxford University Press, 1996.

Rawls, James J. *Chief Red Fox Is Dead: A History of Native Americans since 1945.* New York: Harcourt Brace College Publishing, 1996.

Szasz, Margaret. *Education and the American Indian: The Road to Self-Determination.* Albuquerque: University of New Mexico Press, 1988.

Wunder, John R. *"Retained by the People": A History of American Indians and the Bill of Rights.* New York: Oxford University Press, 1994.

Index